MW01016375

PRAISE FOR *BOXIN*

"No journey in life proceeds without getting one's bearings. Michael Hadley has deftly navigated the cardinal points of a life and revealed their treasures. His charts both musical and navigational are trans-global, his reverence for ancestry and service indelible, and his connecting place and human experience a tangible history—each a literary destination for his reader. Hadley has boxed the compass of a life well-lived and brought us to home port safely again."

TED BARRIS journalist, broadcaster, and author of *Battle of the Atlantic: Gauntlet to Victory*

"What an adventure life can be for those willing to set sail. By turns a mariner, public servant, musician, and scholar, Michael Hadley recounts a rich journey across the eventful twentieth century and into the present with the sea as his throughline. Insightful and inspiring."

ELLIOT RAPPAPORT author of *Reading the Glass: A Captain's View of Weather, Water, and Life on Ships*

"In *Boxing the Compass*, an adventure story and intellectual autobiography, Michael Hadley vividly recounts his travels with the Kitsilano Boys' Band and service as a Canadian naval officer; his experience as student and teacher of German literature and research of submarine warfare; and, fulfilling a life-long spiritual quest, his advocacy of restorative justice in places as far afield as Uganda. Literary and musical allusions, both popular and classic, enhance this elegantly written memoir. *Boxing the Compass* is a tour de force."

PATRICIA E. ROY professor emeritus of History at the University of Victoria

"This memoir is compelling, erudite, and courageously introspective. Hadley's rich and varied experiences lead him to profound insights into the nature of belonging, belief, and justice. Read this and gain a deeper understanding of the world we live in and the roads our humanity takes us down."

DR. DAVID J. HAWKIN author of *Christ and Modernity* and *The Johannine World*, and retired professor of Religious Studies at the Memorial University of Newfoundland

"Michael Hadley takes us on an extraordinary journey offering a profound reflection on life. From his early years growing up on a coastal lighthouse station to the rhythmic world of jazz, the disciplined path of a naval officer, and the halls of academia, his narrative weaves a tapestry enriched with wisdom, compassion, resilience, and an unwavering commitment to humanity."

CATHY CONVERSE award-winning author of *Against the Current: The Remarkable Life of Agnes Deans Cameron*

"Michael Hadley has written an extraordinary book reflecting an extraordinary life. Taking us from his growing up to his retirement (though his inquiring mind will never retire), there is a kaleidoscope of experience. The impetus and insight of his writing on restorative justice has helped move it from being experimental to becoming established in many countries as a natural way to bring healing from extreme harm."

TIM NEWELL author, retired prison governor of HMP Grendon, and cofounder and trustee of the charity Escaping Victimhood

BOXING THE COMPASS

BOXING THE COMPASS

A Life of Seafaring, Music, and Pilgrimage

MICHAEL L. HADLEY

Heritage House Publishing Company Ltd.
heritagehouse.ca

Cataloguing information available from Library and Archives Canada
978-1-77203-473-8 (paperback)
978-1-77203-474-5 (e-book)

Edited by Leslie Kenny
Cover design by Colin Parks and Sara Loos
Interior book design by Setareh Ashrafologhalai
Cover images courtesy of Michael L. Hadley (*front*)
and Akira Hojo/Unsplash.com (*back*)
Interior photographs from author's collection
unless otherwise indicated

The interior of this book was produced on 100%
post-consumer recycled paper, processed chlorine
free, and printed with vegetable-based inks.

Heritage House gratefully acknowledges that the land on which
we live and work is within the traditional territories of the Lkwungen
(Esquimalt and Songhees), Malahat, Pacheedaht, Scia'new, T'Sou-ke,
and W̱SÁNEĆ (Pauquachin, Tsartlip, Tsawout, Tseycum) Peoples.

We acknowledge the financial support of the Government of
Canada through the Canada Book Fund (CBF) and the Canada
Council for the Arts, and the Province of British Columbia through the
British Columbia Arts Council and the Book Publishing Tax Credit.

28 27 26 25 24   1 2 3 4 5

Printed in Canada

For everything there is a season, and
a time for every matter under heaven.
ECCLESIASTES 3:1-2

CONTENTS

PREFACE

I am a part of all that I have met…
ALFRED, LORD TENNYSON, "Ulysses"

A LIGHTHOUSE AND A TRUMPET, a monastery, and a submarine. These strange bedfellows emerge among the many colourful threads woven into the texture of my life. The strands evoke themes as diverse as seafaring, scholarship, pilgrimage, and music. Just how this is so forms the warp and weft of a very personal story.

Take the sea, for instance. It has always been a commanding presence. Through my Newfoundland forebears and my proximity to the ocean, I acquired what Farley Mowat once called "a romantic and Conradian predilection for the sea and ships." Whether through direct experience or my own literary imagination, the sea and seafaring have provided me with reference points, cues, and motifs. They have given shape and context to my reflections. So, too, have the other threads in the weave. In writing these reflections, I have simply connected a few enticing dots.

Why gather my memories, anyway? My sole defence is that I have lived—and lived thoughtfully. By gathering echoes in the twilight of my life I have sought form and pattern from among the remembered fragments of experience.

There are those, of course, who maintain that life is nothing but a rolling crap game. Random and ultimately inconsequential. They take their wins and cope with the losses. Even at its best, life can look like a madcap enterprise out of Alice's Wonderland. Yet others recognize meaningful patterns, or believe they do. At the very least, as one disgruntled writer once confessed, life is just one damned thing after another. That, too, can be a compelling narrative thread.

What shapes a life, I have learned, is not so much the fact that certain events have occurred. The importance lies in their meaning. We search for meaning and engage ourselves in the outcomes. That is ultimately the whole point of our journey. In my case, literature and the active life hold it all together. In an age dominated by the technological mindset, it is important to place humans and their values at the centre. That's why the humanities really matter.

Born in the 1930s, between the much-admired "greatest generation" and the populous baby boomers, my birth cohort is popularly referred to as the silent generation. This is because of our alleged uncritical conformity with inherited customs and traditions. Unfortunately, the label sells us short. Like every generation, we too made choices about the social forces in which we found ourselves. As my father put it, "blessed are those who expect nothing, for they shall not be disappointed." We learned early that life owes us nothing.

In literary terms, a compelling icon of my generation is the titular character in J.R.R. Tolkien's acclaimed fantasy novel *The Hobbit*. Not the tiny, fat-tummied, brightly dressed, and furry-footed Bilbo himself, but his world view. "We are plain quiet folk and have no use for adventures," he famously said when the wizard Gandalf was tempting him to undertake a journey into the Unknown. Parochial and comfortably set in his ways, Bilbo saw adventures as "nasty, disturbing, uncomfortable things! Make you late for dinner!" In whimsical moments, I sometimes think of myself as having started out much like the hobbit. But eventually I too grasped unusual challenges and became someone I hadn't expected.

For these reasons, I adhere to the German notion of "the grace of late birth," a term that positions our generation amidst the social conditions under which we evolved. Born too late to have contributed to the great geopolitical and socio-economic upheavals of the twentieth century, we nonetheless engaged with and were shaped by them. My childhood unfolded under the shadow of two global cataclysms: the Great War, from 1914 to 1918, and the Great Depression of the 1920s and 1930s. For us, the war was the stuff of household lore. Our immediate family and friends were among those who had suffered the horrors of the Western Front, who were gassed at Ypres or machine-gunned at Passchendaele. We lived vicariously through their tales of bravado and derring-do, and later of their struggles in the face of economic hardship brought on by the Depression. Their legacy formed the matrix of our growing-up.

In the same way, from 1939 to 1945 we absorbed the second great clash of global armies. Too young to distinguish propaganda from fact, we saw the Second World War in black and white, a struggle between good and evil. It often felt like evil would win. Yet, when our side dropped an atomic bomb on Hiroshima on 6 August 1945, and another on Nagasaki three days later, we woke up to the "atomic age." Newsreels at the Saturday matinee announced the horror: over a hundred thousand killed with a single bomb. Good had won out, but had it? Certainly, our favourite movie idols—Captain Midnight, Hopalong Cassidy, and Deadwood Dick—had shown us, in their serialized two-gun shoot'em-ups, that we could at least live in hope.

Hiroshima marked the beginning of an era of such rapid and ongoing societal change that my generation has been running ever since just to catch up. Now into our eighties and nineties, even the youngest of us has arguably witnessed more global change than any previous generation to date. The arrival of television linked us visually with the rest of the world, while the jet age revolutionized global travel. Then came the space age, when the launch of Sputnik I in 1957 ignited a race that put humans on the moon just a dozen years later. We discovered ourselves part of an ever-expanding physical universe, with all this implied for the new frontiers of science, philosophy, theology, and politics. In fact, everything—our knowledge, our challenges, and our anxieties—seemed to grow exponentially.

During this time, the Cold War, which lasted from 1947 to 1991, triggered a vicious nuclear arms race against the USSR (Union of Soviet Socialist Republics) based on the principle of mutual assured destruction. Its acronym, MAD, said it all. The rivalry culminated in the Cuban Missile Crisis of October 1962, an event that brought the world the closest it has ever come to complete global annihilation.

Such a result would have been a self-fulfilling prophecy of the highest order.

In the 1970s, the digital age exploded onto the world in the form of informatics and the global communications web. Artificial intelligence, developed during the Second World War, began to exceed human intelligence at certain types of problem solving. Many fear it may one day take control. In the medical domain, researchers were learning how to prevent diseases that had once ravaged humanity, diphtheria and polio among them. In 1950, the birth control pill liberated women in ways previously enjoyed only by men. And in December 2020, scientists developed a vaccine against the virus that caused a global pandemic known as COVID-19. It took them less than a year, a tenth of the time normally required for such innovations. Society and its values were shifting rapidly. From the 1960s on, protests against the status quo became the norm as younger generations learned to challenge everything from politics to sexual mores. Literature and music of the period reflected the general malaise.

Behind these breathtaking events stretched a panorama of savage and seemingly unstoppable proxy wars and conflicts that continue to the present day. Waves of refugees, reminiscent of the massive flows of humanity uprooted during two world wars, still seek safety in foreign lands and are often repulsed. Human despair and suffering still reveal the dark underbelly of powerful political institutions. In the twenty-first century, a failed Arab Spring fundamentally recast the power structures of the Middle East, while corrupt dictatorships in parts of Africa threaten to undermine whatever remains of compassion and hope among the wealthy nations of the world. Add to this the devastating effects of global warming, the rise of Trumpism, and Russia's wanton war against Ukraine, and we might be forgiven for thinking our planet was doomed to self-destruct.

I owe much to serendipity, the seeming interplay of chance occasions. The famous polymath Albert Schweitzer, who inspired much of my early thinking, regarded chance as "the pseudonym that God chooses when he wants to remain incognito." As I have experienced it, however, serendipity involves much more than mere happenchance and perhaps less than divine grace. Rather, it results at critical points from a convergence of four factors: preparation, opportunity, positioning, and calculated risk. An operative principle from my naval training—we called it situational awareness— captures the idea. Without it, you risked becoming a cropper. I arrived at this understanding not only through the devices and desires of my forebears, and in particular the stories of their hazardous migrations, but through my own ambitions and promptings as well. In short, what I have undergone and what I have undertaken spring from a series of intriguing "what-ifs."

Had my immediate forebears not come from the tall ships and dories of Newfoundland, I likely would not have messed about in boats. Had I not met the irascible musician Mr. D., I might not have taken up the trumpet or participated in two remarkable tours of Britain's vaudeville stages while yet in my teens. Had I not been brought up during the Second World War, I likely would not have joined the navy and trained for combat, nor taken up the formal study of German and become a professor and historian of German submarine warfare. Indeed, had the unusual opportunity of the 1958 Brussels World Fair not taken me to work in Europe, I would not have met my future wife and soulmate, Anita Borradaile, who inspired my life and shared in my travels, adventures, and scholarly pursuits. Nor, in my later years, would I have picked up the traces of my earliest teachings and inclinations and set off with Anita on the spiritual path that has marked our life together. Winkling out the meaning of such events required that I first get my bearings and chart my path. In nautical parlance, that meant boxing the compass, mastering it before I could steer the ship.

And so, my weavings began. I picked up one thread, then another, and yet another. The individual strands became textures, and the textures became patterns. The pieces of my narrative fell into place during extraordinary wanderings to holy places in Ireland, the UK, Europe, Asia, the Middle East, and Africa, and in the everyday acts of touching the earth and sea. My experiences crystallized in the course of my writing. Indeed, the act of writing evoked critical waypoints in the weave of my relationships to people, places, and ultimate concerns.

The Ojibway author Richard Wagamese speaks for many of us in his book *What Comes from Spirit*. He writes, "It is only by sharing our stories, by being strong enough to take a risk—both in the telling and the asking—that we make it possible to know, recognize, and understand each other."

In writing my life, as an opening line from Goethe's *Faust* suggests, I have welcomed flickering phantoms and congenial spirits from the past.

MLH

FROM THE LIGHTHOUSE

But we weave ourselves and our lives
around such real and yet mythical places.
AL PURDY, "Reaching for the Beaufort Sea"

"FROM THE TOP of Pachena Point Light the view jus' blows yer away." That's how lighthouse keeper Jack Hunting saw it. The old Yorkshireman's face lit up when speaking of his vantage point at the edge of the world. On clear days, he'd quip that you could see "further than God he-self." But when the weather closed down, "you was backs to the wall, wi' nowt to light yer path." There were days on the light's catwalk when you could barely get your head above the weather. Salt spray from the raging sea 43 metres (150 feet) below could reach up and sting you; dense fog could engulf you. Black, overcast night skies could cast a stifling pall. Yet for Jack, this lonely outpost of empire on Vancouver Island's west coast was a beloved home. "How jammy am I?" he'd grin in his old-country brogue. Jack would spend almost thirty years tending the Pachena light and hearkening to the shifting moods of his splendid isolation. An inveterate storyteller noted for his self-deprecating wit, he quickly became my "Uncle Jack."

I spent my early childhood at Pachena Point Light, one of a chain of "keepers of the coast" that stand along the salient of Vancouver Island's western shore. For thousands of years, the area had been inhabited by the Huu-ay-aht Peoples, but we had little contact with them. Keeping to itself, our tiny community comprised Uncle Jack and his wife, Nan, four radio operators and their families, and a couple of linesmen who patrolled the lifesaving trail in order to maintain the landline. Pachena also housed a lifeboat station. My father had been recruited as a radio operator in 1926, but scarcely had he and my mother arrived than they were reposted to Merry Island, on the Sunshine Coast, and from there to Alert Bay, on Cormorant Island in the Broughton Archipelago, where my sister was born in 1930. This was the traditional territory of the Kwakwa̱ka'wakw Peoples, now home to the 'Na̱mgis First Nation. My parents would have found two distinct societies on the island: the 'Na̱mgis community and the settlers. Prominent on the island stood three institutions: Gilakas'la Christ Church, St. Michael's Residential School, and the marine radio station. (When I visited Alert Bay in 2022, the church seemed abandoned and the school had been razed, while the U'mista Cultural Centre celebrated its peoples' rich heritage.) Our family moved back to Pachena Point in 1931, where my father remained officer-in-charge of the radio and radio-ranging station until 1937.

Secluded and remote, Pachena Point offered us few diversions. The closest settlement was the tiny community at Bamfield cable station, reachable by a sixteen-kilometre (ten mile) hike along a rugged, forested trail. Designed by the architect Francis Rattenbury and built in 1902, the station connected Canada by undersea cable to Australia via Fanning Island, some 5,600 kilometres (3,500 miles) distant. The cable completed a vital link in the All Red Line, the global telegraph loop that enabled electronic communications across the British Empire. Since the earliest days of European trade and exploration on the west coast of North America, the region had posed an ever-present danger to mariners. Indeed, waters off the west coast of Vancouver Island quickly became known as the Graveyard of the Pacific. Reason enough to build lighthouses and lifesaving trails.

Our principal link to the outside world was the passenger-freighter *Princess Maquinna,* on her regular runs from Vancouver and Victoria. Coast dwellers regarded her as a faithful old friend. The sound of *Maquinna*'s whistle on approaching Pachena always bode well, for it meant that the seas were calm enough for her to stand offshore and unload gear into a lifeboat. Typically, however, the weather was grey and snarly. At such times, the ship proceeded further upcoast to Bamfield. The personnel of Pachena Point Light would then hike by land to meet the ship and pack the gear back to Pachena on their backs.

A yellowing photograph shows me as a newborn tucked into the lifeboat's stern as it entered the heaving waters of the Pachena Gap. My mother and I were returning from Campbell River, on the east side of the island, where I had been born at the Anglican mission station of the Columbia Coast Mission. While the *Maquinna* hovered close offshore, Uncle Jack skippered the lifeboat through the narrows to where a deckhand was able to toss the little bundle of me right into Jack's waiting hands. My mother followed behind. Our landing proved a memorable family caper that saw me tumbling from either the lower freight hatch or the upper deck. As we approached the shore, Jack hitched the lifeboat onto the cable-hoist that ran from an outcropping of sea rock to the clifftops above. Fading photos illustrate the precariousness of the highline rig and the steadfast confidence of the rowers, who manoeuvred the laden boat into shore while facing forward in a standing position. Such were the stories of how I reached my first home.

HEADING OUT from the western edge of Vancouver Island, a mariner faces the immensity of the rolling ocean. A restless sense of adventure overtakes him as the land recedes behind the vessel's churning wake, and a momentary shiver of pleasure and apprehension tingles along his spine. Such moments have always affected me this way. In his novel *Lord Jim*, the deep-sea mariner Joseph Conrad wrote of "the spurious menace of wind and seas" and "the magic monotony of existence between sky and water." His words evoke for me "the prayerful mood of Evensong" aboard a ship, when the "nights descended on her like a solitude." My feelings precisely.

As a navigator, I have taken my bearings from Pachena; as a pilgrim through life, I have reflected on its meaning. Pachena was just one lighthouse among many on a rugged and dangerous coast. But symbolically, its beacon marked the starting point of my journey toward youth and maturity. In my imagination, its beam scattered the shadows in every sweep, reaching right across the country to my mother's childhood home in Harbour Grace, Newfoundland. As though bred in the bone, the stories my parents told and retold of our life there merge with older mythologies of the region to form a haunting history—one that reads like a liturgy of my life. The late Robin Skelton, a poet and friend from my teaching days at the University of Victoria, captures the feeling in imagery of the area's earliest inhabitants, "long dead / but still stirring / dark leaves / with spirit," and of the piercing call of seabirds, whose screams echo "from headland to headland."

Indigenous Peoples had occupied these impressive shorelines for thousands of years before newcomers—Spanish, French, English, American, and Russian among them—began arriving in increasing numbers in the eighteenth and nineteenth centuries. Their legacies as settlers and colonizers have taken me a lifetime to comprehend. It has become fashionable to stress the rapaciousness of these new-comers. Yet, through the pattern of interwoven cultures that formed as a result of these encounters, we glimpsed the potential for a new, more compassionate world. Indeed, had the early Europeans read John Donne's *Devotions on Emergent Occasions* prior to their arrival here, they might have recognized in the spiritual kinships of the New World a sacred knowledge that their own cultures had long since forgotten. "No man is an island entire of himself," Donne had written in his *Seventeenth Meditation*. "Every man is a piece of the continent, a part of the main." For Donne, land and sea—continent and main—marked the boundaries of earthbound human life. Yet he believed that everything in creation is spiritually connected. "I am involved in mankind," he had written, words that hint at our current efforts toward reconciliation with Indigenous communities.

As a youngster, I once played the role of Captain George Vancouver in a school pageant. I liked to think of him casting a nostalgic and restless eye over the craggy cliffs of Vancouver Island as he sailed for home in 1793. Departing from Friendly Cove (Yuquot), he would have recalled a magnificent wilderness of small islands; remote, sheltered coves with sandy beaches; and dense rainforest. Dressed in my homemade costume, I cast my theatrical eye over the barren school grounds and beheld coastal waters teeming with wildlife. Had I but known at the time, that was Indigenous wisdom: everything is alive and interrelated. The poet Earle Birney, a professor from my student days at UBC, put his own mark on the moment: "Beat then back past Friendly Cove / past wild sweet song from painted mouths / the great birds wooden on the dugout prows / past the white feathers of peace."

Much later, my parents played their part in the great tapestry of immigration to Canada. Bringing their hopes and dreams, their skills, and their unique understandings of how the world works, they set out to make a new life. My father, Norman, escaped the grimy industrial heartland of Birmingham when he left home in 1922 and immigrated to Canada. The coal-driven Industrial Revolution had long since transformed the "green and pleasant land" of William Blake's great hymn to England; it had become the Black Country of England's midlands, with its "dark, Satanic mills." Meanwhile, the First World War had flung open the door to an era of migrations and new beginnings.

During the war, my father had served with the Royal Navy as signalman, a role that suited him and his technical talents well. At the end of it, the prospect of returning to life in Britain's rigidly class-conscious society held little appeal, and he opted to follow his brother Harold to the Canadian frontier of Vancouver, British Columbia. In departing England, he was leaving behind everything he knew: his childhood haunts; his family home; and his mother, Elizabeth. He would always urge me to break out and "hitch your wagon to a star." But when I ultimately did just that, it caused both him and my mother much pain.

My Uncle Harold had started life in Canada by enlisting in the North West Mounted Police in Regina. Later, he would regale us children with exhilarating stories of chasing robbers and bootleggers across the Prairie on horseback while firing his six-shooter, "smoke wagon," from the saddle. When war was declared, he signed on with the Canadian Expeditionary Forces and headed to battle-torn Europe. He was wounded in the fierce battle for Passchendaele in July 1917 and soon after returned to Canada. Ever the raconteur, Harold made the Western Front sound like a fun-filled "barrel of monkeys." With my mother's broom standing in for a rifle and bayonet, he would crawl across the living room floor and up and over the sofa in a mock attack on the German trenches. Then, turning serious, he'd tell of how he once jumped into a huge bomb crater in the middle of a bombardment, only to find a German soldier taking shelter in the self-same muck. Battle-savvy and cautious, they lay eyeing one another for several hair-raising minutes, only to crawl off in opposite directions once the shelling was over.

Such scenarios were *de rigueur* among the "old sweats," and were dramatically rendered in Erich Maria Remarque's iconic war novel *All Quiet on the Western Front (Im Westen Nichts Neues)*. Certainly, our uncle's antics gave us spellbound youngsters a hint of the humanity, and the tragedy, of war. Upon climbing out of his narrative shell hole, he would belt out the popular trench-song of the day, "We Are Fred Karno's Army." Set to the tune of the venerable Anglican hymn "The Church's One Foundation is Jesus Christ, the Lord," the song adopted the slapstick comedy of a popular music-hall entertainer to poke fun at the farce-like hypocrisy of the British Army.

Not to be outdone, my father would jump in with his own stories of life as a signalman in the Royal Navy, and especially of the time he served during the famous raid on the Belgian port of Zeebrugge, in April 1918. The raid was a desperate attempt by Britain to block the Brugge Canal and prevent German submarines from exiting its inner harbour. My father spun a gripping tale of bravado and derring-do replete with bursting shells and machine-gun fire; flag hoists and signal lights; and the dramatic sight of "old *Vindictive*"—the obsolete Arrogant-class cruiser—as she struggled to plug the narrow waters and put British commandoes ashore. I could almost smell the gunpowder.

Yellowing immigration papers tell a lean story of my father's journey to Canada. Travelling alone, he left his home in Smethwick,

Birmingham, and set off (presumably by train) to Liverpool, where he joined with eight hundred passengers taking third-class passage aboard the ss *Canada*. At 9,472 tons, she was a good deal smaller than the BC Ferries vessel *Spirit of Vancouver Island* that runs between Vancouver Island and the BC mainland. In those days, to attract clientele it was common for the shipping lines to advertise the superior quality of their steerage-class accommodations with phrases like "A new cabin class at the old price!" But photos from the time attest to the dark and spartan conditions that my father would likely have experienced.

It took eight days for the ss *Canada* to cross the Atlantic, pass over the top of Newfoundland via Belle Isle Strait, traverse the Gulf of St. Lawrence to the pilot station at Pointe-au-Père Lighthouse, and complete the final stretch to Quebec City, where she delivered my father on 17 September 1922. It was the same route I would follow decades later on concert tours to Britain with the Kitsilano Boys Band, and to my first professional postings in Europe in 1958 and 1961.

The immigration forms in my father's day asked very few questions; they offered only the barest detail to the border agents whose job it was to evaluate the calibre of the immigrant. If a candidate were British, could read, and was reasonably healthy, he was a shoo-in. (The British remained a preferred class of migrant well into the 1960s, when I was an immigration officer). There were no questions asked of my father's qualifications, education, or training. He declared himself healthy and with no intention of returning home. In short, he was cutting the traces for good and setting off in a new direction. He tackled many different jobs until he found his niche in the government's wireless service. An enterprising man with a robust sense of humour, he would regale us with tales of getting established in Canada, which involved living for a time with his brother on a houseboat in Vancouver's False Creek and going door to door selling Hoover vacuum cleaners and pile ointment. His lifetime career with the Department of Transport proved much more promising. Only when settling his estate forty-two years later in 1964 did I stumble upon an explanation for the forty pounds he had claimed on his immigration landing form, a significant amount at the time. On opening his safety deposit box, I discovered a gold sovereign minted in 1901 and immediately recalled his telling me it had been a farewell gift from his mother, so that he "would never ever be broke." Many immigrant stories are as stark and compelling.

MY MOTHER, Winnifred Sheppard, rarely spoke of her past. She could never seem to get beyond the leanest details. Her childhood in the windswept village of Harbour Grace, Newfoundland, struck us as a bleakness of poverty, sickness, and failing fisheries, allevi-ated only by the stubborn love of her family and the surrounding closely knit community. Not even her greatest adventure—the coast-to-coast journey from Newfoundland (still a British colony at the time) to Vancouver Island as an unaccompanied sixteen-year-old orphan—warranted more than a single sentence. She had been placed in the care of the train conductor, and that was that. Her one-liner expressed as much about her culture's deference to authority as it did about the acceptance of hardship. In her view, society had its hierarchies, and our lot were decidedly at the bottom of the pack. Later, she would admonish us children to "know your place" and "never presume on your betters." She had doubtless wanted to spare us the pain of straying outside our social class.

Born of Grand Banks fishermen, mother had early grasped harsh lessons: life is tough and precarious, and often fraught with danger and sorrow. Taking time out to search for one's soul or delve into one's identity did not come into it. You did what you had to, stayed within your social class, and left everything else in God's hands. She had no opportunity to learn otherwise.

Mother's journey to join her eldest brother, Llewellyn, in Victoria, BC, would have begun with a twenty-two-hour ride on a cantanker-ous narrow-gauge railway from St. John's to Port aux Basques, on the west coast of Newfoundland. With luck, she would have found a seat that pulled down into a sleeper. Then it was on to the steam-driven ferry SS *Kyle* for the eight-hour crossing to North Sydney, Nova Sco-tia. At just over a thousand tons displacement, *Kyle* was a tenth the size of BC Ferries' Spirit-class vessels. From there, she would board a colonist train for the week-long trek to Vancouver, followed by a further five hours by CPR ferry to the port of Victoria. (I understand the rigour of the migration, for in my youth I would cross Canada by colonist car four times.) How my mother experienced those lonely miles and what she thought about or feared, we never learned and never dared ask.

A devout Anglican all her life, my mother's faith gave her strength and solace in the face of life's vicissitudes. I still have her copy of the *Book of Common Prayer*, published in 1907, when she was four years old. The tiny volume fits neatly into the palm of my closed hand. I like to imagine her holding the miniaturized gem of Anglican piety when attending St. Peter's Church, where she had been baptized as a babe on 11 December 1903. She doubtless kept it close during her arduous solo journey across the North American continent.

Her own mother, Emma Sheppard, had died in 1905 at the age of thirty-eight, leaving behind her husband, Alexander, and seven children. Soon after, my mother was placed in the care of her Aunt Susan and Uncle Richard. Such arrangements were not uncommon among families accustomed to poverty, illness, and the dangers of the sea. More unusual, perhaps, was Alexander's nineteen-stanza poem to his wife, "My Kind-Hearted Emmie," that dramatized her dying moments. In the poem, Emma beckons each of her grieving children to her bedside for a final farewell and admonition. They are not to fear death, she assures them, for Christ is the navigator and pilot of all voyages and will lead them safely to heaven. More than a private declaration of simple faith, Alexander's poem is a revealing social document that attests to the centrality of religious practice at the time. It is about love, trust, steadfastness, and hope in the peace of God.

Mother's three brothers all went to work in the Newfoundland fisheries, earned their papers, and became skippers. The two eldest, Llewellyn and Ernest, moved to the West Coast after serving overseas in the First World War. The third brother, Albert, followed along later. They timed their departure well, for by the 1930s,

Newfoundland was in the grip of the Great Depression, and the waterfront of Harbour Grace lay practically deserted, the population having dropped to some two thousand souls. Llewellyn, twenty years my mother's senior, sponsored her move from Harbour Grace to Victoria in 1919. At the time, he was working as a ship's officer aboard the 66.5-metre (218-foot) luxury yacht *Dolaura,* owned by the Vancouver Island coal baron Robert Dunsmuir. The yacht was the same size as the Newfoundland ferry SS *Kyle.* Here he rubbed shoulders with a boss reviled by many for exploiting his poorly paid Asian and Afro-American miners in the up-island Cumberland region.

IT WAS Uncle Llew, nicknamed "Skipper," who kept the Newfoundland lore alive. Tucked up close to him as a young lad, I revelled in his yarns. My mother's stories sometimes echoed them. The colourful names of the seascapes and outports he'd sailed as a youth reflected a lively cast of mind that intrigued me: Conception Bay, Blow Me Down, Heart's Content, Comfort Cove, Pass-My-Can Island, Witless Bay, Tickle Cove, and Come by Chance. He liked to spin tales about navigation hazards such as the hidden reefs, or sunkers, that dot the coast and lie in wait for the unwary mariner; and of the serendipity of hidden coves and openings—in places like Chimney Tickle and Muddy Hole—where you could hunker down when pressed by weather or sea.

"Now, let me tell ye, me b'y," he'd begin, as he settled into his armchair by the fire and tapped his old briar pipe. (My mother called it his "dudeen" after the Irish clay pipe *dúidín.* She applied the same term to any old pipe that exuded comfortable domesticity and nautical bliss. This included each of my own pipes—the upmarket Birks Commander I puffed as a young sea officer and the stubby nose-warmer and quirky meerschaum-lined calabash I chewed on in my later navy years.) "Now, let me tell ye," my uncle began again, his dudeen sending aromatic curls into the air. "We was in our dory, fishin' the Banks. Even before the fog rolled in, we could smell 'er. She was like cold steel and tangy salt, b'y. Why, she sticks in the nose 'n chills the spine. Ye couldn'a miss 'er." He paused for effect, drawing me into the spell he always cast. "No wind to heist a sail, b'y, so we took our bearin's on the mother ship and began to row. 'Twern't long afore the fogbank overtook us. Swirls of it, so thick we couldn'a see the other boats nearby, though we sometimes heard a shout or a bit'a conversation. Fog does that, ye know, b'y. Wraps you up and makes you feel disoriented 'n right proper alone. And so we were."

Leaning further into his chair, his eyes gazing toward the mantelpiece with its odd collection of mementos and keepsakes, he'd work his way to the end of the story: "Now, if ye ever gets caught," he'd say, with a suspenseful pause that left me to ponder matters beyond my ken. "If ye ever does get caught... keep yer eyes on the sea 'n hearken to her sounds. If ye do that, then a well-found boat will never let yer down. Trust yer sea sense, 'n she'll see ye through." Skipper often left his lengthier tales unfinished, but he always included a nugget of wisdom for the seafarer I aspired to be. Fog... alone... well-found boat... sea sense. It had obviously worked for him. And now, this long-in-the-tooth sea captain was confiding his wisdom to *me*.

One family character loomed larger than life. My mother's Uncle Richard, a retired schooner skipper who had spent a lifetime fishing on the Grand Banks, blustered his way through many stories. Now shore-bound at home in Harbour Grace, he would pace back and forth, second-guessing the manoeuvres of ships entering and leaving harbour under sail. To his mind, no one but he could get the drill down quite right. With his flaming red beard and sinewed stride, Richard would pace back and forth while calling out to Aunt Susan about the inexcusable incompetence of homecoming skippers. "Hell, Lord, Damn, Susan!" he'd shout, in a burst of consternation. "Hell, Lord, Damn! Jes' look at 'em. Brail up! Brail up! Why, he ain't even catted the anchor yet! And take a look o' that, will you now, Susan. Take a look o' that! He's not even braced up, and his t'gallant's still drawin'. I tell ye, if the dumb bugger don't come to wind right away, he'll land on our damned door!" For whatever else Richard might have been famous, he was renowned in our family for his oaths. I

like to picture him in frustrated high dudgeon. He comforts me in
the knowledge that if I ever wish to cuss my own stupidity or that of
others, I have my inherited mantra to draw on. "Hell, Lord, Damn,
Susan" lay at the soul of it all. Apart from that, he was an altogether
hospitable man. He had, after all, taken my mother in.

THE OUTPORT communities of Newfoundland might well have
served as a template for our tiny community on the west coast of BC
in the 1930s. At least socially, that is. Pachena was an outpost that
gleaned its knowledge of the outside world from the crackling voices
on the station's wireless radio. The wireless operators spoke with
all the passing ships—or at least those with radios. News might also
arrive with the occasional visitor to the outpost, who always found
a ready welcome be they a disgruntled rain-soaked and trail-worn
linesman or a passing missionary. The grey seascape conditioned
all of our lives, as did the mournful foghorn, a constant reminder of
our unusual life at the edge of the world.

But living in isolation didn't mean wearing dungarees all day. My
parents' wedding photo from 22 June 1926 shows the finely dressed
couple in Bamfield, with the cable station in the background; he in
a three-piece blue serge suit and dapper boutonnière, and she in
a white flounced dress reaching just below the knee, with white
kid gloves to above the elbow and a large, broad-brimmed bonnet.
Though formally posed for the portraitist, they appear relaxed and
happy, yet characteristically muted. Mother's large and careless bou-
quet had the air of having just been picked from an English country
garden. In a sense, the scene seems out of synch with the rugged-
ness of the location. Before hiking the trail to their new home—a
little white cabin with government-ordained orange trim perched on
a rock at Pachena—they changed into outdoor gear. Another photo
shows the jaunty couple on the Telegraph Trail, in hardy clothing
and tall leather hiking boots. Ever the proper Englishman, my father
sports a tie and tweed jacket.

Stories and box-camera photos gleaned over the years reveal a
fading record. One browned and curling photo shows the Pachena

staff gathered on the beach in their swimsuits. Nothing in the photo suggests they actually swam in the dangerous waters, though on good summer days the sand of Pachena Bay could look enticing. The upbeat picture shows my mother as youthful, attractive, even coy. One doesn't generally think of one's mother that way, or as someone with a playful private life. Yet there she is, the vivacious young bride, long before my existence was even a twinkle in my father's eye. Written in her own hand on the back of the photo are the breathless words "Boys at the station! My 'brand new husband' was on duty at the time, but came along after four o'clock." They had a whole life ahead of them, but for now, the lighthouse at Pachena was home.

I am often struck by the fondness with which people speak of the lighthouses they have known or admired. Their words invariably include terms of endearment, caution, or enlightened concern. They speak with fondness of the "old Pachena light," or "old Merry Island." Transformed by an arabesque of the pen, the stalwart lights are said to "keep watch," to "stand guard," and to "hold an anchor to windward." In Eastern Canada, the famous Lighthouse Trail along Quebec's St. Lawrence River—La Route des Phares—echoes these thoughts. Promotional material for the forty or more lighthouses that dot the trail, which extends from Rivière du Loup to Gaspé on the south shore and from Tadoussac to Havre Saint-Pierre on the north shore, proudly states: "Since we inhabit a land of the sea, lighthouses are part of our heritage." I have experienced this fascinating region both ashore and afloat.

In poetic terms, these eastern shores watched the passage of Indigenous Peoples for thousands of years, just as they silently witnessed the arrival of explorers like Jacques Cartier and James Cook in the seventeenth and eighteenth centuries. In wartime, lighthouses installed along the river—many now decommissioned and turned into B&Bs—stood guard against the intrusions of German submarines in the Battle of the St. Lawrence, in 1942. Yet as the ads explain, "Once sentinels of our shores, they are now guardians of our maritime culture." Certainly, the ads for Pot à l'Eau-de-Vie (I'll call it Brandy Pot Light) invite us to "stand watch at the gateway to the continent like the last lighthouse keepers." (The French versions merely invite us to spend the night "in the spirit of the last century.") Whether "shining or wrapped in a mysterious haze," the lighthouses beckon the visitor to contemplate the region's history and culture. So too, out here on the Western coast, where I now live.

PACHENA POINT attracted occasional visitors, missionaries among them. It was likely United Church clergy who first broke the ice with us. They had opened the first mission at Bamfield in 1925. We may also have been visited by the Shantymen, an evangelical Christian association who operated a small hospital at Esperanza and regularly braved the BC waters in search of souls. Always dependent on the winds and weather when travelling from their home base in Victoria, the Shantymen would run for shelter wherever they could. If a storm struck in the Strait of Juan de Fuca, they might duck through "The Narrows" into Nitinat Lake; if well past Tofino when adverse weather set in, the idyllic refuge on Hurst Island known as "God's Pocket" offered safe harbour.

On one occasion, a mission boat arrived on a day of unusually quiet waters in the Gap. The skipper-pastor invited the children to sing a hymn. To the pastor's delight, two lads, well schooled by their evangelical parents, gave a lilting rendition of the Sunday school favourite "Jesus Loves Me, This I Know, For the Bible Tells Me So." (The hymn originated in a sentimental 1860 novel in which a character sings it to console a dying child). Then came my sister's turn. Pulling herself up tall and taking a deep breath, she belted out her own home-grown favourite: "Puddin' puddin' puddin', good old Yorkshire puddin' / When it gets too stale to eat, put it in yer boots to warm yer feet." It was a little on the secular side, to be sure, but it had a ring of truth to it. Pressed on the question of where she had learned her hymns, she retorted, "Well, Mommy plays the hymns but Daddy plays the hot stuff." Puddin' was clearly of the hot variety. As for me, I was too young to partake in the hymn-singing.

The yachtsman and travel writer Jonathan Raban once observed that "for people who live on islands, especially small islands, the sea is always the beginning." That was my impression, too, when listening to the grown-ups around me. For them, the sea was the beginning of any journey away from the confines of Pachena and Bamfield. It was the first hurdle to be overcome on any trip out, be it for medical care or for broader human contact. For those left behind, however, the sea held a different meaning. "Islanders also know how the sea goes on and on, in a continuous loop of shoreline and life, without a terminus," Raban wrote. Between these two options—endless ocean and escape from it—lay a dimension that was rarely intimated or discussed—the inscape, or interior life. These were big concepts for a child's mind. Yet strangely, incrementally, I grasped them well, as the process of inwardness had from my earliest days taken form in my body. My first clear childhood memory is of endless pain. Born with a congenital club foot, I underwent numerous operations throughout my childhood and more than a few trips with my mother on the "ol' *Maquinna*" to Victoria and back. In those days, doctors had few options when treating this birth defect, especially as we lived in isolation and couldn't access the necessary regular medical intervention. I wore a heavy cast until the age of three or four and often felt like an outsider, or, in Newfoundland parlance, like someone come from Away. My mother once told me that at the end of many treatments, the orthopedic surgeon came to see me at my Uncle Llew's home in Victoria, where we were staying. When he asked me to walk toward him, I refused. I was frightened, for doctors always meant pain. In all innocence, the story goes, I made a deal. "If I walk to you, will you go away and never come back again?" I asked. The surgeon agreed, and I walked. I never saw him again.

ISLAND LIFE, I learned as a mariner, has a unique and elusive quality to it. The Nova Scotia poet Charles Bruce puts it bluntly: islands, he writes, "are a different country." Bruce's meditations hint at the idea of spiritual independence, a distinct quality of being that distinguishes an islander's way of life. How else, I wondered, could lightkeeper Jack Hunting and his wife, Nan, have survived their twenty-seven years at Pachena light, from 1931 to 1958? Was it the soothing rhythms of daily routines that appealed to them? Or the almost monastic austerity, but without the religion? I have found little evidence of the lighthouse life having produced any contemplatives. Certainly, for Jack it was straightforward, or so it seemed: rise and shine, check and tune the diesel generator, climb the concrete stairs up the hundred-foot tower to polish the lenses, paint the stairs, gaze to seaward, watch the fog, toss at night with the moaning foghorn in one's ear, rise and shine. There might be a birthday party to break the monotony or a hike down the trail to Bamfield to gather supplies. Otherwise, day in and day out, it's the same routine: generator, stairs, lens, gazing, fog, sleep. Each day brought a new tale or two that would grow with every telling. Years later, when I caught sight of Jack at his retirement home in Victoria, I found him repainting the front steps, as a prelude to polishing his shiny windows.

When Jack and his wife Nan took annual leave, they would visit us in Vancouver after we had moved there in 1937. Always jovial and crisply dressed in his three-piece walking-out suit, his ankle boots polished like the lenses of Pachena light, he would talk incessantly, mostly about the ups and downs of lighthouse life. Some said that both he and Nan could talk the hind legs off a jack rabbit. One of his stories—heavy and steeped in sorrow—recounted the unexpected death of his son, Jack. Like other children at the station, young Jack had schooled himself through correspondence courses, twelve years of them, and gone off to study at the University of British Columbia. He was returning home one day aboard the *Maquinna* at the end of one of his terms. On reaching Bamfield, he suddenly collapsed and died. His father told that story again and again, always with increasing amounts of detail as he tried to relive what he had not witnessed, and grasp what he could never quite understand. The depth of his grief calls again to my mind Charles Bruce's poem about the inwardness of islanders: "An absent look, a listening in the eyes / As if they heard, in blood and flesh and bone / Between the breakers' rise and fall and rise / Some word let fall between the sea and stone." The death of a child is a parent's deepest sorrow. Having lost my son to an early and unexpected death, I know that now. Jack Hunting bore his bitter loss, and relived it, handsomely.

STORYTELLING FORMED part of the coastal matrix, and each light station spawned its own tales, fanciful and quixotic, tragic and foreboding. Like a folk song where singers borrow themes where they find them and add and subtract verses on a whim, the lightkeepers' stories were told and retold, endlessly embellished, and ascribed from one light to another. The first assistant-keeper of Pachena—a woman—suffered from depression and threw herself off a cliff in despair; the keeper of another light went mad and painted all the rooms in his house bright red. Yet another chased his supposedly sex-starved female companion out of the house with an axe. And then, in 1942, a Japanese submarine attacked Estevan Light on the tip of Hesquiat Peninsula. The surprising act set off the conspiracy theorists, who spread rumours of its being the work of the Germans, or possibly the Americans, acting under clandestine orders. But as the record shows, the incident was no more than the opportunistic flourish of Japanese submarine I-26 as it passed by on its way back from an otherwise unremarkable deployment near the Aleutian Islands. Following the Japanese custom of shooting up a shore station when leaving a battle zone, the Estevan attack was a case of "farewell with fire." It was a slapstick operation that ultimately tied down a Canadian battalion that might otherwise have been sent to Europe. But it certainly put the wind up the locals, while promoting the image of lightkeepers as gallant guardians of the coast.

Such were the stories and wisdom passed along by the people who wove their way into my earliest years. Given my connection to Canada's two great islands—Newfoundland and Vancouver Island—east and west intertwined at the centre of my being. The East Coast tales I heard as a child, always told in the vernacular, cast a spell. I learned about barren seas, seal hunts, and the cod fishery; and of houses in the outports with widow's walks, from which the women would gaze out to sea to search for their overdue men. I learned how, in an instant, the ocean can change from enticing calm to a voracious and implacable enemy. In time, the Arctic Ocean and the Great Lakes would weave their mythologies as well.

A NEW world of wonders along the Fraser River Estuary greeted me when my family settled in the Marpole neighbourhood of Vancouver in 1937. Here, the Fraser pulsed with marine traffic: deep-sea tramps and coastal freighters puffing upstream to New Westminster, and self-dumping barges and brawny tugs bringing logs to the Eburne mills. Fish boats chuffed everywhere, and the estuary was alive with millions of migratory birds. By contrast, Marpole was slow-paced and bucolic, a place where everyone knew their neighbours, where chickens foraged in back gardens, and where children could range freely wherever they wished. Deliveries of milk, vegetables, and bread arrived each week by horse-cart, though the iceman had a truck. To make a phone call, you'd telephone the operator (whom you knew by name) on a party line, and after a few minutes of friendly banter she'd put you through. Common in the 1930s and 1940s, party lines linked many homes together such that anyone along the network could listen to their neighbours' conversations. The lonely and inquisitive often did.

This little world of Marpole formed a safe if somewhat circumscribed haven in which to grow up. Like many BC towns at the time, it comprised primarily white, Anglo-Saxon Protestants. In short, we were WASPs, though years would pass before the acronym would enter into our evolving multicultural vocabulary. In hindsight, our self-understandings were narrow and parochial, but as far as we and our neighbourhood friends were concerned, we were simply ordinary Canadians.

Until the early 1950s, Marpole was a quiet and sparsely populated suburb of modest, working-class homes. Bushland predominated, or so it seemed to us children as we played freely among the vacant and timbered lots. An eight-block hike down Hudson Street took us to school, to church, and to the shops at the intersections of Oak, Hudson, and Granville streets. Life seemed so casual and safe. A pungent pall from the burners at Eburne Sawmill hung over a cluster of businesses huddled along the river's edge. The mill, crouching beside the wooden bridge that linked Marpole to the agricultural lands of Lulu Island, formed an awkward counterpoint to the ugly Marpole Infirmary next door. On warm days, wheelchair patients, some severely disabled, took the air on the sidewalk. I recall casting furtive glances through ground-floor windows at polio patients encased in the iron lung. They were among the 11,000 Canadians paralyzed by the polio virus between 1949 and 1955, before the Salk vaccine came into use. The thought of spending my life lying encased in a mechanical respirator terrified me, and I rushed off to other vistas.

One of these vistas was the Fraser crossing. From the earliest days of industrial development on the Fraser, wooden swing bridges connected the various deltas, pivoting on demand to allow fish boats and tugs to pass through. One of the fifteen bridges led to Lulu Island and another to the airport on Sea Island. Sea Island was by far the more interesting, for in the 1940s it featured not only an airport but a Boeing aircraft factory producing war planes, or "Bombers to smash the Hun," according to local wisdom. Happy was the child who stopped by as the pendulating wigwag alarm signalled a bridge was about to open, offering a front row view of the parade of splendid vessels, among them seiners and trollers with their narrow pilot houses and "one lung" Easthope diesel engines typical of the West Coast style. For reasons of imitative harmony—a term we didn't know, of course—we children called these jaunty craft putt-putt boats. Nearby, the tiny fire hall, with its two shiny fire engines, lured us into taking detours home from school. On lucky days we caught sight of the firemen as they slid down the magnificent brass pole and dashed off in a wail of sirens. But our fears were not of house fires so much as enemy air attacks. Here, atop the hose tower, stood the air raid siren that so often sent the bitter taste of adrenaline into our throats.

The war years from 1939 to 1945 shaped my childhood understandings in subtle and not so subtle ways. Indeed, the period crystallized in our imaginations what it meant to be a patriot in

Canada. Wartime news and propaganda confirmed our views. The war was quite simply a battle between good and evil. In his radio address to the nation in October 1939, Prime Minister Mackenzie King described it as a "crusade to save Christian civilization." His words stayed with us through the years. We heard the grown-ups talk about it at table. Faced with the fear of invasion by Germany or Japan, our Protestant environment nurtured in us a binary view of virtually everything. Wartime propaganda dealt easily in stereotypes. We shared a low tolerance for human differences simply because everything around us was English. After all, so local arguments ran, hadn't Roman Catholic France "gone down to defeat" in June 1940 without having put up "a real fight?" Wasn't Popish Italy fighting on Germany's side? Didn't Catholic Ireland allow German submarines to land and refuel, and didn't she keep her cities illuminated at night as beacons to guide the German bombers to Britain? And right here at home, weren't the French Canadians refusing to take up arms in defence of the Crown? (In fact, Quebec battalions fought with distinction in this war as they had in the First World War. But no one ever enquired into the sterling record of such Quebec regiments as the famed "Van Doos," the Royal 22nd Regiment.) In our neighbourhood, the war was entirely about saving Protestant Christianity. Historical facts had little to do with it. Fed by a facile and obtuse cast of mind, the civic catechism of prejudice insinuated itself into our childhood world.

MY FIRST school, David Lloyd George Elementary, was a red-bricked Victorian building topped by a Union Jack. I don't recall hearing much about the school's namesake except that he had once been a British prime minister. In fact, Lloyd George had served in that position from 1916 to 1922, the first and only Welshman to do so. Famous for his scathing wit and radical views, he once shook the British establishment by arguing for a tax on land. He was even credited with having single-handedly won the First World War for Britain. Lloyd George is known to have admired the Canadian

Expeditionary Force, particularly after the defining Battle of Vimy Ridge in April 1917. Not surprisingly, none of this seemed to have trickled down to us youngsters.

Each school day began with readings from the Bible, followed by the recitation of the Lord's Prayer (required by the provincial Department of Education) and an uplifting song or two, usually lusty hymns of God and Empire. "The Maple Leaf Forever," considered a Canadian anthem at the time, was about British imperial conquest and told of James Wolfe's planting the Britannic flag on the Plains of Abraham in Quebec City, in 1759. The powers behind that victory had been three: England, Scotland, and Ireland, a truth trumpeted forth through the national symbols of thistle, shamrock, and rose that came to entwine the maple leaf, which symbolized the unity of English and French in British North America. The Battle of the Plains of Abraham, we learned, had been essentially a grand naval victory. None other than Captain James Cook (he didn't hold that rank at the time) had navigated the Royal Navy's fleet up the difficult channels of the St. Lawrence to land the British army and rout General Montcalm and the colony of New France.

"Rule Britannia, Britannia Rule the Waves" was another staple in our song book, and on special occasions we sang Edward Elgar's "Land of Hope and Glory," from his *Pomp and Circumstance* series of patriotic marches. Premiered in Liverpool in 1901, the stirring lyrics instilled in generations of colonials a fiery and unquestioning allegiance to Britain, the "mother of the free." (Conveniently overlooked was Britain's former role in the slave trade and her ruthless exploitation of the land and peoples of India, Africa, and North America.) Naively, but with the utmost conviction, our squeaky little voices proclaimed, "God, who made thee mighty, make thee mightier yet!" This was imperial propaganda at its best.

Sea power was never far from our sense of identity. The dominant figure in our dark, wood-trimmed schoolroom was the oversized, heavily framed portrait of our king, George vi, in naval uniform. All day long, he gazed down at us, bestowing a sense of peace and authority. The ubiquitous Mercator maps of the world that decorated every classroom documented the extent of Britain's influence in huge swathes of pink that marked its dominance over nearly every part of the world. Clearly, being English was a very good thing. And the Royal Navy, we learned, had made it all possible. All of this, we children thought, must have made God very happy indeed.

MY FATHER'S work, in the construction of radio-range stations in communities around the province, kept him away on lengthy absences during the 1940s. As a result, my sister and I grew particularly close to our mother. She quite literally kept the home fires burning. Her daily tasks included cooking and cleaning, hauling wood to the basement, splitting kindling, banking up the furnace for hot water and heating, and filling the role of two parents. The burden of handling heavy domestic chores with few modern conveniences left little scope for what we now call personal development. But she took pride in creating a sanctuary for our childhood. One day, in our absence, a drifter who had just murdered the local pharmacist broke into our home in search of valuables. (We had none.) Our neighbours urged mother to move in with them until the murderer was caught, but she insisted on remaining. She would let nothing jeopardize the sanctity and security of our home.

The little mission church of St. Augustine's in Marpole nourished our mother and became her spiritual home and the centre of her social life. It was here where I first learned the formalities of Anglican devotion, starting with Sunday school at ten o'clock, and Mattins at eleven. Except for the joyous festivals of Christmas and Easter, when we celebrated new life and new beginnings, I found the Anglican liturgy of the day to be a dreary business. The stilted sixteenth-century language of the *Book of Common Prayer* seemed obsessively focused on guilt and the sinfulness of the body, deficiencies attributed to even very young children, whom it also cast as "miserable offenders." Nestled in the pew against the warmth of mother's arm, I could never understand how this brave and loving woman could be so convinced of her unworthiness. Of course, it was all about underscoring the great gulf between us and the perfection of God. Perversely, the church reinforced how godliness and Englishness were one. The Union Jacks at the altar, the memorial plaques with the names of parishioners who had fallen for God, King, and Country, the emphasis on ancient hymns with English motifs, not to mention the obligatory prayers for members of the Royal Family—all converged to remind us of the essential truth that St. Augustine's was, after all, a colonial church.

I recall at age eleven sitting for my written exam in the Anglican catechism, following weeks of after-school instruction. Successful candidates would be permitted to take Communion. It was heavy stuff for a wee lad. "What is thy duty toward God? What meanest thou by this word Sacrament? What are the benefits whereof we are partakers thereby?" I'm sure I hadn't a clue. There is no way I should have passed, yet I did. Our priest must have looked the other way and pushed me through. I came to view these customs as the expression of an already tired and out-of-touch Anglicanism, though, in fairness, we youngsters did gather an understanding of compassion and forgiveness, of a world that was essentially good, and of our moral obligations toward all of creation. Only in the 1960s would I engage in a liturgical and linguistic renewal of my faith that focused on these same moral principles—peace, compassion, reconciliation, love, community, and service—that nourished me throughout my life. Around this time, I put this into action by serving as a lay reader to help prepare *The Book of Alternative Services of the Anglican Church of Canada.*

Significantly, long after the theological conflicts of my childhood had passed, I found that it was the music of the church, particularly the rich hymnody of my upbringing, that sustained my spiritual imagination. From the eighth-century Irish melody "Be Thou My Vision," to the sixteenth-century harvest songs of German poets like Matthias Claudius and Martin Rinckart and the narrative Christmas carols and uplifting hymns of Eastertide, music had slipped into my memory and marked the pathways of my life. I would later play hymns like "Abide with Me" in a concert band that showcased its deep brass harmonies, and find myself uplifted by my children's performance in their school choir of the compelling melody and lyrics of "Morning Has Broken." I was deeply moved by Holst's "Jupiter" (from *The Planets*), the theme song for the 1991 World Rugby Cup, in which our late son Norman played for the Canadian team. The famous hymn opened every game and drew upon the Biblical theme of justice: "Let streams of living justice flow down upon the earth." The music expressed concepts familiar in the restorative justice movement, a cause to which I would later commit myself in full. In sum, music was both medium and message.

As I look back at the comfortable but parochial world of Marpole of the 1940s, I recognize elements of the fringe cultures that even then unsettled me and challenged my world view. Our treatment of Ol' Yip is one such example. Each week, the Chinese gardener would peddle his vegetables door to door in his tinny Model T Ford truck, which he drove up and down the grassy back lanes in silent isolation. We children regarded Ol' Yip, and the other Chinese market gardeners in the area, with a combination of fascination and suspicion, and carelessly referred to them with unfriendly slurs that were common at the time, instead of using their actual names.

Then there was the Jewish family who ran the little bakery near the Odeon Cinema. Curiously, they bore the name Gentile— Gentile's Bakery. I knew from Sunday school that Jews and Gentiles were connected in some difficult historical way, and that Jesus had come into the world to be a "light to lighten the Gentiles" (Gospel of Luke 2:32). But the Gentile family were not Christians, they were Jews. It was all very confusing.

Our racial prejudices had international dimensions. A salient case, the details of which were well known but never discussed, was the refugee ship MS *St. Louis*. One of the last passenger ships to leave Germany in May 1939, the ship set out carrying over nine hundred Jews trying to flee the rising tide of Nazi terror. The *St. Louis* attempted to find a safe country for the refugees—first in Cuba, then in the USA, then in Canada—but was refused at each port. With nowhere else to turn, she was forced to return the passengers to Nazi Germany, where many lost their lives in the death camps. When asked how many Jews might be welcomed to Canada after the war, a senior member of the Canadian government replied, "None is too many." Forty-five years later, those words became the title of Irving Abella and Harold Troper's compelling study of Canada and the Jews of Europe in the years from 1933 to 1945. Despite interventions by many influential Canadians (including the members of several Protestant congregations) in support of Jewish immigration, Canada's antisemitic politics prevailed. Had the citizens of BC been aware of the words in support of Jewish immigration being expressed in such papers as the *Globe and Mail*, *Toronto Daily Star*, and *Winnipeg Free Press*, I believe they would not have been moved by them.

The East Asian residents of British Columbia fared little better. Two of our Marpole neighbours, the Bantu brothers, lived an ascetic life in a shack beside the Japanese Language School and made a living trucking firewood from the Eburne Mill to customers in the Marpole area. They lived their entire lives on the margins, never really trusted by the locals and without hope of ever being accepted by white society. It was the same for the Japanese families who dotted the shores of the estuary, and worse, in fact, once the country was at war. Soon, the school would be "abandoned" by the Japanese and taken over by the local Boy Scout troop. As a member of St. Augustine's 22nd Cub Pack, I entered the school one day shortly after its owners had left. Vandals had wreaked havoc. The terrible images still grip me to this day: broken furniture, doors ripped off their hinges, and savaged blackboards with Japanese writing. It was a desecration both disturbing and enigmatic.

Of course, we cautiously tolerated the German-speaking gardeners who worked at the nursery near the fire hall. Written in large letters across the wall of the lofted stable that served as their barn were the words "The Swiss Gardeners," signalling that they were not the enemy aliens many suspected them of being, but Swiss neutrals. Outside the boundaries of home, school, and parish, the world seemed a threatening place.

SHAPING STEREOTYPED images of the enemy was not just the work of officials. Cartoonists, comic book writers, and filmmakers played their part. As young boys immersed in pulp literature aimed at children, we had few doubts about what would happen if either the Germans or the Japanese should invade Canada. It would be pure terror—a hellscape of heads crushed under Nazi jackboots or bellies slit open with samurai swords and bayonets. Publications like G.A. Henty's jingoistic and racist stories for youth promoted the British imperial ethos of world domination, while the *Chums Own Annual* fed us exquisite adventures of clever British schoolboys capable of outsmarting the most cunning German spies. American comic books highlighted the prowess of the all-American soldier at defeating the attacks of German and Japanese forces. In Canada, the Johnny Canuck comic series dished up a home-grown version of wartime action stories, except you had to colour each "action-packed" edition yourself.

There were other signals as well. The funnies in the daily news-paper, the newsreels at the Saturday movie matinees, and Hollywood's formulaic war movies all propagated crude stereotypes of the enemy Other that inflamed our suspicion of non-British cultures.

The endless barrage of substandard information underscored for me the need for watchfulness and preparation. Above all else, we feared air raids. School exercises prepared us for them. The front page of *The Star Weekly* newspaper of 28 March 1942, for example, boasted a coloured map demonstrating how Canadian cities, including Vancouver, could be the target of attacks by German aircraft launched from carriers on the Atlantic coast. The hype was sheer nonsense, for Germany had no aircraft carriers. And in any event, such long-range aircraft were beyond imagining. The more realistic air threat came from Japan, or so the propagandists would have us believe.

The day the war-bomb salesman knocked on our door further raised my level of alarm. Had I realized he was selling war *bonds,* on behalf of the Canadian government, I would not have paid it much attention. But war bombs were another matter. Peering out from behind the kitchen door, I observed the agent and my mother sitting together at the dining room table discussing the different types of bombs she could purchase to help us win the war. I shivered with excitement as I began formulating plans for where we might hide them.

We all felt we were in the fight—even at school. On Friday mornings we'd march to the teacher's desk to receive iodine pills to combat goiter and war-savings stamps to combat the Hun. Twenty-five cents got you a postage-stamp–sized picture of a tank; a soldier with fixed bayonet; a fighter plane; or, best of all, a battleship. We'd paste the stamps into a little booklet as a record of our contribution of the war effort. Our teacher was the purveyor of stamps and pills alike. Government bulletins urged us to "get in the scrap" by contributing to donation drives organized to collect kitchen utensils and other scrap metal for the manufacture of warplanes, while across the nation, families tended their backyard "victory gardens" to produce food for themselves and our troops overseas. The rationing of foodstuffs and gasoline, another government imperative, caused hardship for many, but this too we learned to accept as a necessary wartime sacrifice. Meanwhile, King George, from his elegant frame, beamed down approvingly upon all that we did.

As the war progressed, our fear of air attacks grew, and our days were occupied with preparing for such an event. At school, pails of water, stirrup pumps, and buckets filled with sand were positioned at strategic points along the hallways. In regular air raid drills, we learned how to take shelter beneath desks and tables and to evacuate the building in single file lines along the schoolyard hedge. The warning siren at the fire hall was sounded regularly to accustom us to responding without panic. At home, we kept emergency supplies in the basement and covered the windows with tarpaper at night to create a blackout, a practice that brought the threat uncomfortably close to home.

Once evening stands out. Returning home from a church gathering, mother and I walked alone in eerie darkness, the streetlights and houses completely blacked out. At one point, we were stopped short by the alarming sight of our neighbour in an ARP (Air Raid Patrol) outfit. His ARP equipment was rudimentary: steel helmet, flashlight, whistle, ARP armband, and a wooden ratchet-wheel noisemaker (like the kind rattled at New Year's Eve celebrations). Around his neck hung a gas mask, suspended in a little cardboard box. The mask disturbed me. It reminded me of the stories I'd heard from relatives about mustard gas attacks in the First World War and the violent deaths and disfiguring injuries our soldiers had suffered. Could the Japanese do the same thing in Marpole? The grown-ups seemed to think they would.

Japanese Canadians paid the price for this myth making. The confiscation by the Canadian government of their homes and businesses, and their relocation to detention camps in the British Columbia Interior, is a matter of historical record. For me, the episode caused another layer of distress brought on by the war, one that I struggled to make sense of. I recall a family outing to Burnaby one Sunday by streetcar. While changing trams near the exhibition grounds at Hastings Park, we chanced upon the shocking sight of Japanese internees enclosed behind a barbed wire fence. Alighting from the rail car, I saw Canadian soldiers with fixed bayonets marching up and down in front of the barrier. We were so close I could have touched them! The memory haunts me to this day, its horror muted by time and the uncertainty of early childhood impressions. On that day I saw faces, some desperate or blank, some that stared with questioning eyes. I saw fingers clutching the wire grids of the sharp and imposing fence. I remember feeling reassured by the presence of my parents, yet from among the crowd I heard the voices of people who seemed keen to put the situation into its "proper" focus: "They're traitors and spies," someone shouted. "They kept naval uniforms and rifles on their fish boats," said another. "They were going to invade us!" "Serves 'em right." But the faces I saw on the other side of the fence weren't the distorted caricatures of comic books and movies. Here, for the first time, I was seeing the real face of the enemy, only to discover a group of people who seemed compellingly similar to my own family. These citizens were "the enemy that never was." Those words formed the title of the Canadian historian and former internee Ken Adachi's definitive study of the Japanese Canadians.

Shortly thereafter, we made a visit to the former Japanese fishing village of Steveston, at the mouth of the Fraser River. The Japanese called it Sutebuseton, a pronunciation more amenable to their spoken language. I still have a vivid memory of that day. The reason for the trip was to celebrate with one of our Marpole neighbours who had brokered the deal of a lifetime by acquiring a lovely fish boat at a bargain-basement price. In fact, the vessel was one of thousands seized or abandoned during the Japanese internment. Steveston resident Unosuke Sakamoto later spoke about the panic that descended on the Japanese community in 1942 as the government officials closed in: "By that time," Sakamoto said, "they all knew they had to sell their boats cheap, so they sold them, with tears." He spoke of other vessels being peddled by government agents to their preferred customers: "White men and Indians chose the boats they liked."

During this time, an entire fleet of impounded boats lay moored at the village floats in Steveston and upstream at Annie Dyke. Another resident, Hideo Kokubo, lamented stoically, "all those years of work just gone. But as it was the war, there was nothing anyone could do, was there?" Like Ken Adachi, Sakamoto and Kokubo were Canadians of my generation. The experience of having their boats taken away, Kokubo said, "was like being cut off at the root."

As we picked our way along the boardwalk on that sunny spring day, I was struck by the unsettling silence in the village. At one point we passed an old fisherman seated on a wooden bench outside his shack, moaning with grief. His keening both startled and frightened me, evoking a loss I could not fathom. I had never seen a grown-up weep. I felt the hand of one of my parents pull me up short. "He won't hurt you," someone said. "He's old and weak." Behind us, the broad, muddy arm of the river lapped at the hulls that bobbed in the current while members of our party laughed and toasted our success at having gotten "the Japs" out.

JOURNEYS BETWEEN Vancouver and Victoria on the CPR Princess ships always reminded us of the enemy's omnipresence. We travelled the route quite frequently in those days. The sense of danger aside, the five-and-a-half-hour voyage delighted us youngsters, giving us a taste of seafaring in a grand liner. The ships were beautifully appointed, with elegant staterooms and panelled lounges, silver-service meals, and liveried stewards and waiters. During the war, vessels like the SS *Princess Joan, Princess Charlotte,* and *Princess Nora* were painted grey and armed with a deck gun, in case of attack by the Japanese. They reminded us of the troopships often featured in newsreels. War seemed thrillingly close to our secure world. If the enemy ever came, we youngsters agreed, we'd surely be ready. When the war finally ended in 1945, it did not spell the end of bigotry. Happily, society changed for the better in the postwar years, as legislation on immigration, multiculturalism, and bilingualism was introduced that opened up new ways of seeing and experiencing our world.

I needed perspective in my early adolescence, and I got it when my dad introduced me to flying. At twelve years of age, I admired my pilot-father enormously. Technically gifted, he had since the late 1930s been engaged in building radio-range and glide-path systems for instrument navigation on the coast and in the Interior of the province. Later he would become officer-in-charge of Vancouver Aeradio, part of the network of air and marine communications stations operated by the Canadian Department of Transport. I loved his stories of "flying the beam," a major innovation at the time that involved using a low-frequency signal to safely guide pilots through low-visibility conditions. Dad would set up the signal and then fly each station's radio-range to check its accuracy. I was in awe of the work he did building range stations at places with intriguing names like Penticton, Princeton, Keremeos, Sidney, and Sandspit. I visited them all in later years. Each had its own personality and call-sign and, like the lighthouses, its own collection of catchy yarns. I can still hear the sounds of the radio transmitters clicking away in automated Morse code, sending out their station's call signs and the As and Ns that marked the edges of the beam.

Early on, I read with my father Wolfgang Langewiesche's famous instructional manual *Stick and Rudder: An Explanation of the Art of Flying*. Published in 1944, it was arguably the first book to reveal in graphic and accessible language the mysteries of piloting an aircraft. Among the insights I gleaned from it was the intriguing mantra "Flying is done largely with the imagination." The manual stressed the importance of foreseeing the consequences of one's decisions and actions. With only the most basic instrumentation, pilots had to learn to fly intuitively, "by the seat of your pants," it counselled. Indeed, the pressure on your butt was a surefire aid for gauging whether you were rising or falling. The aircraft became an extension of the pilot's senses. On winter evenings, my father would set up in our living room a mock console of a two-seater aircraft, complete with stick and rudder, for me to practise with under his watchful eye.

One day in the spring of 1948 we took to the air in a double-winged de Havilland Tiger Moth. We set off from a grassy field at what is today the Vancouver International Airport. I can still smell the wax on the gleaming, canvas-covered fuselage and recall the anticipation I felt as I buckled into the cramped cockpit and closed the canopy over my head. Dad took the Moth's aft cockpit, while I, in splendid isolation, sat up front. Both seats contained instrumentation and equipment for flying the aircraft, but I was to keep my hands off it unless otherwise instructed. We communicated through a rubber hose. "Brakes set ... gas on ... throttle set ... trim set," Dad recited as he ran through the checklist in preparation for the taxi and takeoff. At the word "contact," the ground crew spun the propeller of the 1931-designed biplane, and the 150-horsepower single engine sprang into life. It was all I could do to contain my excitement and anticipation. All revved up, we awaited clearance from the tower. Soon, an air traffic controller flashed his green light at us. Dad acknowledged by wagging the rudder, for in those days light aircraft didn't carry radios. Then he opened the throttle, and we rushed full bore down the grassy stretch until, at a speed of forty knots, we lifted off. Alone with my thoughts and feelings, I watched the needles on the gauges move as we rose above the airport and headed westward over the Strait of Georgia. Gradually we edged into the left-hand circuit and overflew the Fraser River estuary at our maximum cruising speed of sixty-seven knots.

Marvelling at the vista unfolding below me, I gazed over the fabled estuary where a powerful river meets the sea. Plumes of billowing silt rose from the river mouth to extend as far as six nautical miles westward toward Vancouver Island. Tumbling down from waterways and ledges high in the Rocky Mountains some 1,300 kilometres (808 miles) to the east, the silt had accumulated over centuries to form huge alluvial deltas. One of the largest, Sea Island, was the home of Vancouver Airport, at just 1.8 metres (6 feet) above sea level.

On another occasion, we flew eastward to participate in an aero club jamboree. As the Tiger Moths were all in use, we flew a Fleet Canuck. Like the Moth, the Canuck was Canadian–built. I liked its feature of side-by-side seating, which made our conversation and companionship so much easier. We had much to chat about as we wended our way over the broad area of the Fraser. Dad instructed me in the principles of flight and of interpreting the readings on the dials, and answered my pressing questions. "Always keep an eye out for suitable landing spots for an emergency landing in case of engine failure," he counselled with a conniving wink, while explaining the fine art of gliding. I never doubted his skill and competence at flying. Indeed, I took pride in scanning the ground for possible landing sites and presuming to offer him my advice. Flying together made for wonderful bonding.

Meeting up later at the pre-arranged farmer's field, now known as Langley Field, the club members would indulge in some old-fashioned barnstorming and hijinks. The Tiger Moths, which always upstaged the others with their daring antics, would line up six abreast along the start line for the relay race, engines growling and pilots keen. At the starting gun they would roar forward into a short-distance takeoff, make a deft loop of the field, and return to mid-field, landing as close to the starting line as possible. Then, with the brake set and engine still running, the pilot would quickly unbuckle his shoulder harness and scramble out of the tight-fitting cockpit to make room for his teammate to jump in and complete his own circuit, followed by the third pilot and the fourth, until each member of the team had had a go. The team with the shortest time won.

Then came the balloon-busting competition: toss a balloon out at a predetermined height and dive about while trying to bust it with the propeller until (if I recall correctly) the aircraft reached five hundred feet. The toilet roll contest came next, which involved tossing out a roll at an altitude of fifteen hundred feet and trying to cut it into as many ribbons as possible as it unrolled its way down. It was all quite madcap. Surprisingly, I don't recall any mishaps. At the end of the day, the participants received mock heroic certificates praising their skills as kings of the ground loop and knights of the rubber stick. Flying home, my father and I would recap the day's fun while relishing the stunning views of the river, strait, and island, and the unknown worlds that lay beyond.

A rich palette of colours interweaves BC's coastal waters. Their textured interplay constantly heralds a coming change of mood or shift in the cross-currents of wind and water. Experiencing them ignites in me a strong desire to venture away from the shore, past bays and passes, to channels and straits, and outward to the open sea. Coastal sailors frequently dream of going deep-sea. I still do, even in my eighties. Seafaring invites you on a two-fold voyage: one to the external world of the senses and another into the human soul. Such thoughts come easily when sailing a taut little yacht point-to-point under ideal conditions, or while creaming along with finely tuned rigging and sails through sun-soaked, shore-lined waters. In my dream, this magnificent experience could last forever, until reaching exotic lands.

2

CHORD PROGRESSIONS

But I struck one chord of music,
Like the sound of a great Amen.
ADELAIDE A. PROCTER, "A Lost Chord"

MYTH AND magic were the furthest things from our minds as our ship churned and twisted its way across the Atlantic in May 1950. Scarcely recovered from her service as a troopship in the Second World War, the twenty-thousand-ton RMS *Samaria* was now a well-worn, thirty-year-old Cunard passenger liner, pounding her way through heaving and darkening seas. As I looked out past the French doors of the tourist class lounge and across the stern, I could see nothing but an eternity of grey and growling waves. And to make matters worse, Mr. D. had just brought down his baton on the overture to Wagner's opera *The Flying Dutchman*.

I was travelling as part of a thirty-nine-piece concert band of musicians, aged fourteen to twenty, en route for a four-month tour of concert halls in Britain and Holland. Green around the gills and fighting the ship's heaving motion, we were now tightening every nerve to capture the passion of Wagner's theme: a ghost ship doomed to sail the seas forever with a captain who gambles his soul's salvation. The score of *Der fliegende Holländer* had never felt so demanding. Whoever laid eyes upon this phantom ship, legend had it, would die. Feeling as we did, the sighting would have been a blessing. But there we were, a powerful musical score before us and a wretched sea all around.

The Kitsilano Boys Band—known as the Vancouver Boys Band during its European tours—was and remains a Canadian legend. Billed as "The Most Famous Boys Band in the World," it was a Canadian phenomenon from its founding in 1928 to the death of its founder in 1982. The band performed a breathtaking range of music, covering everything, as the glittering advertising promised, "from Sousa to Boogie-Woogie." Classical works from Bach to Grieg and Rachmaninoff to Holst spotlighted brass and woodwinds playing passages originally scored for symphonic strings, all of it backed by rich ensemble playing.

Our band always featured brilliant soloists. I still recall the soaring and vivacious triple-tongued trios of trumpets and the stellar performances of the trombone and euphonium. Audiences thrilled to jazz numbers that featured ensembles of masterful instrumentalists on tenor saxophone, trombone, trumpet, clarinet, and drums. Critics from London to Glasgow and Dublin to Scheveningen praised the band's brilliance. "They can swing a hot number with Benny Goodman at his best, and follow it with a classic from Chopin," wrote one. "The versatility of the band is as remarkable as the extensiveness of their repertoire," another proclaimed. Admired everywhere we went for our maturity, professionalism, and superb showmanship, the band bore witness to the potential of youth and to the inspired leadership of its founder, Arthur W. Delamont.

"Mr. D.," as his boys have always called him, was an extraordinary character. With his shock of white hair, his commanding presence, and his firm and expressive baton, he was at once charming and irascible. Scowling and overbearing during a tough musical passage, he could burst into a beatific smile once we had gotten it right. He projected a mix of wit, cutting criticism, good humour, understated praise, and artistic vision. He was demanding. It was said that he could get music out of a stone, and God help you if you were the stone. You always felt you had little choice; it was either shape up or ship out. I did my damnedest to shape up. I had just turned fourteen, and this was my first concert tour.

My parents had always kept me close to home. I was a scrawny little fellow who walked with a marked limp. My vulnerability, which I would soon outgrow, had made them overly protective. Except for a week of church camp, I had never been away from home. Now they were letting me go for the first time. Really letting go. With courage and foresight, my parents were giving me room to grow. My musical career had begun rather inauspiciously a few years earlier, when my school music teacher had tried me out on an old cello and judged me bereft of talent. She would have been astonished at my success as a brass player under Mr. D.'s baton.

Brass had always been my inspiration anyway. I had begun with an old bugle from among my Uncle Harold's First World War memorabilia, then graduated to a well-worn valve trumpet from a neighbour whose son had given up in disgust. That old trumpet served me well in my school band and helped prepare me for my first meeting with Mr. D., which turned out to be a life changer. It happened during one of his ensemble lessons at Point Grey Junior High. He was a demanding teacher, and one day he pulled an old upright alto horn out of a canvas bag that reeked of garlic and old boots, and urged me to have a go. It was more of a directive than an invitation. Unknown to me at the time, this was his style when he wanted to rebalance his bands by shifting a player from one section of instruments to another—from alto to bass, for example, or from trumpet to alto or baritone. Alto had a different embouchure and pitch than the trumpet, but the fingering was the same. On this occasion, I gave it my best and found that I loved the horn's full-bodied tone and its alto-tenor range that made it well suited for the French horn parts in symphonic works. Mr. D. pushed me to levels I could barely manage, and after some months I traded the upright horn for a French-made concert mellophone.

I soon realized that Mr. D. was grooming me for the Kitsilano Boys Band and its 1950 concert tour of the UK. The trip would be the band's first tour since its heydays in the 1930s, before the war. And I would be among the youngest in the group, and the least experienced. I needed ensemble experience, fast. Immediately, I found myself rehearsing five evenings a week with four different concert bands: the Kitsilano Boys Band, the West Vancouver and North Vancouver concert bands, and the Keefer Street Band in East End Vancouver. The latter three were feeder bands from which Mr. D. drew his talent. All the while, my private lessons and daily home practice continued. I made the cut.

THUS BEGAN one of the most formative experiences of my life. I had never travelled by train before—much less by colonist car. Yet this had been the band's mode of travel in the overseas tours of 1934, 1936, and 1939. Designed for the transport of immigrants arriving in East Coast ports from Europe, colonist cars provided a no-frills option for transcontinental train travel by offering only the most basic facilities. They were essentially rolling-stock live-aboards. Our group of forty, plus the mothers of two of the boys who would serve as cooks, travelled as a self-contained unit in two rail cars turned end on end to join their galley kitchens together for a larger cooking space. The rail cars struck us as rather quaint. A combination wash place and gentleman's lounge, it offered communal washing and toilet facilities, a padded smokers' bench, and large brass spittoons for tobacco chewers. It was right out of the nineteenth century.

Life aboard the train quickly fell into a daily routine. In the morning, Mr. D. would wake us with a rousing reveille on the cornet as he passed through our cars. While we washed and dressed, the porters would arrive to fold the bunks into sitting compartments, trailed by a contingent of boys whose turn it was to set up the folding tables and put out the cutlery and plates. To lighten the cooks' unenviable load, we limited our fare to cold meals. Then, it was on to our first practice of the day, which entailed a period of individual practice and section rehearsals, a discipline we called woodshedding. The term made sense, for we were well accustomed at home to chopping blocks of wood into kindling for the stove and furnace. Woodshedding meant hard slogging, sweat, and occasionally tears. The rest of the day would include at least one and sometimes two rehearsals.

It was essential that we stay sharp for the performances scheduled along the way.

Crossing the country by train for eight days afforded a rich introduction to our nation's vast and largely uninhabited regions, its scattered settlements, and isolated way stations. I was so preoccupied with the view that I quite forgot I was leaving home and family for almost half a year. As we rolled along, I thought of the early settlers who had travelled the same route by steam train, ox cart, and horse, but in reverse order to our eastward passage, which took us through Revelstoke, Calgary, Swift Current, Regina, Brandon, Kenora, Port Arthur, Toronto, and Montreal, before our final stop in Quebec City. In cities where we stopped to play a concert, the CPR trainmen would shunt our two cars onto a siding. Here the railyard became our home patch until, at the end of the evening concert, we'd hitch up to the next train passing through and continue our journey.

At stations with a planned stop of an hour or more, the band would tumble onto the platform to perform a few numbers for a break. We young ones, known as the little fellas, hustled about selling our souvenir postcards of the band on the steps of Vancouver's courthouse. Whistle stops were brief community affairs, bustling hubs of activity where locals could "see what's up," get a fresh newspaper, and socialize with their friends while passengers and freight were loading and unloading. The stops gave us a taste of local culture and of the frontier mindsets that formed our national mosaic. Compared with what we were about to encounter abroad, Canada was a rough-cut work in progress.

We reached Quebec City on 23 May 1950 and boarded the RMS *Samaria*. None of the band members had travelled deep-sea before, and the ship was the largest most of us had ever seen. Launched in 1920 and converted into a troopship in 1941, some of her amenities had been restored when she returned to passenger use in 1948. Yet she retained much of her wartime character. Our tourist-class accommodation offered large dormitory-style cabins furnished with two-tiered curtained bunks. Long tables in the dining hall seated upwards of twenty per table. Fourteen hundred passengers dined in two sittings. We were a colourful group of travellers. Among us were pilgrims en route to Rome, shepherded by a group of priests and nuns; and war brides with their young children in tow, anticipating their first visit home to meet grandma and grandpa since the end of the war.

After years of wartime rationing, the food was munificent. For lads like me who had rarely eaten out except for a rare trip to the fish-and-chip shop, the splendid menus with their multiple courses and range of choice were paradise. Some boys attempted to sample everything, only to be admonished by our cockney waiter: "'t'isn't done, sir; 't'isn't done." He regarded it as part of his job to instruct us in the behaviours appropriate for young gentlemen. My first dining experience became a fiasco when I noticed the menu had no prices. I knew the items would be well beyond my pocket change and became seized with anxiety. While the other lads indulged their appetites, I quietly nibbled at the abundant crusty rolls and pats of butter that graced the table. Finally, on the second day, a senior lad asked why I wasn't digging in like the others. "Don't have the money," I shrugged, embarrassed. "Good heavens, man," he guffawed. "It comes with the ticket!" I dined lavishly thereafter.

With all lines cast off, our ship headed down the grand St. Lawrence toward the pilot station at Pointe-au-Père (Father Point), about a hundred nautical miles away near Rimouski. Standing 31.4 metres (103 feet) tall, the famous Pointe-au-Père light beckoned us on our outbound voyage. There, we would drop our pilot and head to the open Atlantic via the Strait of Belle Isle that stretches between Labrador and Newfoundland. Little could we have known what this part of the journey meant to Mr. D. As we departed from Quebec, a darkness seemed to weigh on him that was still noticeable the next morning at rehearsal, after we'd left Pointe-au-Père. Finally, we learned the reason for his distress. "Boys," he admonished us quietly, "remember the *Empress of Ireland*."

Mr. D. himself would never forget it. Thirty-six years earlier, he was among the survivors of the worst marine disaster ever to occur in Canada, when over a thousand people died. On 28 May 1914, the

28,000-ton CPR steamship *Empress of Ireland* had steamed out of
Quebec City en route to London, England. Like our own trajectory
aboard RMS *Samaria,* the *Empress* would have proceeded down-
stream to the pilot station at Pointe-au-Père Lighthouse and on to
the Atlantic. Among the thousand or more passengers on board
were 170 members of the Salvation Army, including a thirty-nine-
piece concert band. They were travelling to London to attend the
Third International Congress of the Salvation Army. Twenty-two-
year-old Arthur W. Delamont and his twenty-five-year-old brother,
Leonard, both accomplished cornet players, were among them. On
departing Quebec City, the band had performed an impromptu concert on deck—just as we would do years later. They had ended with
the old Salvationist hymn "God Be with You Till We Meet Again," by
Jeremiah Rankin. The hymn was a declaration of the guiding power
of faith and hope through the human journey: beginnings, anticipation, crisis, and closure. It was a prayer that God might "Keep
love's banner floating o'er you [and] Smite death's threat'ning wave
before you."

The hymn was both a blessing and a foreshadowing of all that
followed. Thick fog blanketed the lower St. Lawrence that day.
Before the advent of radar, gyro compasses, and GPS, ships would
"feel their way" through the fog by means of dead reckoning, or
"deduced reckoning," sounding their warning foghorn as they went.
The method involved calculating the ship's position based on its
rate of speed, the direction of its course, and the time elapsed from
one point to the next. By vectoring in the effect of tides and current,
the navigator would arrive at an estimated position on his chart. It
was an exacting procedure that demanded the utmost in skill and
concentration from the navigator and from every member of the
watch-on-deck, as they strained to penetrate the murk while listening intently for the sounds of other vessels.

By this means, having dropped off her pilot, the *Empress of Ireland* was still groping her way through the fog near Pointe-au-Père
at 2:30 AM on 29 May when she was struck abaft the starboard bow
by the inbound collier *Storstad.* The crash proved fatal. The collier

penetrated the *Empress's* hull to a depth of 4.6 metres (15 feet), and within fourteen minutes she went to the bottom, taking 1,015 passengers and crew to their graves. Unimaginable horrors beset the passengers and crew as they tried to escape. Asleep on the lowest decks of the ship, the Salvation Army group and other third-class passengers faced a virtually hopeless situation. A few, like Mr. D., managed to scramble to the boat deck and over the side; others, as divers later discovered, became stuck while attempting to escape through the portholes, and drowned. Mr. D.'s brother Leonard gave his life jacket to his mother, who survived. He was never seen again.

Divers who first descended on the wreck, 39.5 metres (130 feet) down, reported sights of unspeakable horror as they attempted to retrieve the bodies. Word of the disaster spread quickly, triggering shockwaves across the country. News reports focused on the unexpectedness and the swiftness of the ship's death-plunge to the seabed. Eventually, through survivors' recollections and reports of the Board of Inquiry, a fuller picture emerged of the events of that fateful night in May 1914. Yet, sooner than expected, the story of the catastrophic loss of the *Empress of Ireland* began to fade from public memory. War was afoot, and news of the slaughter on the Western Front soon dominated the media scene. And like today, the *Titanic* disaster of 1912 held stronger news appeal.

Some, like the directors of the Maritime Museum of Rimouski at Pointe-au-Père, held on to the memory and found creative ways to honour the victims. For his part, Mr. D. took a very personal approach. For the rest of his life, he saw to it that the spirit and tradition of the lost musicians would live on in new generations of concert bands. He achieved this with an outstanding blend of Salvation Army musicianship and North American showmanship. Together, these became the distinctive trademark of Canada's Kitsilano Boys Band.

THE RICH brass and woodwind sound of the Kitsilano band was conditioned as much by instrumentation as by style. In North America, to choose but one example, concert bands tended to prefer the trumpet as the lead solo instrument, as exemplified in the clarion brassiness of the "Sousa style" popularized by the American band-leader John Philip Sousa. British bands, by contrast, chose the cornet, which delivered a softer, more mellifluous sound. Mr. D.'s genius lay in blending the two approaches. He drilled his boys in the art of hymnic playing by insisting they practise long, sustained tones, and by selecting from among our repertoire numbers that featured sostenuto playing—the performance of sustained notes and phrases stretched to their fullest value. Our instrumental sections became skilled at forming a single, unified "voice" and never breaking a phrase, not even for a breath. Mr. D. encouraged his young musicians to listen intently to each voice in the ensemble. And while emphasizing the importance of maintaining a full range of tonal colour, he also insisted on brilliant attack, sensitive interpretations, and dynamics, dynamics, dynamics. It was this blend of "Sousa" and the British band style that made the Vancouver Boys Band stand out from the others. We drew our strength from our demanding teacher and by paying tribute to our predecessors of the 1930s by passing their legacy forward to new generations of young players.

I can imagine how, on departing Montreal for the band's first tour of the UK in June 1934, Mr. D. would have hinted at the story of the *Empress of Ireland* as they passed by the Pointe-au-Père light. He never, ever, spoke about it at length. Once in Britain, the band would distinguish itself grandly by winning a high-level national competition against adult musicians in some twenty-one bands. One of the assigned test pieces was Handel Parker's hymn "Denton Park." On listening to the boys' performance, Parker is said to have observed, "Let me hear a band play a hymn tune, and I will tell you what kind of band it is." He judged the Canadian boys superb.

In 1936 (the year I was born), the band returned to the UK for a second concert tour. As in 1934, the program combined a blend of vaudeville, Salvation Army, jazz, and the classics. Again, the ship would pass by the site of the *Empress of Ireland* wreck, and again Mr. D. would speak in serious tones to the young musicians of the deeper meaning behind their performances. This time, the National

Brass Band Competition took place at the Crystal Palace in London. Thirty-five bands competed with a test piece by Tchaikovsky. All except the Canadians were adult musicians. The Canadian boys won. They returned home by sea along the same route.

The clouds of an impending world war were already gathering over Europe in June 1939, when Mr. D. took a third group of young musicians to the UK. A promising schedule of engagements and competitions lay before them. This time, after leaving Quebec City, they set course across the Atlantic via Belfast to Greenock, Scotland, near the mouth of the Clyde. The band's fame had preceded them, for they were greeted with excitement at every stop. But throughout the hot summer, anxiety about the tense relations with Germany was escalating. Anticipating the worst, Mr. D. cut the tour short and scrambled to get a booking home on the SS *Athenia*. But by then, all overseas transport had been committed to emergency use. The *Athenia* left without them and met her death when sunk by German submarine U-30. Back in Canada, amidst the confusion caused by the war and diminished communications, the boys' anxious parents feared that their children had perished on the *Athenia*. In fact, while their families despaired, their boys were voyaging homeward in secrecy aboard the *Empress of Britain*. It was a harrowing trip. Expecting a torpedo attack at any moment, they spent most of their time huddled in life jackets on the upper decks. Yet, they made it home safely.

Such were the legacies that impressed themselves upon us in 1950 as we crossed the Atlantic aboard *Samaria*. The war had ended just five years earlier, but its memory remained fresh in our imaginations, and our travels through the UK that year were coloured by it. I set off again in 1953 for my second—and the band's fifth—overseas tour. Like many others, I regard the 1930s, '40s, and '50s as the halcyon days of the Kitsilano Boys Band experience. They marked the final pre television years when vaudeville was big business and the grand old theatres—like those in the Moss-Empire chain in which we performed twice nightly—dominated the entertainment scene.

From its earliest days, the band had been represented by Harold Fielding Agencies. Our personal agent was Chris "Stocky" Stockwell, a dapper Englishman, impeccably dressed in the "morning formal" style of suit popular among bankers and other professionals in London. The outfit consisted of a black jacket and waistcoat, grey vertically striped trousers, black shiny shoes, a folded walking-cane umbrella, and a bowler hat. The bowler was for a long time the ultimate symbol of what was called "effortless English style." We all acquired one in 1953, just for fun; it made for a comical accessory to our travelling outfit of blue turtleneck sweaters and corduroy pants. But oh, to be young.

Travelling to Britain for the first time was more than just a cultural excursion for me. In an unsettling sense, it was a homecoming. That was certainly how my family and my larger community regarded the journey. All my life, the people closest to me had spoken fondly of England as the "old country." It was "our island home," "our Mother England," images that included all of Great Britain. Despite that pull toward what my Anglo upbringing said I *should* feel, I knew I was Canadian. That meant being a colonial.

But for all that, it was the concept of England as an island that attracted me. The historic ports of Portsmouth, Southampton, and Liverpool beckoned me, and I marvelled at the chalk cliffs of Dover and Beachy Head. Our travels took us to the south-coast seaside resorts of Bournemouth and Eastbourne, with their exotic white sands, and along broad coastal stretches of the Irish Sea at Blackpool and Holyhead. Concert dates in Holland took us across the English Channel, where I caught views of the grey North Sea coast that bordered Scotland and Northern England. The effect of Britain's seascapes upon me was transformative. Images imprinted in my schoolboy's mind over years of Anglocentric schooling now materialized before me like a spiritual awakening. These scenes, I realized with the wisdom of my fourteen years, were not just the imaginings of nostalgic colonials. They were vividly alive and real. That summer, though nearly fifty years had passed since the debut of Edward Elgar's *Pomp and Circumstance*, which he had composed for the coronation of King Edward VII in 1902, we could still play it to great acclaim. Performances of it in parks and music halls drew spontaneous singing and explosions of applause from our audiences. That the British Empire was in slow decline was no longer in doubt. Yet, so powerful were these anthems that even the BBC, as part of its popular London Pops series, continued the tradition of the audiences joining together to sing "Rule Britannia" and "Land of Hope and Glory" at the end of each concert right up to 2020. Someone then had finally realized that the hymns held too many associations with colonialism and slavery to be fit for public performance. In any event, the COVID pandemic closed the concert halls that year, so this left no audiences around to complain when the virtual concerts broadcast from the venerable Albert Hall concluded without the imperialistic singalongs. Even in 1950, the dream of empire was falling out of favour. Yet, as *Samaria* steamed up the River Thames and landed at Tilbury Docks, just forty kilometres (twenty-five miles) from London's Tower Bridge, we felt we had indeed arrived home.

THE 1950S were exciting times to be in the professional entertainment business—though to be precise some of us were below the legal age for professional stage work. Almost every city and town had its variety theatre. They bore regal names like the Palladium and the Hippodrome in Golder's Green, in London; the Embassy in Peterborough; Theatre Royal in Portsmouth and Dublin; and the Grand Theatre in Bolton. Their ornate architecture and lush interiors lent prestige to the entertainers who performed there. From acrobats and jugglers to comedians, lion tamers, dancers, contortionists, magicians, and funambulists, these were consummate show people who performed their art with dazzling virtuosity. Below the stage, the pit orchestras brilliantly supported each act with bravura performances of their own. (Vancouver's Pantages Theatre produced similar shows during the vaudeville era in Canada, when Mr. D. played trumpet in the pit orchestra.) Among these many popular acts, the Vancouver Boys Band received top billing.

Once in the UK, we fell into a regular touring routine. Sundays were spent travelling by bus or smoke-belching steam train and settling into the new city. Mondays, we'd gather at the theatre with the director and other acts for a quick run-through, after which we'd rehearse each morning and play twice-nightly shows. When the gruelling week was over, it was on to another town. Over four months, we criss-crossed the entire UK, with stops at London, Weymouth, Bournemouth, Exeter, Torquay, Edinburgh, Aberdeen, Bolton, Bath, Peterborough, Manchester, Newcastle, Dublin, and many more. Our concert tour three years later in 1953 maintained the same fast pace.

Since its nationalization in 1948, British Railways was still relying on coal-driven engines, though electrification had begun. The second-class carriages we travelled in smelled of smoke, and the upholstery reeked of soot. If a window happened to be open as the train raced unexpectedly through a tunnel, you risked choking on fumes. The walls of the stations—including famous ones like Paddington, St. Pancras, Euston, and King's Cross—were blackened throughout. After an all-night journey spent trying to sleep upright in a compartment for six, one felt rather grubby. I recall one time waiting for a connection in the wee hours of the morning and searching around in the dark, grimy station for a used cup before lining up on the platform for a cuppa from the tea-wagon. If the train arrived in the morning, you could get the advertised "Wash & Brush Up" in the public washroom for thruppence (a small brass coin worth three pence in the old reckoning). We soon grew accustomed to travel culture and became expert trainspotters. The Flying Scotsman, the Brighton Belle, the Comet, and Golden Arrow all cast their spell.

If second-class train travel provided one form of education, the meagre lodgings we were provided with among the working-class districts of Britain added another rich dimension to our learnings. Each Sunday, on arriving at a strange town, we would be given our billet's address and would set off with our bags to find it. My buddy Ron Wood and I always billeted together. I remember the two of us, barely turned fourteen, heading off into the night with Mr. D.'s admonition: "We meet for rehearsal tomorrow, ten o'clock AM, at the Hippodrome!" And that was it, we were on our own.

With few exceptions, our digs stood in dreary, coal-stained streets of row houses with rooms that rented by the week to "theatre people" and other transients. With their soot-stained windows and front doors that stood flush against the narrow sidewalk, these dank and melancholy homes were how we came to know England. The atmosphere was right out of Dickens—no central heating, no bathtub, no running water (we had a wash stand with a pitcher of cold water and a bowl), and an outdoor "wee hoose" set at the back of a tiny brick-walled yard. Wartime rationing was still in force. At the start of the week, we'd present our ration books to the landlady so she could purchase butter, sugar, or meat, whatever she needed to prepare our breakfast and a late-night supper for after the show. On Saturdays, we'd head to the public baths, comprising twenty-four or thirty cubicles, each furnished with a bathtub and stool. The water pipe came through the wall from the hallway, where the bath master controlled how much warm water you got. For a few pence, plus a penny for a towel, you got your dip and a piece of soap. It was a far cry from the comforts of home that we so casually took for granted.

We loved vaudeville; the smell of the theatre, the history, and the drama quite intoxicated us. We especially anticipated Monday mornings. All the acts would arrive, including the members of the impressive pit orchestra (amazing sight readers!). One by one the performers would mount the stage, hand their well-thumbed scores down to the conductor in the pit, who distributed them to the musicians, and together they would run through the act and work out the necessary cues. Maybe the juggler needed some special dynamics when all the red balls were in the air, or the female contortionist expected a particular crescendo from Tchaikovsky's *Swan Lake*. We'd watch mesmerized as the trapeze artist signalled to the percussionist for some especially dazzling effect. "This is what I want you to do when I hang from the trapeze by my teeth," she'd explain. When our turn came, the orchestra would take a break while we set up our instruments, worked out the lighting, and played through some repertoire to test the acoustics. The vaudeville rehearsals were remarkable things—fast-paced, precise, and very efficient.

While the performers were perfecting their sequences, the backstage area would be teeming with theatre crews unpacking the costumes and equipment—even guiding elephants and tigers down from their trucks. As we travelled on similar circuits, we came to know many of these performers and soon learned to recognize the difference between their stage personas and their authentic selves. One character we came to know well was a female gymnast and contortionist. Bursting onto the stage under specially designed lighting in a bikini with long tassels on her bra twirling in opposite directions, she gave every impression of a vivacious eighteen-year-old. That was the illusion. In fact, she was a very tired-looking middle-aged woman. Despite her tough life on the stage, or perhaps because of it, she took a motherly interest in four of us seventeen-year-olds on the '53 trip. I recall one time when we "four musketeers," as we called ourselves, were heading to Paris for a four-day leave prior to sailing home from Southampton. Before we left, she recommended a cheap hotel in Montmartre, where "nice boys" like us would be entirely safe. Our guardian angel certainly knew her Paris.

Working with travelling players gave us glimpses into the theatre life. One of the acts featured a superb soprano. She had the mature voice of an adult in the body of a twelve-year-old child. Billed as a child prodigy, the tiny singer's stage act was electrifying. From the darkened theatre, a crescendo of light and sound would suddenly fill the space, and the girlish figure, in a child's frock and with bows in her hair, would appear centre stage. Her mature voice was genuine, but her stage personality was an illusion, for she was about thirty years old. Backstage, we knew her as an adult and came to appreciate the loneliness of the life she led. One Monday during the morning rehearsal, one of the actors picked her up, stood her on a table, and gave her a hug. As they chatted, we realized that the two friends were sharing a precious moment as members of a great family of travelling players, one whose way of life would soon disappear. We experienced many such poignant moments. By 1953, we were witnessing the disappearance of vaudeville. Television was coming into vogue, and some theatres were already boarded up. The dying vaudeville scene gave us insight into the vulnerability of the human condition.

The vaudeville performers were but one dimension of our UK travels. Another was our exposure to the British tradition of working-class brass and concert bands made up of players from collieries, motor works, and other industries. They played to the highest standards. Their matched instruments, largely from the famous British music company Boosey & Hawkes, produced a uniquely mellow tone and intonation unlike anything we'd heard in Canada. (That brass band tradition continues today in such brilliant ensembles as the Salvation Army, the Grimethorpe Colliery Band, and the Black Dyke Band.) Then, too, as part of the Moss-Empire chain we had free access to the great jazz shows of the day, featuring sparkling stage bands conducted by performers like Ted Heath, one of the most famous swing band leaders in Britain, and the matinee idol Jack Parnell. Some of us sat in on their rehearsals. Another British tradition—concerts in the parks—rounded out our musical experience. The outdoor concerts we played at London Embankment, in Edinburgh, and in the spa towns of Bournemouth, Weymouth, and Bath were an exhilarating way to perform our huge repertoire of twenty-one different programs. It was a daunting repertoire for us boys to master.

OUR TRAVELS across Britain by boat, bus, or train often caused us to reflect upon the lives of our forebears. A particularly stormy voyage from Holyhead, Wales, to the Port of Dublin (Dún Laoghaire), and our deepening engagement with the coastal and interior regions of the UK, drew us into their world. It seemed that wherever we turned, places and people reminded us of what our own culture owed to England. A highlight for me was our visit to the grand naval harbour of Portsmouth, a place that had been calling me my entire life. There, I laid eyes on Admiral Nelson's flagship, HMS *Victory*, at rest in the dockyard. The sight of her cast a lifelong spell on me. The ship is a magnificent example of the 104-gun, first-rate, line-of-battle ships of the Royal Navy. HMS *Victory* embodied the quintessential naval tradition captured in the notion "the Nelson touch." I took in the full sweep of her sheer lines and then looked upward through her complicated rigging to where the t'gallants and royals would have flown, and to the mainmast cap standing sixty-one metres (two hundred feet) above the waterline. I was struck by what she meant for British culture. She exemplified the most advanced and complex piece of technology of her day. I imagined her being brought to life by her crew of 850 men, and the majesty of her 560 square metres (6,000 square feet) of sail filling full taut in a driving gale.

HMS *Victory* was, like all tall ships of her day, a "wooden world," as I would later learn when studying naval history and N.A.M. Rodger's masterful book *The Wooden World*. This was a self-contained seagoing world with its own language, laws, customs, skilled professions, and unique social relationships. Her keel had been laid in 1759, the same year Generals Wolfe and Montcalm faced one another in Quebec on the Plains of Abraham. Their battle had determined the course of Canadian history. As I strolled *Victory*'s decks, I imagined Admiral Lord Nelson himself audaciously pacing the quarterdeck in full-dress uniform, taunting the enemy with his undisguised contempt for danger and his unperturbed sense of invincibility. Deeply moved, I stood at the spot where he was fatally struck by a French sniper's bullet during close-quarters combat on 21 October 1805. Later in my travels, I came upon J.M.W. Turner's painting *The Battle of Trafalgar*, from 1824. With unerring insight, Turner had recreated the organized chaos of naval warfare. Conjuring up the mood of apocalypse, his masterpiece decries for me the madness of mortal combat.

Portsmouth dockyard provided yet another surprise, for the Canadian cruiser HMCS *Ontario*—carrying her own concert band— lay in port at the same time as our Theatre Royal appearance, where we were playing twice nightly to packed houses. *Ontario* had been launched in Belfast in 1945 as HMS *Minotaur*, and then transferred to Canada. Her bandsmen met with us during our stay at Portsmouth and invited us aboard for a reception and tour. Again, the naval world and its culture impressed me, as did the ship's capacity for battle. The experience was formative, for five years later I would ship aboard *Ontario*'s sister ship, HMCS *Quebec* (formerly HMS *Uganda*, launched in 1943 from Newcastle-on-Tyne). I would be training to become a sea officer (and taking every opportunity to sit in with the ship's concert band and enjoy a riff). In truth, it was not only *Quebec*'s naval connection that appealed to me, but the knowledge of her former incarnation as *Uganda*, after the remote East African country, a name that for reasons unknown lurked at the back of my mind. (But that is a different thread in the complex weave of my life that I'll keep for later.)

Partway through our UK tour, our trajectory took us to Holland, where we performed nine concerts in eight days. There we learned about Canada's role in the liberation of the Netherlands from German occupation in May 1945, and of the special relationship that had formed between our two countries as a result. We boys only began to grasp the depth of this bond during this profoundly moving visit. The ship that took us from Harwich, England, to Hoek van Holland, *Koningin Emma* (Queen Emma), had been named after the popular Queen Consort of the Netherlands, who died in 1934. Launched in 1939 for passenger service between the UK and Holland, she had been requisitioned by the British government to transport commandos following the German occupation of Holland in 1940. Her speed (over twenty-four knots) and versatility made her ideal for covert operations under the most hazardous conditions. Thus, she was among the ships present at the ill-fated Dieppe Raid of August 1942, involving some five thousand Canadian troops—at a cost of over nine hundred Canadian lives.

The warmth of the reception we received in Holland overwhelmed us. It made each stop feel like a homecoming. On arriving at a town, a marching band would greet us and lead us through a throng of cheering citizens to the city hall, where the mayor would welcome us with a version of the local liberation story. In towns like

Hillegom, Scheveningen, Zandvoort, Hilversum, and Amersvoort (the site of a former concentration camp), local families billeted us in their homes. The stories they shared sharpened our understanding of the horrors of life under German occupation, but inevitably ended with descriptions of the Canadian troops' jubilant arrival into their town and of how the children climbed aboard their tanks and jeeps in celebration. The liberation was completed on 5 May 1945, and two days later, Germany signed an unconditional surrender at Reims, in northeastern France. The Instrument of Surrender took full effect on 8 May. The war was over at last. Over 7,600 Canadians had died in the effort, which is why the mayor of Hillegom presented us with a Dutch flag bearing the words "Hillegom dankt Canada" (Thank You, Canada). We received the thanks as though we ourselves had earned it. The memories we took home from that visit enlarged our world beyond imagining.

The military and naval connections struck me in 1953 when I embarked RMS *Samaria* for my second UK concert tour. It was the band's second postwar tour. This time, our destination was not London's Tilbury Docks but the Port of Southampton, about 130 kilometres (80 miles) away. One of our first stops on arriving was the BBC studios in London to announce the start of our four-month tour. During our approach to Southampton that June, we had passed by Spithead, near the Isle of Wight, and found ourselves threading our way through one of the largest fleet reviews in history. Some four hundred warships from Britain, the Commonwealth, and the Allied countries had gathered to celebrate the coronation of Queen Elizabeth II. Above us, three hundred aircraft overflew the anchorages under brilliant skies. Formed up on *Samaria*'s promenade deck, we set about playing the national anthems of the warships that passed close aboard. As our course into Southampton took us through squadrons of predominately British ships, we joined the celebration with sequences of "God Save the Queen," "Rule Britannia," and "Land of Hope and Glory." When we tired of that, we played the Royal Navy's rousing official march "Heart of Oak," with its stirring sentiments from the days of Nelson: "Come, cheer up my lads /

'tis to glory we steer / to add something more to this wonderful year." The final line said it all: "We'll fight, and we'll conquer, again and again." The review was tradition in action, an overwhelming demonstration of sea power.

OUR TRAVELS across Britain and Europe opened our world enormously, for we experienced a depth of culture and history through art, architecture, music, and the hard knocks of living that we could never have garnered from school or books. On arriving home, we faced something of a culture shock. As the old stage song had it, "how're you going to keep them down on the farm, once they've seen 'Paree'?" Like the farm boys, we had come back changed. Our understanding of life had been broadened, and we had experienced a rare kind of freedom, rambling through Piccadilly Circus on our own late at night, enjoying the glory of the reveal-all *Folies Bergère* in London and Paris, and setting off on cross-country train journeys on our own. We had known the world of show business and had lived among working-class Brits; performed at sports events in Twickenham and motorcycle races at Wembley; toured factories in Manchester and Bolton; explored castles, cathedrals, and museums; and savoured the night life and the taste of fine ale. After all this, home seemed narrow and confining.

Not until many years later did any of us speak about the meta-narrative—what the experience was really about. Only later did we begin to look back at the deeper meaning of what we had lived. Memories of the music can still haunt. I can still feel the thrill of anticipation in the moments before the curtain rises. I recall being seized at times with the extraordinary specialness of it all, the sense that I was part of some grand purpose. "I am never going to hear these sounds again," I would say to myself, or, "never again will I live inside this musical passage, or play these difficult horn passages on a British stage." "Finally, this moment is *it*," I once exclaimed to myself. It was like a spiritual journey. If this was life, you didn't want to grow up, and wished only to live in suspended animation in this exact moment forever. I was reminded of this feeling many years later, as a professor of German literature. I was teaching a particularly poignant passage in Goethe's *Faust,* the scene where the beguiling Mephistopheles says to Faustus, who is forever craving one new experience after another, "When you say to the moment, 'tarry a while, you are so beautiful'—then I've caught you!" To escape stagnation, we must always take the next step onward.

AFTER THE 1953 tour, I began studies at the University of British Columbia and switched from horn back to the trumpet, a better fit for playing with jazz groups and the UBC Big Band. My father, always ready to give me a leg up, presented me with one of the finest trumpets on the market—a Holton Stratodyne. I soon formed my own gig band and began playing in Vancouver's downtown venues. This was just as the era of old-time popular music was giving way to new musical styles. Around this time, two of my favourite jazz stars came to town and took Vancouver's music scene by storm: Louis Armstrong and his Dixieland All-Stars at the Cave Supper Club; and Harry James's Big Band, with the incomparable drummer Buddy Rich, at the Vancouver Arena. Their performances were dazzling; my musical idols, whom I knew only through vinyl records, now stood within touching distance, playing their hearts out. I felt humbled. Having experienced these all-stars up close, how could I ever pick up my trumpet again? But I had been to the mountain top, and I did.

By the early 1960s, guitars, folk, and rock were overtaking my preferred genres of Dixie, West Coast, and New York jazz, and the luscious big band sounds of Tommy Dorsey, Glenn Miller, Duke Ellington, Count Basie, Benny Goodman, and Harry James. The new wave of protest music, with its raging and ranting, seemed bent on making up for its lack of finesse by raising the volume. Whether as a musician or a listener, I couldn't make the transition. I feared the demise of what I still call the good old days of fine instrumental playing, subtle composition, and sensitive interpretations by gifted musicians. I grieved the loss of melodic lines, skillful command of chord progressions, and intelligently executed rhythmical patterns. When Louis Armstrong released the hugely popular *Hello, Dolly!,* in

1964, he played the final number in a long tradition of lyrical jazz as my generation had known it.

On the other hand, the 1960s did see the rise of exciting artists like trumpeter Herb Alpert with his Tijuana Brass. The brassy and melodious mix of jazz, Brazilian bossa nova, and Mexican pizzazz was happy, feel-good music. But then this music too began to slip off the charts. Alpert consoled himself with the claim that music styles are cyclical, while we graduates of the Kitsilano Boys Band did our best to keep the big band sound alive. Prominent among our alumni was Vancouver's own "king of swing," Dal Richards. A saxophonist from the early 1930s, Richards led the house band at the Vancouver Hotel's legendary Panorama Roof Ballroom for twenty-five years, from 1940 to 1965. Many of our "old boys" played leading roles alongside him, but despite the fine musicianship, the band's popularity declined, unable to withstand the assault from what Dal called the "sham music" of rock. During the 1990s, while in his seventies, his radio show "Dal's Place" continued to promote the big band sounds, but to waning audiences. Meanwhile, in Toronto, trombonist Ron Collogrosso, who had played stunning trombone solos while touring with us in the 1950s, enjoyed a successful career as a composer and arranger under the name Ron Collier, and played with jazz greats like Duke Ellington. Other young musicians, like Arnie Chycoski from the 1955 UK tour played with Montreal's Guido Basso, who, at the age of thirteen had backed Ella Fitzgerald professionally. Basso went on to play trumpet and flugelhorn with virtuosos like Woody Herman and Count Basie. Another child of the 1930s, trombonist Rob McConnell, of the famous McConnell and the Boss Brass, for years set the standard for the so-called Canadian sound in big band music. Had either Basso or McConnell lived in Vancouver as youths, they would certainly have been among the talented teens of the Kitsilano Boys Band.

By this time, the Parisian pianist and composer Jacques Loussier, who had launched a successful trio in 1959 and would go on to a perform for another fifty years, was blending jazz piano with works by Bach, including the *Goldberg Variations*. His countryman Claude

Bolling, a pianist, composer, and big band leader, also blended sophisticated classical and jazz stylings. Bolling's 1975 album with flautist Jean-Pierre Rampal, *Suite for Flute and Jazz Piano*, dominated the pop charts for a decade. Musical imagination in the popular performing arts was still alive and well.

Amidst these developments, I had failed to recognize that the new wave of popular music in the 1960s and '70s was about producing music with an ethic. For this younger, postwar generation the '60s was a time of personal discovery that drew them into a new world of feeling and a desire to radically change the world. In 1967, the popular folk trio Peter, Paul and Mary launched their album titled *Album 1700*. Dressed in suits and ties right out of the 1950s—though with pants and jackets much more skin-tight than we ever wore them—they belted out lyrics like "rock and roll music I could really get it," and "I figure it's about the happiest sound goin' down today." Then came the socially critical songs, like Pete Seeger's "Where Have All the Flowers Gone" that led the anti-war protests. In any event, by the end of the 1950s, my days in performing music were numbered. It was time to move on to other things.

Yet I would play my coda—the thematic conclusion to my musical career—on two more occasions, once during the Brussels World Fair in 1958 while working in the Canadian Pavilion, and again in 1961 while serving as an immigration officer at the Canadian Embassy in Cologne, Germany. The Kitsilano Boys Band was alive and touring in those years, and on two occasions, Mr. D. had telegrammed me on short notice to request my assistance with bookings and accommodation for forty-five people for the group's tours of Belgium and Germany. There was no "would you please," or "could you try" about it. I knew his style and made things happen. The performances were everything I expected: a new cadre of exuberant young musicians playing brilliant music under Mr. D.'s dynamic leadership. No longer under his tutelage, I enjoyed a hearty relationship with my former mentor. Together we negotiated the musical programs with our Belgian or German hosts. The tour was not without logistic challenges, such as having to transport boys and instruments across the Rhine River in tiny excursion ferries for a concert in the park, and wrangling a contract with West German Radio in Cologne for a live broadcast.

Our bonding experience played itself out with flair. On the final day of their stay in Germany, the band marched down Deutscher Ring in downtown Cologne (where I was living with my wife, Anita, and baby daughter, Pauline) to right where our road met the shoreline drive along the river. As we watched from our ground-floor balcony, Mr. D. struck up the band and saluted us as they marched off toward the Rhine.

Thus, my long relationship with the Kitsilano Boys Band reached its end. The band was heading home to Vancouver. But the expressive sea route would not be part of their experience, for the conveyance of choice was now by aircraft via the polar route. The boys' understanding of Canada would necessarily be different from mine, as they would not have experienced the thrill of crossing the country by train. Nor would they have encountered the old pilot station at Pointe-au-Père Lighthouse or passed by the wreck of the *Empress of Ireland* before facing the daunting Atlantic.

My years with the band had laid the foundation for how I would live the rest of my life. From Mr. D., I learned that at any given stage of my life, I always had more music in me than I ever thought; that with discipline and the courage to accept competent criticism I could make that music sing; and that, whatever form my "music" might take through my many careers as a naval officer, foreign service officer, author, professor, and parent, it would become richer by my listening closely to the other players around me. Finally, Mr. D. taught me that investing in the raw potential of fellow human beings is always worth the risk. How else can I account for the uncanny life successes achieved by this retiring and unremarkable lad from Pachena?

3

SHIPPING OUT

When you have been tossed and wracked and
chilled, any wharf looks good, even a rickety one...
EMILY CARR, *Klee Wyck*

"I'S THE b'y that builds the boat / And I's the b'y that sails her / I's the b'y that catches the fish / And brings 'em home to Lizer." The words of the old Newfoundland ballad echoed throughout our kitchen. My favourite Newfoundland uncle, Captain Llewellyn Sheppard, a wizened old salt whom I deeply admired, had indeed brought a fish—fresh from the locker of the Department of Fisheries patrol vessel *Laurier*, which he skippered while patrolling the fishing grounds of the Pacific Coast. Singing out the song's zesty lyrics in hoedown style, he would take my mother by the waist and lead her across the kitchen floor and back, with a turn past the four-legged woodstove. During the years of my father's long absences for work in the BC Interior, Uncle Llew's surprise visits were happy, cherished occasions for my mother that broke the monotony of long days spent caring for children on her own. She beamed the moment he stepped through the garden gate.

I too welcomed Uncle Llew's visits. He built me my first model sailboat of West Coast cedar that still retains its woody scent eighty years later. Next came a model destroyer, followed by an apple-box sailboat with a broom-handle mast for exploring the pirate-infested seas at the foot of the garden. I watched with astonishment when he demonstrated his old sailor's craft of putting model ships into bottles. And there were always the stories, endless tales of the sea-kindly boats of Newfoundland, with their strange sounding names like bully boat, longliner, swamp bottom, and tramp skiff. Listening to his tales and admiring his craftsmanship made me think that Newfoundland was the most wonderful glory hole a person could ever leave.

I recall the fantasy vessels and fictional oceans of childhood for their carefree innocence. Other ships I remember for their individual character or personality. The famous yacht *Dolaura*, on which Uncle Llew served as an officer on first arriving in BC, set my mind awhirl. Built in Scotland in 1908 for the coal baron Robert Dunsmuir, the 66.5-metre (218-foot) steamship, with her clipper bow and stern and her raked masts and funnel, exuded luxury, classical style, and speed surpassing anything that had been seen on the BC coast before. As far as I know, the only memento left of this ship is her mahogany-framed barometer, which I inherited from my uncle years ago. I also recall the SS *Princess Maquinna*, the "old faithful" of popular lore, that took me to my first home at Pachena Point Light Station. Built in Esquimalt in 1912 for the British Columbia Railway, the *Maquinna* was the first major commercial ship constructed in local waters. The well-designed and sea-kindly vessel sliced through the frequently harsh and stormy offshore waters of the West Coast to reach the isolated communities that depended on her. To the loggers, fishermen, and lighthouse personnel who took passage, *Maquinna*'s luxurious interior offered a reprieve from the rough living they were accustomed to. Some said she brought civilization into their lives. Then there was Skipper's *Laurier*, which he had brought from Halifax, through the Panama Canal, to Victoria. Meticulously cared for in "Bristol fashion," as naval parlance has it, she was beautiful. Her classic lines and cruiser stern, her gun-mounting on the foredeck and glistening brightwork projected her naval origins. She took me on my first voyage as a youngster of ten. I still see the old man on the bridge, crisply turned out in his blue uniform, smoke curling from his briar pipe, conning his ship through the Fraser River's constantly silting and shifting channels and out into the Strait of Georgia, as the Salish Sea was then called.

I was fifteen in 1951, when I first signed on a ship and went to sea for pay. There was a touch of nepotism involved in my being hired. My second Newfoundland uncle, Captain Ernest Sheppard, was skipper of the Union Steamship Company's senior ship, *Catala*. When her sister ship, the passenger-freighter *Cardena*, posted an opening for a day porter, "Uncle Ern" had seen to it that I got the job. And so I became the ship's general factotum and all-round gofer, while being on call to do the chief steward's bidding. I threw myself into it wholeheartedly, thrilled to be finally learning the ways of ships and the sea. I was also learning about remote—and sometimes transient—coastal ports and passages that until then had meant little more to me than exotic names: Bella Coola, Bella Bella, Namu, Duncan Bay Landing, Blind Channel, Queen Charlotte Sound, and—before the Ripple Rock explosion in 1958—the treacherous Seymour Narrows.

My stroll to work on the *Cardena* took me through a rundown part of the city known as Skid Road. To the people in our comfortable, blue-collar neighbourhood of Marpole, Skid Road was the slippery slope on the fringes of society down which drunks, derelicts, and the "dregs of society" skidded until they hit rock bottom. Passing through these harbour haunts opened a strange new world for me. There I witnessed the bustle of lorries and drays shifting cargo, and the hubbub of the overcrowded employment office on Carroll Street, where clerks called out bids for casual day labour. I breathed in the aroma of wholesale houses packing coffee and tea and the briny tang of the docks at low water. All round me, I heard the cry of seabirds, the querulous screech of ships' whistles, and the echoing, deep-throated responses of deep-sea vessels about to depart. Deep in memory lies the apprehension I felt at the end of each voyage, when I would walk back through the same twilight streets, clutching my pay-packet tightly in my pocket as I passed the swinging doors of beer halls, the mocking winks of prostitutes, and a revolving cast of Dickensian underworld characters.

But my ship was quite another world. Union Steamships provided a lifeline to the inhabitants and seasonal workers of BC's isolated inner coastal communities. Travel aboard the *Cardena* and her sister ship *Catala* meant high living. Both passenger-freighters boasted the attributes of deep-sea liners: heavy wood panelling throughout and excellent food in the silver-service dining salon served by waiters in white jackets and dark trousers. The ships offered a panelled observation lounge forward and a smokers' lounge aft. While most of the cabins had double-tiered bunks, a few larger cabins near the officers' quarters opened onto the upper deck and were decidedly more expensive.

By contrast, my ascetic quarters in the 'tween decks, up forward by the cable locker, were cramped. I shared a tiny pie-shaped cabin with two young Chinese cooks. Our cabin opened onto the ship's austere steerage accommodation: multiple rows of doubled-tiered metal bunks standing on uncarpeted metal plates. On joining ship, I found the bunks already filling up with loggers and fishermen returning upcoast—most of them penniless after their revels among the beer parlours and flesh pots of waterfront Vancouver. The revolving-door syndrome hit them every time they came into town: in flush and out broke.

I quickly warmed to the colourful shipboard life. It was the very man's world to which I aspired: the ship's winch operator loading and unloading tons of cargo at every port; the "ky-yiying" of the Chinese cooks toiling in the hot and crowded galley despite frequent attacks of seasickness; and the focused proficiency of engineers and seamen. Being part of such a motley group of shipmates was sheer joy. Many of them offered unsolicited advice to this scrawny, white-haired kid. "Keep away from wimmin 'n likker" topped the list. "Stay in school and get a good job" came the next. And sometimes, strange as it seems, I was the one sought out by junior crew for my own supposedly wise counsel. Perhaps it was because I had been at school longer than most. They even approached me with their intimate problems: "How many times d'ya gotta do it before yer wife gets a baby?" one recently married dishwasher asked. At fifteen years old, I had wondered about how one would set about doing it; but for the life of me, I hadn't a clue about the details.

In the course of my shipboard duties, I developed an affinity for the radio officer, whose cabin I cleaned each day. Our association arose in part because my father had been a sparker (radioman) in the Royal Navy during the First World War and had gone on to make a career in wireless telegraphy at light stations in Alert Bay, Merry Island, and Pachena Point. At the time of my *Cardena* experience, he was the officer-in-charge of the burgeoning technical operations of Vancouver Aeradio, at Vancouver Airport. Dusting off the equipment in *Cardena*'s radio shack, I felt a connection not only to my family, but to the entire coastal radio network as well. I enjoyed my chats here and there with the radio officer, which covered a variety of nautical themes, and quickly came to view him as a mentor. One day, I put my cards on the table. I didn't want to get stuck, like some of the crew I had met, spending the next twenty or thirty years scrubbing washrooms and decks and making up beds. I wanted to become a sea officer. And I wanted to start right away by learning to steer the *Cardena* as a quartermaster. "Fine," he said. "But first you must learn to box the compass."

Boxing the compass is a lost art from the days when magnetic compasses were the primary aid to navigation. In my day, the magnetic compass was still in use. Boxing it was a technique for teaching young seamen to master the "compass rose," in order to be able to execute steering commands. This compass rose, or compass circle, was marked off in thirty-two points, from north through east, south, and west and back around to north. These were known as the "cardinal points." A candidate had to be able to recite them in clockwise and anticlockwise sequence and name all the intermediate points and quarter points in between. Whereas nowadays the helmsman might be ordered to steer a specific number of degrees on the gyro compass—for example, "steer zero six seven"—the helmsmen of older times would be ordered to steer "northeast by east a quarter east." Nowadays, the term boxing the compass is more likely to be used figuratively, in the sense of "getting one's bearings" or "making sense of one's life"—something I have been trying to do ever since.

Within a short time, I had mastered the compass and was spending my scarce free time at *Cardena*'s helm. Once my work as a day porter was done, I would cast off my white jacket and black bow tie and climb up to the wheelhouse. This was the ship's nerve centre, from which all aspects of navigation and ship safety were controlled. I recall glorious summer evenings at the wheel, listening to the quiet conversations of the ship's officers and observing the serious business of navigating. I delighted in my small role in sharing responsibility for the ship as we threaded our way through the labyrinthine fjords and channels of the Broughton Archipelago.

My shifts aboard the *Cardena* took me to historic settlements like Namu, Bella Bella (Waglisla), Klemtu, and others on the BC coast that had once formed the heart of a thriving fishing and fish-packing industry. These foreign-sounding names beckoned me into a distant, unfamiliar world I had never met before, a world largely unknown to most Canadians. The lure of the deep inner coast has never left me. From the 1880s to the 1950s, up to 150 canneries dotted the BC coast. The Skeena River alone hosted twelve busy plants. Canneries operated around the clock, and many a time we pulled alongside a rain-soaked wharf in the middle of the night to unload supplies and hoist aboard crates of fish for delivery in Vancouver. At the height of a salmon run, when the smell of salmon roe hung in the air and throngs of the deeply coloured fish struggled against nets that stretched from boat to boat across main navigation channels, steamers like ours had to pick their way gingerly through the overlapping nets—"backing and filling" in nautical jargon—to cede right of way to the fishers. Navigation and docking were always a challenge, particularly in places like Inverness Cannery on the Skeena, with its seven-metre (twenty-three-foot) range of tide.

Many Indigenous Peoples worked the cannery trade. I soon learned that coastal First Nations had their own well-established traditions for harvesting and honouring the sea's bounty. The Nisga'a Nation, for example, had for thousands of years been greeting the arrival each spring of millions of small oolichan (eulachon, or *Thaleichthys pacificus*). Known variously as the life-giving fish, the saviour fish, or the candle fish, the oily creatures provided a rich supply of

food, oil, and medicine. The Nass River, with its tidal range sometimes exceeding six metres (twenty feet), once had the largest
Indigenous oolichan fishery of any river on the coast.

Cardena's calls in upcoast outports exposed me to the craftsmanship of the wooden gillnetters, trollers, halibut boats, and live-tank
cod boats that so often cluttered our route and converged with us at
our cannery calls. From our dockside vantage point, I could admire
up close the complexity of their rigging, the aesthetics of their hulls,
their manoeuvrability, and their rugged sea-keeping qualities. I
learned to prize the exquisite craftsmanship of boats built at the
Wahl family's boatyard in Prince Rupert. At the height of the Second World War, when demand was at its highest, the Wahl family
was completing a boat a day.

Along the BC coast, generations of traditional craftsmen had
become so skilled at blending the grain, texture, and hues of wood
with sea-kindly hydrodynamics that their craft seemed married to
the sea. In this great legacy, the Wahl-built boats excelled. They
were beautiful, graceful, and functional. I saw this same marriage
of form and function in the Indigenous canoe, which symbolized the
wealth of relationships that bind First Nations to what they called
the Creator's world.

MY GRADUATION from high school in 1954 ended my summers
with the Union Steamship Company. Next, it was on to studies at
the University of British Columbia, but I still had ships on my mind.
One day, near the beginning of my first year, I came home from
campus and brazenly announced that I had "joined the navy." I had
signed up with the University Naval Training Division. My mother
was shocked that I had done so without first consulting her. Her concerns may have been well founded, for the Cold War with the USSR
was raising new international tensions. The USA had detonated a
hydrogen bomb in Bikini Atoll that year and was now in talks with
Canada over the construction of the DEW (Distant Early Warning) Line in the Canadian Arctic, as a defence against anticipated
ballistic missile attacks from the USSR. Newsreels had repeatedly

shown images of the terrifying, radiation-laden mushroom cloud as it roiled above the coral islands. With two world wars behind her, mother doubtless feared the worst. But I was living my own life, and I knew what I wanted.

I began my navy career in 1954 as an officer cadet in the Naval Training Division at HMCS *Discovery*, in Vancouver's Coal Harbour. I was a naval reservist and that was my home port. The instruction there involved one evening a week plus additional weekends to learn the basics of seamanship, navigation, and platoon drills. The UNTD's robust program called for us to attend a civilian university for two terms per year, from September to April, and to spend our summer terms with the fleet, both ashore and afloat. At the end of a four-year BA or BSc degree, we were granted a commission in the Royal Canadian Navy. Given the anglophile origins of most of us, we readily embraced a naval culture rooted in the British naval tradition and the growing reputation of Canada's military on the world stage. Besides, Britain's Royal Navy was considered the most experienced navy in the world, so why would you not want to follow its lead? (Although francophone cadets joined, and excelled, in great numbers, their adaptation both culturally and linguistically was more difficult.) But whatever our origins, UNTD provided us the opportunity to learn the seafaring trades with others our own age from across the country—all while earning good money. Our instructors worked us hard. Excellent mentors, they held us to standards many of us had not quite expected. The Traditions of the Service, they assured us, were higher than those on "civvy street." Rule Number One came down with a slam almost as soon as we arrived at the naval base in Halifax for our first summer of intensive training: "Leave is a privilege; not a right." It seemed we would be permanently on duty until specifically told otherwise. So began our introduction to navigation, naval gunnery, and communications, a series of "character-building" indoctrinations meant to transform us "Untidies" (the nickname for UNTD) into "officers and gentlemen."

My first ship was the cruiser HMCS *Quebec,* based, at the time, in Halifax. Together with her sister ship HMCS *Ontario,* she formed part of Canada's ambitious postwar dream of the "all big-ship, big-gun navy." We would have had some inkling of her exploits from our study of Joseph Schull's *The Far Distant Ships*. Published in 1950, it was the only book available on Canadian naval history during the Second World War. We had relied on it earlier when preparing for our final selection board. Just as expected, we had been probed on our grasp of Canadian naval traditions.

HMCS *Quebec* was the largest warship most of us had ever seen, let alone lived aboard. Over 168 metres (550 feet) in length, she carried a wartime crew of 750 men and could reach a speed of 30 knots. She boasted nine 6-inch guns and ten 4-inchers. The gunnery instructor liked to remind us landlubbers that the inches referred not to the length of the barrel but to the diameter of the shell. First launched in August 1941 as the British warship HMS *Uganda,* she was recommissioned into Canada's navy in October 1944 and renamed. In her heyday, she was regarded as the most advanced naval weapon in Allied hands; the perfect fighting machine. My old uncle was impressed: "Well, b'y, you must be real proud of her." Indeed, I was, and especially so as I remembered Skipper's tales of the First World War. Pride in one's ship was part of the package.

It was an exciting moment that day in 1955 when my platoon marched down to the Halifax docks to board our own ship for the first time. We were finally going to sea for full-calibre shoots in the Virgin Islands. Talk of warfighting among the NATO partners was in the air. That year had seen our former enemy, Germany, join the alliance, following the birth of West Germany's armed forces after a ten-year postwar hiatus. Together, we now had our sights on the USSR. Thus, with our kit bags over one shoulder and a rolled-up hammock over the other, we moved with a certain awkward jauntiness up the brow to find our locker and where to sling our mick.

The mick, or hammock, was a wondrous, all-purpose piece of gear. Rolled up tightly with its taut, evenly spaced, seven-seas lashings, it could plug a hole in the hull or keep you afloat if your ship went down. And if you were really tired, you could even sleep in it. Each morning at six o'clock, a shrill, twittering bos'n's call would startle us from sleep, and a petty officer would rouse us with the stentorian call, "Wakey, wakey, rise and shine, lash and stow!" It was the signal to hit the deck running. Ten minutes to roll up your hot mick, detach it from the overhead hooks, and stow it upright in the communal rack. There it would spend the rest of the day—all steamy and personal—as a damage-control resource. From there, we mustered on the fo'c'sle (forward deck) for morning exercises, followed by a quick wash, breakfast, cleaning stations, training classes, and standing our watches. Life was purposeful, with little time for relaxing, or what our mentors disparagingly called lollygagging. Lucky the trainee who managed five hours of sleep a day, for in addition to our classes we worked watches of four hours on, eight hours off.

The training cruise in 1955 provided a lifetime of memories—of the great ship's plunging movements as green swells rolled over the bow; of the eruption of spray and spume as a beam sea struck her sides; of ice-cold night watches on deck as a member of the emergency seaboat crew (hoping we'd never have to launch); and of the gradual shifts in colour as the North Atlantic's angry grey merged with the azure and topaz shades of the Caribbean. There, I experienced for the first time the cresting, deep-blue waves of the southern sea under brilliant sunshine, and had my first sightings of flying fish, kittiwakes, and long-haul frigate birds. The images always bring me back to John Masefield's poem "Sea Fever." "And all I ask is a windy day / with the white clouds flying / And the flung spray and the blown spume, / And the seagulls' crying." Less poetic was the technical training we received. Under the critical eye of a master seaman, we learned how to splice flexible steel-wire rope, chip paint off weather-worn steel decks, correctly handle cables and anchors, and prepare the battle stations for a full-calibre shoot. The goal was to be able to perform these skills like second nature in even the most unfamiliar situations.

The Battle of the Atlantic (1939–45) was fresh in the nostrils of the experienced crew as we exercised battle stations under wartime conditions. With the ship running darkened and the action-alarm's high-pitched, undulating squeal pulsing incessantly, we worked our way hastily and silently from one watertight compartment to the next, guided only by the occasional red or green lamp. Drawing on his wartime experience at sea, Alistair MacLean had captured the sound of the ear-splitting alarm in his newly released potboiler HMS *Ulysses*: "A whistle pitched near the upper limits of audio-frequency, alternating, piercing, atonic, alive with a desperate urgency and sense of danger." Indeed, he wrote, the screech, "knife-like, sears through the most sleep-drugged brain." The exercise was eerie and unsettling even though we trainees knew it was just a war game. But it could have become real, for the Cold War mentality was increasingly permeating military and naval thinking of the day. The strategic doctrine of mutual assured destruction—MAD—hung in the air. We spoke of détente, but really regarded it as wishful thinking. Expecting the worst, we underwent ABCD training in how to prepare for atomic, biological, and chemical warfare. The D in the acronym stood for damage control, once the worst had happened.

Navy readers of those years will recall Nicholas Monsarrat's *The Cruel Sea* as the quintessential expression of the wartime experience of a whole seagoing generation of combatants, Germans included. It is eloquent, nuanced, vivid, and thoughtful. We steeped ourselves in the novel for its accurate portrayal of our own naval tradition. Rich in its understanding of the human condition and of the broad dynamics of naval life, the book draws it all together when two exhausted officers ponder what they had experienced. "There must be a special kind of war-memory—showing mercy in fading quickly, drowning for ever under the weight of sorrow." Somehow, the stories of combat we read blended into the war games we played.

My war station was in A-turret's shell-handling room, near the bow of the ship and well below the waterline. Getting there was like descending a series of submarine conning towers piled one on top of the other. The long and narrow chamber led from the upper deck through a series of watertight compartments and hatches to the shell-handling room below. Our procedure was quick and precise. The lead man in our line opened the upper deck watertight hatch and descended a narrow ladder encased in a grey tube, at the bottom of which was a second hatch that the last man down would close and batten behind him. We climbed through one hatch after another until finally we all reached the bottom. There we would stand, in the artificial twilight, on a greased deck to prevent sparks from igniting the explosives. Around us were the "bottling works"— the hoists that would lift the shells up to the gun turret. Our task was to heave the heavy shells from storage and hump them onto the hoists for delivery to the guns. It was exhausting, especially for young bodies unaccustomed to heavy labour. We could imagine the guns way overhead, and feel their powerful recoil.

We shell handlers were a motley bunch; young trainees like me and old hands with little hope of promotion. The navy ungraciously referred to such a gaggle as "odds and sods" or "dog's bodies." In the sweaty conditions of the handling room, the epithets seemed to fit. On one occasion, we assumed the ship must have fired an all-calibre broadside to starboard—four turrets of six-inch guns—for she suddenly rolled to port, where she hung anxiously for a moment before clawing herself back into an upright position. "One more like that and she'll break apart," said the twice-demoted wardroom steward. We found his gallows humour unsettling, though his tales of raunchy love in one exotic port after another helped to relieve the gloom.

After a wonderful passage from the dark Atlantic into the aquamarine waters of the Caribbean, we came alongside in San Juan, Puerto Rico. Our guileless expectations had triggered fantasies of dusky maidens, palm trees, and rum. But before any shore leave, we had to "turn to" and attend to the daily tasks of scrubbing, polishing, and waxing. A twitter of pipes summoned our platoon to muster for work assignment, and we quickly formed up three-deep on the boat deck to await instructions. "Alright me lads, now which of you lot have driving licences?" the coxswain barked. Excitement rippled through the platoon as volunteers raised their hands in expectation of a cushy job swanning about town at the wheel of a shiny staff car. "Right," smiled the cox. "Then you ten," he said, counting off the heads, "will scrub out the heads and wash-places—that's bathrooms and toilets to you landlubbers." With casual conceit, he sorted the ten into various work parties. Then, like Captain Hook eyeing his victims, the cox enquired again: "And which of you can dance?" Fearing a stint scrubbing out the bilges, nobody moved. "Dance with Puerto Rican girls, in a posh club, with goodies to eat and drink?" No takers. At this point, the coxswain lost all credibility and numbered off a dozen of us for our marching orders: "At 1600 hours you will appear at the brow in your wings and strings, where a US navy bus will take you to the club for a formal social engagement. And you *will* behave like gentlemen—which you ain't. But first," he intoned, "you'll be chipping paint below decks, where the crowds on shore can't see you."

"Wings and strings"—jargon for the wing collar and black bow tie—were the accessories we used to upgrade our battle dress into formal attire. A flick of the wrist, and voilà. That evening, our fantasy became a glorious reality: fancy drinks and canapés and dancing with lovely young ladies (albeit under the watchful eye of their *dueñas*). The glamorous event put paid to the rollicking verses of our old drinking song that pilloried the seeming duplicities of navy life: "They say that in the navy / the girls are mighty fine. / You ask for Betty Grable / and they give you Frankenstein." Not so in Puerto Rico.

Our naval training covered everything from the art of living as a team in close quarters to the technical crafts involved in maintaining the complex machine on which we utterly depended. I had always inclined more to the Muses than to Techne, but once I began working engine-room watches on the Algerine-class minesweeper HMCS *Oshawa*, on the West Coast, I had to grasp—physically grasp—the interworkings of all her parts. I was, after all, living inside a machine with its mechanical, electronic, and hydraulic systems. Oiling and wiping the huge pistons and testing the temperature of the eccentrics with my bare hands was hot, dirty work. Good for the soul, the engineers told us. Certainly, it was very good for learning how a warship's engine room worked. Shoreside, we took courses in naval gunnery, communications, navigation, and fleet and flotilla manoeuvres, and gradually developed professional skill sets. I can still hear our instructors saying, "Pay close attention, lads. You may never hear this again—and may one day really need it." This admonition was never more telling than years later when I commanded a naval vessel in challenging circumstances and found myself having to draw upon resources which I had forgotten I actually had. We needed reminding about just how critical each phase of our training actually was. When shipping aboard a submarine many years later—a machine completely surrounded by the threatening sea—contemplating my dependence upon the technology that supported its watertight integrity could send a shiver down my spine.

IT WAS during my training in celestial navigation that Muse and Techne really converged. The Esquimalt Navigation School seemed particularly hot that year as we sweltered over star globes, nautical almanacs, and sextants and pondered the intriguing mathematical relationships between the earth and the heavens. When studying coastal pilotage, we had learned to fix the ship's position by taking bearings of geographical points ashore and using them to plot and project the ship's onward course to destination. So, we now learned how to navigate when on the high seas out of sight of land. We learned to take bearings and angular altitudes of celestial bodies, like the sun, moon, stars, and planets. After making a series of mathematical calculations known as sight reductions, we would work out a line of position, somewhere along which our ship lay. We took sights of other celestial bodies for accuracy. The point where all the lines met marked our position. We then projected course tracks onward to where we wanted to arrive, and when. Classroom theory and practice introduced us to the cosmos, with its fascinating clusters of light. Their names intrigued me: Cassiopeia, Andromeda, Alpha Centauri, Betelgeuse. Once at sea aboard the frigate HMCS *New Glasgow*, these celestial wonders came alive for me.

Sailing between Esquimalt and Pearl Harbor, Hawaii, provided me my first opportunity to put the theory I'd learned into practice. With my sextant and deck watch in hand, I took running fixes of the sun—morning, high noon, and afternoon. Far from the loom of land, I took multiple sights at crisp moments of morning and evening twilight. During night watches under resplendent skies, I identified the celestial bodies and took my sextant shots. All these swarming, luminous bodies in our ever-expanding universe drew my mind into both mathematical calculations and spiritual meditations. A psalmist in the fifth century BCE had been moved to proclaim (19:1): "The heavens declare the glory of God; and the firmament sheweth his handy-work." Yet again, the same sage posed an eternal question to Yahweh, the creator of the universe: "When I consider Your heavens, / the work of Your fingers, / The moon and the stars, which You have ordained; / What is man that You take thought of him ...?" (8:4) What is the human being, indeed.

Standing on the ship's bridge at night put me in mind of other early conceptions of the cosmic order. The ancient Greeks, I recalled, also believed in a coherent universe, the mysteries of which could be penetrated by human reason. Ulysses, the gifted hero of Homeric legends, expresses this idea in Shakespeare's play *Troilus and Cressida* (1.3.85): "The heavens themselves, the planets and this centre / Observe degree, priority, and place, / Insisture, course, proportion, season, form / Office, and custom, in all line of order." Shakespeare had put these words on the lips of the astrologer-king for whom the stars held meaning for human action. Yet, Shakespeare would also have been aware of the ancient theory of *musica universalis*, the music of the spheres, a system hearkening back to Pythagoras and Plato and to the earth-centred Ptolemaic view of the universe adopted in the first century CE. The idea of musical spheres had evolved from ancient philosophical accounts of proportion in the movements of the heavenly bodies, concepts also found in classical Greek architecture. For the ancients, this proportionality reflected an underlying harmony. Relationships in the physical world were not random but systematic, and it was because of this stability, with its qualities of "insisture, course, proportion, and season," as Shakespeare had put it, that we learned we could reliably navigate by tracking the stars. To any who doubted it, the first *Nautical Almanac*, the name given to the series of British astronomical and navigational guides first published in 1767, laid it all out with unprecedented mathematical accuracy. It was an act of remarkable scientific achievement.

Stargazing is an experience unique to those who can escape the intrusive glare of human habitation. As my friend Philip Teece, himself an astronomer and yachtsman, once put it, the glut of artificial light has cut us off from "a Universe beyond our perpetually floodlit world." Teece rightly regarded darkness "as a privilege." In pondering the immensity of the cosmos from his own darkened boat, he spoke of the "cosmic display" as a "rare spectacle." He realized when scanning the cluster of Hercules that his "binoculars were a time machine." Indeed, he confessed, "I peered 25,000 years back into the long-past epoch in which the light from the Hercules Cluster began its journey to reach my eye on this night." Light travels at the rate of 300,000 kilometres per second, and Betelgeuse, the closest of the supergiant stars, is four hundred light years away. Others are millions of light years away. One is humbled by a profound sense of reverence. In the words of Teece: "From this vantage point I began to see beyond mere appearance, and to grasp the multidimensional reality of what I was looking at."

Teece's impressions, and my own sense of wonder at the immensity of the universe in contrast to the Lilliputian reach of human endeavour, invariably strike me whenever I put to sea in a small boat. In fact, I have often thought that the small-boat drills I practised during my training as a junior officer were designed as an antidote to the often-brash presumptions of youth. "So, you want to be an officer, do you, *sir*?" (In order to avoid being charged with insubordination, lower-deck mentors always added the "sir"—with heavy emphasis—when challenging us.) As midshipmen and cadets, we were officers only in a technical sense and still had to shape up when under the tutelage of our more experienced lower-deck instructors. But that was the least of our comeuppance.

One of the tools for either shaping up or shipping out was the naval whaler. Commonly called the seaboat, its mid-eighteenth-century design had been officially embraced by the Royal Navy in 1810. A hundred years later, Canada adopted it for the Royal Canadian Navy, where it remained in use until the 1960s. Clinker-built of elm and oak, and propelled by oar and sail, the seaboat was eminently seaworthy and manoeuvrable, though the oarsmen, with their 5.2-metre (17-foot) sweeps, could find it hard slogging in a heavy seaway or on a long pull in a regatta. Weighing 1,225 kilograms (2,700 pounds), the 8.2-metre-long (27-foot) boat had many uses: as a lifeboat aboard ships; a messenger boat, both at sea and in harbour; and a vessel for running armed units from ship to shore. Launching it from the boat deck in the days before automated hoists (still common in my day) required old-fashioned seamanship. The operation began with the summons, "Away, seaboat's crew." An officer then ordered "clear lower decks," to muster muscle from all off-watch personnel. The boat's crew would then clamber aboard the boat while it was hanging in the davits, set the blocks and tackles (pronounced "taykles"), and prepare the boat for sea. Finally, when the spare hands had tumbled up to the boat deck, the fully crewed boat would be swung outboard and lowered into the sea by means of brute manhandling of the falls (ropes). It all required skill and judgement, and we drilled constantly until the orders and routines became second nature. The launching involved quite another vocabulary: "Take the strain," or "marry the falls," the boat-launcher would bark, while everyone else worked in silence. "Ease to the brake, easy, now; handsomely, lads; light-to; avast!" The pitch, pattern, and pressure of the drills tumble into memory like the sting of salt over a rolling deck.

I was once set to sea with others in a seaboat from the deck of the frigate HMCS *New Glasgow*. We were in the mid-Pacific, en route to Pearl Harbor. As we descended to the water, brilliant sunshine and long, rhythmical swells greeted our launch. "Ship your oars," the cox'n called, prompting us to begin sliding our heavy sweeps through the thole pins and over the sea; then, "Stand by," whereupon we gripped the oars and leaned far forward to dig into the sea and propel the hull. Then the hard part began, as the call "Give way together" signalled us to pull like a team of galley slaves. Steadily, our rhythm increased. And as we pulled, our ship steamed away from us under streaks of black smoke, leaving us entirely on our own. The cox'n's sharp order, "Eyes in the boat," would call us back to our task whenever we turned to look back at the ship or survey the heaving waters aswirl around us. And so, we pulled and ached, pulled and ached, until the waters churned astern. Humouring us with attempts at levity, the cox'n regaled us with yarns featuring Mediterranean galley slaves. "First the good news," he shouted over our gasping breaths. "There's double lashings of steak and lobster for lunch." (Groan.) Then the bad news: "Pharaoh wants to water ski." At the order "Lay on oars" he gave us a brief respite from our sweaty labours. As we searched the horizon to look for our ship amidst the swells, I could not help but recall the Breton fisherman's prayer: "Oh God, thy sea is so great and my boat is so small." It was at this unguarded moment that I heard Uncle Llew's jaunty, storytelling voice break upon me from aboard his First World War ship, HMS *Vienna*:

Well, me b'y, we was off in the North Sea. Great times to be at sea with wonderful shipmates. Mind you, lad, there was a war on, and we had to keep a sharp eye out for the Germans. Well, one day the captain says to me, "Canada," he says (the English always called me Canada), "the ol' wireless be broken down, and we're too far for ships in the flotilla to read our flag hoists. So, I wants yer to take the whaler and crew and run some errands."

A dramatic pause here while my uncle stuffs his pipe and luxuriates in the memory of his younger days.

Well, me b'y, the seas was buildin' up   not yet into greybeards, mind ye, but angry, churning, and nasty-like. So, we called out the seaboat's crew, lowered away, slipped our gripes, heisted sail, and took off into the spume. Well now, let me tell ye [pause, ponder, puff], there we was in that blusterin' blow, racing under full sail, chasing down, from crest to trough and trough to crest; taking our sights of the ships in our flotilla, all boisterous and bucking along the rollers and taking the occasional green one over the bow. We felt so wondrously alive we could have taken on the whole German fleet.

And then he smiled at the folly of his last remark and leaned back into his chair, knowing he would never again live those uplifting moments of daring, dash, and danger.

The order "Stand by!" broke me out of my reverie and into a more pressing reality. Before the cox'n could bark "Eyes in the boat!" I had caught sight of our frigate returning, with a bone in her teeth, to pick us up. Cirrocumulus clouds arched across the sky and hinted at the approach of a frontal system that could make us very uncomfortable. So we set-to with a will to meet our rendezvous. Once alongside our mother ship, we reversed the hoisting procedure by hooking the boat back into the Robinson disengaging gear and connecting to the falls that tumbled down to us from the ship's davits. High above us, the crew handled the lines amidst murmured calls of "down slack the falls, easy... marry the falls... walk away handsomely"—like a reassuring liturgy as they pulled us up to the deck.

I SHIPPED aboard HMCS *Fortune* in July 1957, on receiving my commission. She was the senior ship in a squadron of four Bay-class wooden minesweepers. Naval doctrine of the day regarded mines as the covert weapon of choice. They were cheap and nasty. Unfriendly forces (code for "Soviet") could employ them to alter an opponent's marine geography to their own advantage. They could block harbours and alter the shape of channels and seaways. Indeed, they could literally undermine the opponent's confidence in navigating safely in home waters. Ultimately, they could destroy ships. Mines could be "contact" (bump into them and blow up) or magnetic and acoustic (pass over them and your magnetism or your noise will trigger your destruction). In short, they could create havoc on their own terms. Ships like *Fortune* were designed to sweep the channels clear.

My posting in *Fortune* marked a time of rapid maturation as a sea officer, for during my bridge watches I had to oversee control of a fast-moving vessel while following the navigator's passage plan. I was responsible for executing squadron manoeuvres and for conducting my own ship when sweeping for mines. In those days, our own friendly forces laid the mines and used live ammunition. I recall one time having the watch during a sweeping exercise upcoast when we had deployed sweeping gear. The gear consisted of a large electrical loop of pulsing alternating current that created an even larger magnetic field. We would steam up and down the presumed minefield in parallel sweeps, navigating precisely in order to define the areas we had travelled. Busily conning my ship under the captain's watchful eye, I began to realize that strong currents at the change of tide were catching my loop, just as I was approaching the point of the field where I had to make a 180-degree turn and settle into the new search pattern. A wind was coming up, and I was standing off a lee shore. The situation was dicey. I made suggestions to the captain about our next course of action, and sought his advice. Quietly and unflustered, he said: "You're the officer of the watch." So, I handled it my own way. Once I had turned the ship and the towed array and settled into the new course, the captain sidled over to me with the words, "That was good; but I myself would have done differently." His approach meant much to me, and I later used it myself in my teaching. Provided safety is not an issue, let the student take the stress and learn.

Back alongside at summer's end, I invited Skipper Llew to an "at-home" evening at CFB Esquimalt aboard the ships to which my classmates and I had been posted. This was a "gentlemen's evening," hosted in the gracious style to which we had been inculcated over the years. Skipper would have recognized the customary civility of the officers from his days aboard HMS *Vienna*, as naval traditions like this had remained virtually unchanged. Earlier that evening, with all the flair of youth, I had picked him up in my green 1931 Ford

Coupe (with its rumble seat, imitation leopard-skin seat cover, and yellow-spoked wire wheels). At the naval base in Esquimalt, we tippled at each ship, met with fellow officers, and tucked into a relaxed collegiality he had not experienced in years. Life can be very good, and that evening with my special mentor filled me with profound gratitude and joy.

AMONG MY postings in the navy, I had never experienced seafaring on a freshwater lake. But in 1964, I landed in the Great Lakes Training Centre in Hamilton, Ontario. A lot had transpired in the years since my graduation in 1958. I had married, passed my foreign service exams, and spent three years in Europe with the Canadian Department of Citizenship and Immigration before changing course to pursue postgraduate studies and a teaching career at the University of Winnipeg. Ships and seafaring were still a going concern, of course, and having maintained my navy status as a reservist throughout this time, I had happily answered the call to assist with teaching new recruits the basics of seamanship.

I arrived at my new home base at the Naval Reserve Division of HMCS *Star*, in Hamilton, only to find three dreary-looking vessels in need of new life: the Porte-class training ships HMCS *Porte St. Jean* and *Porte St. Louis*, and the former air force supply ship HMCS *Scatari*. A frigate would later join us from Halifax. The Porte-class vessels had been named after two of the main gates of the old town of Quebec City. At that stage in the evolution of the Canadian Navy, giving a French name to a ship was as close as anyone came to acknowledging francophone Canadians in what was fundamentally a British naval culture. Little attempt was made even to pronounce the ships' names correctly. The *Saint Jeen* and the *Loois* they remained.

Nothing looks drearier, nor more jaded and forlorn, than a boat left unattended for long periods during winter and early spring. These ships were no exception. Having overwintered unmanned in the dock basin, with only a ragged layer of straw bales in place to buffer their hulls against the winter ice, they needed refurbishing, and it was up to us in the permanent crews to get them into shape in time for the program. For the first phase of my posting, cleaning, fine tuning, and provisioning the ships would be the order of the day. We were preparing to take groups of new recruits in two-week batches and teach them basic seamanship. These brief but intense voyages through the Great Lakes waterways would turn them from a ragtag-and-bobtail group into disciplined seamen who could stand tall among their peers. The trainees came to our squadron from across Canada. They were young, in search of adventure, and eager to learn.

As I never tired of reminding our sailors that summer, they would be passage-making in one of the most remarkable seaways in the world. The St. Lawrence seaway had begun as a vision in the eighteenth century and ended in June 1959 as an astounding reality: deep-sea ships from the open Atlantic penetrating deep into the Great Lakes, thus adding an eighth great sea to the legendary seven.

These waters experience all the conditions for which the high seas have long been known: calms and storms, shipbuilding and shipwrecks, commerce and combat, audacious exploration and discovery, and high-performance sailing competitions. Having overflown the Lakes years earlier, I had grasped first-hand the vastness of the largest body of fresh water in the world, encompassing 240,000 square kilometres (150,000 square miles) of "inland sea" and a breathtaking 17,700-kilometre (11,000-mile) coastline harbouring cities and towns on both sides of the Canada-US border. The Great Lakes boast over two hundred lighthouses. Famous ones, like Toronto's Gibraltar Point Lighthouse, built in 1808, and the Buffalo Point Light, built in Lake Erie in 1833, tell stories of hauntings, murder, marine disasters, and war. Viewing these lakes from the air, I could visualize the forces that shape weather and sea conditions. During the hot summer months, the Great Lakes absorb heat, somewhat like a storage battery charging itself on external energy. With the onset of autumn, surges of polar air mix with the radiant energy rising from the water to produce cyclonic gyres—systems of rotating ocean currents that, by twisting at a high velocity, stir up the surface of the water, creating huge waves and formidable storms.

The Great Lakes are the home of commercial ships called "lakers." Local mariners simply call them boats. Hundreds of feet long, with their wheelhouses perched at the very tip of their bow and their aft deckhouses at the farthest edge of the stern, these "straight deckers," as locals also call them, look ungainly. An uncluttered upper deck stretches from the pilothouse up forward to the boiler house aft. Flat hatches cover the access points to the vessels' huge holds. But ship designs are not the only distinguishing feature of Great Lakes maritime culture. The Lake sailors talk differently from deep-sea salties. Where ocean mariners undertake voyages steered by quartermasters or helmsmen, lakers take trips and are steered by a wheelsman. In Great Lake parlance, watchkeepers are called watchmen, funnels become smokestacks, and breakwaters become breakwalls. Differences in language suggest intriguing historical differences between nautical cultures and practices, but at bottom—which no vessel ever hopes to touch—they are all creatures of the sea. There was, as Henry James wrote when steaming on the Lakes in 1871, no "ambiguity of vision."

I had first cast eyes on the Great Lakes during my cross-Canada journey in 1950 with the Kitsilano Boys Band. During a stop in Toronto, I had visited the site of one of the greatest marine disasters in Canadian history, which had happened on Lake Ontario just six months previous. In the early hours of 17 September 1949, the six-thousand-ton tourist ship ss *Noronic*, the "Queen of the Lakes," had burst into flame alongside Pier 9, killing 119 of its 512 passengers in a matter of minutes. By the time I came upon the scene in the spring of 1950, the anguish of the *Noronic* was still fresh in the city's memory, and the skeletal hulk lay dead for all to see. Design flaws in the ship and an inadequately trained crew were the cause. Set against Toronto's rich seafaring history, the fate of the *Noronic* and its aftermath served as a cautionary tale. I used it when giving my recruits firefighting training as part of their seamanship curriculum. I had recently completed a hands-on fire-leaders course in the Damage Control School at the Esquimalt Naval Base, in which we faced a range of emergencies. Unusually, we were a class of mixed ranks of trainees. That made good pedagogical sense, for aboard ship survival is everybody's business. First came the theory; then the serious practice. Dressed in protective clothing and wearing a self-contained breathing apparatus, I stood one day on the top deck of what some wag had dubbed HMCS Tumult, a three-deck hulk regularly subjected to withering flames. My task was to lead a hose-team down through a series of hatches and compartments and extinguish an oil fire raging below. We'd be groping all the way, for the hulk was filled with black smoke and we'd be unable to see. As clouds of billowing smoke swirled about me, the chief petty officer instructor grasped me by the shoulder and asked with a shout whether I got claustrophobic. "I haven't a clue, Chief," I blurted through my mask. "Well then," he replied with a wicked glance, "today's the day we're gonna find out." Faced with new experiences and major tasks in the navy, you simply got on with things. Anyway, I was too busy putting out fires to concern myself with how I felt (I wasn't claustrophobic). It was all part of being a seaman.

Seamanship, in the glory days of square-rigged sailing ships in the seventeenth and eighteenth centuries, comprised all the arts of caring for, managing, and working the ship. A sailor was considered "marked trained" once he had proven himself able to "hand, reef, and steer." That meant he could reef and handle the sails and steer the ship in all weather. This would have required mastering every kind of rope work, anchor work, and splicing, and knowing all of the ship's gear—her blocks and tackle, shimmies and sheaves, and boats and rigging. Though the technology of seafaring has changed radically since those days, the fundamentals remain the same. Seamanship as I was taught it—and as I went on to teach others—is as much about practicality and ingenuity as it is about self-reliance and teamwork. It is about maximizing human effort and imagination and shaping them to set purposes. It was these principles that moved Admiral Patrick Budge to remind us, in his own version of Nicholas Monsarrat, that "sailors, with their sense of order and discipline, should rule the world." In misquoting *The Cruel Sea*, he may well have overstated his case, but we never doubted his loyalty to the principles of the Service.

My work with training the recruits kept me busy that summer, but I always made time to appreciate the pleasures of the inland sea. Repeatedly, we were treated to some of the most remarkable star scapes I had ever experienced. The middle watch, the period from midnight to four o'clock, was always my favourite. While the ship slept, silence reigned and darkness surrounded our small watch-on-deck, which comprised myself on the bridge (with an eye to the radar in the wheelhouse); the lookouts on the darkened bridge; the helmsman, his face illuminated by faint light from the binnacle; and the fire watchman making his rounds. Morning always crept up on me too soon, the dawn light etching the horizon and breaking into my quiet train of thought. I sometimes felt, like Coleridge's ancient mariner, "Alone, alone, all, all alone, / alone on a wide wide sea!" Yet, beneath the peaceful scene lay a silent threat.

From its early beginnings, locals had expressed concerns about the seaway's potential for destroying the native ecology, a fear that was eventually realized. The first signs of the pestilential zebra and quagga mussels native to the Black, Caspian, and Azov Seas appeared in 1986. They had been introduced by ballast water discharged from foreign-going vessels. In addition to invasive species, the area's fish and wildlife habitats had become contaminated by runoff from industrial development in the surrounding communities. This perhaps explains why during my time on the Lakes I never saw any marine creatures—neither the much-touted lake trout and perch, nor the splendid ten-pound trophy walleye. While the Great Lakes offered a unique experience of Canada, I missed the salt water, with its playful seals and sea lions and its powerful orcas. I missed the sight of dolphins teasing the bow of the ship, and cavorting and lolling in its wake. Perhaps Henry James had it right after all when he described the Lakes as "the sea, and yet just not the sea." Yet for all that, the Lakes have a character and a magnificence all their own.

Reflecting on my summer on the Great Lakes reinforces for me how deeply my rigorous naval training, together with the Traditions of Service, nourished me and prepared me for life. Wherever I went, the values of camaraderie, trust, and fellowship always marked my journey. Certainly, while working in public relations at the Canadian embassy in Germany, I had always worn the naval officer's crest on my blue blazer: a crown and anchor on a maple leaf background. It was an image I was proud to project.

MY CURIOSITY about ships and seafaring, which had begun in childhood, led me to pursue naval history and the exploits of mariners in peace and war. In cities from Vancouver to Halifax, Greenwich to Hamburg, and Sydney to Tokyo, I gravitated to maritime museums. Historic museum ships welcomed me aboard: the RCMP's arctic patrol vessel *St. Roch* in Vancouver; Nelson's flagship HMS *Victory* in Portsmouth; Canada's doughty corvette HMCS *Sackville*, of Battle of the Atlantic fame, in Halifax; the tea clipper *Cutty Sark* in Greenwich; the type XXI submarine U-2540 ("Wilhelm Bauer") in Bremerhaven; and the type VIIC "Atlantikboot" submarine U-995 in Laboe. I liked to imagine the crew members of these historic vessels as they approached their ship for the first time with the same anticipation I myself had felt on first going to sea. Since time immemorial, sailors have regarded their ships with an air of romantic realism—an overwhelming sense of adventure mixed with twinges of apprehension as they faced the harsh realities of living in a machine embraced by the sea. It was ever so, whatever the ship or country.

And then, there was Greece, which I visited when I was in my fifties, though I had first encountered it thirty years earlier as an undergraduate studying Western culture and philosophy. My studies of Greek culture—and especially philosophy—were transformative, yet it was the 1964 film version of Nikos Kazantzakis's 1952 novel *Zorba the Greek* that first fired in me the sensuous imagination for Greece. Anthony Quinn's brilliant portrayal of the boisterous antihero Zorba and his world made it all so palpable. These were the halcyon days of the 1960s with their unique brand of protest and personal encounter. The era exuded a spirit of revolt, individualism, of nihilism and self-indulgent sensuality.

Only later did I go to the roots of the film by steeping myself in the novel. Even now, I can imagine the crafty Zorba admonishing me for taking so long to embrace his written story. "What, boss? You mean, after seeing that movie you waited ten years before reading the book? You are some lazy devil." Lazy or not, I eventually made the journey to Greece, and found myself in August 1987 at sunrise in Piraeus Harbour, near Athens. The sun was already caressing the Aegean Sea with promises of mists and mid-morning heat. The sensuous experience of standing on those storied shores coalesced the present and the past, and broadened my mind to new horizons. The words of Kazantzakis's nameless narrator capture my sentiments on that day: "The sea, autumn mildness, islands bathed in light, fine rain spreading a diaphanous veil over the immortal nakedness of Greece. Happy is the man, I thought, who, before dying, has the good fortune to sail the Aegean Sea."

The occasion that brought me to Athens was an international conference of naval historians that had been scheduled to coincide with the launching of the *Olympias*, a reconstructed Athenian warship from the fifth century BCE. The project was a proof-of-concept initiative to test the viability of the trireme, a superior ship design of the period that featured three banks of rowers. It was in all respects a remarkable example of experimental marine archeology, for the reconstruction had drawn upon the talents and insights of a broad spectrum of professionals from ship architects to literary historians. Presiding over the event and its many celebrations was the charismatic singer, movie actress, and political activist Melina Mercouri. She had gained recognition in the '60s with such popular songs as "A Ship Is Coming" and for her starring role in *Never on Sunday*, a romantic comedy about a free-spirited call girl. At the time of our visit, she was the Minister of State for Culture and Science. Her presence added zest and vivaciousness to an already charged event.

On the appointed morning, we gathered at 6:00 AM on the dock at Piraeus and boarded the 37-metre (121-foot) vessel *Olympias*. The ship would be powered that day by 170 oarsmen and oarswomen, including junior officers from the Hellenic Navy and rowing teams from Oxford and Cambridge along with volunteers from countries that had contributed to the project. As the ship pulled away from shore under the barked orders of the *Triarchos* (Commander of Trireme) and the increasing drumbeat of the *auletes* (flautist), we passengers or *epibatai* (spearmen and archers) strode about with airs of feigned command. Each of us—one from each nation attending the conference—found himself lifted back in time to the dramatic naval wars between Athens and Sparta during the years from 431 to 404 BCE. Pacing up and down the wooden upper deck, we looked down between the boards onto the banks of rowers: sixty-two on the upper bank (*thranitai*), fifty-four on the middle bank (*zygitai*), and fifty-four on the lower bank (*thalamite*). Contemporary accounts in Thucydides's multivolume *History of the Peloponnesian War* had described the trireme as an especially swift, nimble, and effective warship. Some later historians had been inclined to doubt his objectivity, and tended to speak of his rich imagination. With *Olympias*, however, there could now be no doubt whatever. On that day, she demonstrated her manoeuvrability and reached a speed of ten knots. Later trials showed she could reach ramming speeds in excess of that and reverse course 180 degrees in one minute.

The sun stood well past high noon when we returned to Piraeus. We had stepped back in time almost 2,500 years and felt an ancient warship come alive under our feet. We had gazed upon the same harbour and coasts as had the Spartans and Athenians of old; gained insight into their remarkable skills at ship construction and engineering; and—except that the rowers of antiquity would had been slaves chained to the boat—felt the same sun, wind, and waves. Kazantzakis had observed in *Zorba the Greek* that human beings tend only to recognize happiness once it is past; that we are often only later overtaken by thoughts of how happy we once had been. But right now, in Greece, the novel's narrator confesses, "I was experiencing happiness and knew I was happy." That's how it was for me in Piraeus.

4

QUESTING

There's that wanderlust first, that itch in the sole, that hankering in the soul that puffs out the sails for a journey into the totally unknown.
M.G. VASSANJI, *The In-Between World of Vikram Lall*

LONG BEFORE I voyaged through North German waters, I had entered them in my imagination as a student discovering nineteenth-century German writers. Theodor Storm's vivid descriptions of the northern coastal seascapes, with their mists and dykes and brooding rural isolation, captivated me, while his imagery of the marshes and mud flats surrounding his hometown of Husum, his "gray town by the sea," reminded me of the Fraser estuary in winter. Reading Storm's poetry late into the night, my mind would be set alight with spooky scenes of foggy nights and uncanny storms, images that had animated me since early childhood. Later, Heinrich Heine's cycle of poems *North Sea Images* (*Nordseebilder*), and Emanuel Geibel's *Baltic Songs* (*Ostseelieder*) evoked for me the romanticism of evening mists and distant lighthouses; of the landlubber's yearning for alluring ports of call and the sailor's longing for home. I felt a kinship with the people of Northern Germany. Their hearths and firesides exuded the same warmth as mine, and the more I learned of their world, the more it resonated with my experience of the BC coast.

My fascination with things German goes back to my growing up in Vancouver in the 1940s, during the second of two gruelling wars with Germany within living memory that together accounted for ten years of vicious combat. I wanted to look into the face of the enemy Other and explore German culture in depth through the medium of literature and language. The propaganda I was exposed to as a youngster had shaped my quest, high school and university studies in the 1950s gave it substance, and working abroad in my twenties matured it. The more I understood, the more I felt driven to understand. In 1964, the German-Canadian writer Walter Bauer, a former prisoner of war, captured the continuity of my own journey through life with a collection of writings entitled *The Road Counts, Not the Hostels* (*Der Weg zählt, nicht die Herberge*). That was how I understood questing.

My undergraduate years at UBC marked a critical rite of passage, which I embraced wholeheartedly. In the 1950s, the university was still an exclusive domain, available to only a minority of high school graduates who had undergone the enriched, three-year "university program" that prepared them for post-secondary study. Indeed, UBC at the time numbered only four or five thousand students. Admission to university signalled our entrance into what we felt was the adult professional life, and we dressed accordingly. The dress of the day was blazer and slacks with a shirt and tie for the men, and tailored skirts and jackets for the women. In today's terms we'd call it business casual and then some. We carried briefcases and polished our shoes. The teaching staff addressed us formally as Mr. or Miss. Many of us in the armed services frequently attended in uniform. As in the old ad for razor blades popular at the time, we aimed to "look sharp, feel sharp, and be sharp." We called it looking "snazzy," men and women alike. When playing band gigs, I inclined to the fur-felt fedora hat and multicoloured diamond socks to set off my blue suede shoes. But these were the last remnants of the showbiz style I had acquired on concert tours abroad.

At this early stage in my studies, the three threads of my undergraduate development—academics, the naval service, and jazz—were almost more than I could handle. I steeped myself in book learning (though my marks were modest), while playing the trumpet and keeping up with my naval-training activities, which involved both work and play. We navy types had our own diversions, such as racing whalers whatever the weather in Coal Harbour on training weekends, and enjoying formal mess dinners at our base at HMCS *Discovery* in Stanley Park. "Let us rejoice while we are young!"— *Gaudeamus igitur!*—German students had been singing since medieval days. But underpinning my studious approach to academe was a fourth thread—an almost unconscious inclination toward a personal spiritual exploration. Medieval monks, I later learned, called this urge "the love of learning and the desire for God." In effect, it actually linked the love of learning with *the search* for God—a notion more to my taste. At the time, I could articulate none of this.

The university campus still bore traces of the Second World War, when it had housed an army camp. Rows of single-storey barrack blocks—still painted in wartime green—served as faculty offices and classrooms. Others at the old Fort Camp and Acadia Camp provided student residences. At the centre of campus, the large armoury building housed the offices (and the Officers' Mess) of the university's three military contingents that trained students for the permanent force and the reserves. Significantly, faculty members with wartime service commanded each of the units. My home department, German, boasted a well-decorated veteran among its instructors. Robert Farquharson, a recently graduated PhD, had joined the Royal Canadian Air Force in 1941, at the age of twenty-two. Within a short time, he was regularly piloting one of the famous C-47 Douglas Dakotas on covert operations behind enemy lines in Burma. Each year on November 11, long columns of uniformed students would march to the Memorial Gymnasium for Remembrance Day services, led by the university's Scottish Pipe Band. One year, we were joined by the entire faculty and student body of the School of Forestry at Sopron University in Hungary. They had escaped the Hungarian Revolution of 1956. For me, their presence lent poignancy to my playing of "The Last Post."

The study of German was popular at university, quite apart from the fact that everyone had to take two years of a foreign language. The curriculum covered grammar, composition, and translation, as well as literary works that introduced us to the culture of Germany. Many of us would have begun studying German in high school with the appropriately titled *First Book in German*. First published in 1942, in the middle of the war, it was still in use over twenty years later. Textbooks for school and university enjoyed a long shelf life in those days. H.G. Fiedler's *Oxford Book of German Verse* is a case in point. Known among students simply as "Fiedler," it had been reprinted ten times between 1916 and 1951, without updating. Steeped in nostalgia, the anthology reflected what the Germans call *eine heile Welt*, a morally intact, pristine world. Its conservative and somewhat dated selection of works never stretched beyond the verse of a long-forgotten poet who had died in 1909. The Gothic font itself made an ideological statement about unchanging cultural values. Perhaps that reflected Fiedler's intended purpose. The anthology certainly looks like an attempt to reassure learners that strong humanistic traditions always survive the ravages of war.

Yet throughout the life span of Fiedler's anthology, the European world had been tearing itself apart. In the First World War, machine guns and poison gas at the Battle of Ypres had turned the front into what Robert L. O'Connell has called "an automated corpse factory," signalling a new era of industrialized murder. By Christmas 1914, as the *Oxford Book* was entering its first printing, some 1.6 million dead and wounded had "fallen." Of course, we students already knew these realities from the Allied perspective. We had read the English war poets in high school—angry writers like Wilfred Owen and Siegfried Sassoon—and were moved by their disgust with the generals and politicians who proclaimed the nobility of death on the battlefield. The myth-making at Remembrance Day ceremonies that claimed to honour the "fallen" who had sacrificed themselves for "God, King, and Country" struck many of us as sham. I bristled at the dishonesty of Laurence Binyon's poem "For the Fallen": "They shall not grow old, as we that are left grow old; / Age shall not weary them, nor the years condemn. / At the going down of the sun and in the morning / we shall remember them." Even as an undergrad, I rejected the sentimental lie. I soon learned that German youth had largely rejected their country's myths too.

Almost seventy years now separate me from my first encounter with Fiedler's *Oxford Book*. When a battered copy recently came into my hands, I was reminded of the attractive antiquarian literary world it had once created for me. Old professor Fiedler, I thought, had gotten much right. The book opens with Martin Luther's great hymn of the Reformation, "A Mighty Fortress Is Our God" (*Eine feste Burg ist unser Gott),* then proceeds through dimensions of the human spirit of which I had had little notion at the time. Of course, his literary canon has long since become familiar to me, as have the many works which his conservative cast of mind had excluded. But on taking up my well-worn copy—scuffed and marked up by generations of eager students— I rediscovered a nostalgic link between the callow youth I once was and the senior citizen I have become. Fiedler's examples of forest and meadow romanticism, its celebration of folksong and ballad, meditation and myth, and obscure historical motifs, still move me strangely. So, too, do his echoes of a parochial and nostalgic Christianity. As a place marker in history, Fiedler is a gem.

Later in my undergraduate years, I closed an important gap in my survey of German poetry with Jethro Bithell's *An Anthology of German Poetry, 1880-1940*. Published in 1941, two years into the Second World War, the anthology focused on the social upheavals brought about by industrialization and war. These were the urgent themes facing the youth of today, his preface insisted. Students of the 1940s were his intended readers, yet in the 1950s, we found the voices in Bithell's anthology as relevant as ever. With vigorous and sharp-edged language, they took up the subject of modernity with a vengeance. A central theme was the idea of "the new mankind" (*Der neue Mensch*) and the unique possibilities of a new generation. Its stirring strains were revolutionary. "March, march, march... Join the ranks. March. We will conquer the world! The New Man is on the move," calls the narrator of Heinrich Lersch's once-popular poem "Man in Iron" (*Mensch im Eisen*). A boilermaker by trade and a faithful Roman Catholic, Lersch supported the Nazi Party from 1933 until his death in 1936. Like so many of his generation, he never saw where these Nazi notions were leading.

Jump-started by Fiedler's collection and emboldened by Bithell, I continued my investigations of German literature through the centuries, from Luther to Friedrich Schiller's classical dramas and on to modern theatre. A common pattern emerged of writers committed to understanding the personalities and dynamics of their changing societies. With a journalist's eye for political and social issues, the North German poet Richard Dehmel attacked widespread injustices in German society and the coming storm of the First World War. His protests led to a German court ordering his poem *Der Arbeitsmann* ("The Worker") to be burned. Discovering his work in 1956, at the height of the Hungarian Revolution and the movement of refugees to Canada, we found Dehmel's language to be both refreshing and relevant, yet he is virtually unknown today.

We students encountered many other literary approaches that deepened our grasp of the human condition. Thus, the contemplative poetry of Rainer Maria Rilke provided a rich counterpoint. Influenced by the work of the French sculptor Auguste Rodin while in Paris, Rilke's "object-poems" (*Dinggedichte*) meditated with simplicity and clarity upon the essential nature of objects, gestures, and emotions. His writing revealed startling aspects of the everyday world as captured in scenes such as a carousel in the Jardin du Luxembourg, or a caged panther in the Jardin des Plantes. Rilke's approach was both experimental and mystical, and it opened my mind to the infinite possibilities of language. His *Book of Hours* (*Das Stundenbuch*), in which a medieval monk meditates on monastic life, on pilgrimage, and on poverty and death, remains among my favourites because of his brilliant poetic approach to the Ineffable.

The early 1950s drew me into the minds of German veterans. The genre known as home-comer, or rubble literature (*Heimkehrer- und Trümmerliteratur*), laid bare the savage, shell-shocked worlds of soldiers as they struggled home from the front. In his acclaimed radio play *Outside the Door* (*Draußen vor der Tür*), Wolfgang Borchert paints a dark picture of the devastation he encountered on his return home to bomb-shattered Hamburg in 1946. In the preface to the play, he writes, "This is the story of one of those who come home, but don't really come home, because there is no longer any home. Their home is outside the door. Germany itself is outside the door." After its total defeat in May 1945, Germany was an outcast among the nations. Faced with hopelessness and loss, the characters in Borchert's play struggle to find answers to the existential questions of modern German history. His stories undergirded my desire to encounter that Germany and to know it intimately. Borchert himself had been broken by the war and died young.

My study of German literature soon took me beyond philosophy and politics to the realm of what I later called personal inscapes. Thomas Mann's famous novella *Tonio Kröger* in particular introduced me to new regions of introspection and self-evaluation and played a key role in my intellectual and emotional development. Significantly, I read it in my second or third year of undergraduate studies, at perhaps one of the most crucial periods in my life. Its linguistic and intellectual challenges were huge, not to mention its daunting level of vocabulary. That was especially so in the lengthy philosophical discussions that occur later in the book between the adult Tonio and the Russian artist Lisaweta Iwanowna. I still have the 1932 American school edition we used, which, as the preface explains, had been published for students who had completed three semesters of college German or two years of high school German. Twenty-five years later, when I taught it as a university teacher, the book would have been well beyond the reach of the average Canadian undergraduate let alone a high school student. How sad that the scope of my profession had so markedly declined over the years.

Tonio Kröger presents the engaging, if sentimental, tale of a young man caught within the tensions created by his double heritage as both a bourgeois and an artist. Born of a stolid North German father and an artistic South American mother, the character must work out a path that balances the expectations of a "normal" life with that of a non-conforming outsider. Unusually sensitive to literature and the arts, Tonio yet feels attracted to the practical-minded people around him who never question the human condition or the meanings of things. Shaped by a romantic desire for a spiritual home, Tonio felt tossed between loneliness and the desire for community. His struggle captured for me the essence of adolescent self-consciousness, and I took it to heart.

Tonio Kröger provided me with a vocabulary for exploring my inner thoughts and conflicts. I felt that Tonio's life resonated with my own search for purpose and meaning. Where did I stand in matters of talent and calling? What was I capable of achieving? And what of the abiding sense of alienation I felt? By venturing into the world of the intellect, was I, like Tonio, nothing more than *ein Bürger auf Irrwegen* (a bourgeois gone astray)? Recently, while rereading my old school copy of the book, I experienced a wistful reunion with my younger self when the person I once was welcomed me back into his world of intellectual and emotional struggle. I came upon a passage that I had marked all those decades ago for closer attention—not in erasable pencil, but in dark black ink: "A few people necessarily go astray, because for them there is no right way." I had been determined that that would never be the case with *me*.

All the while, I was reading widely in English, French, and Polish. While these studies never fired me up as German did, the English language—my West Germanic mother tongue—impressed me with its evocative power and capacity for creative innovation. I fell in love with the linguistic gymnastics of Dylan Thomas's poem "Fern Hill": "Now as I was young and easy under the apple boughs / About the lilting house and happy as the grass was green"; and the brooding bite and directness of Shakespeare's *Hamlet*: "To be or not to be, that is the question."

German, I found, was equally graphic. Early on I was reminded that in crafting his translation of the Bible into German in the 1520s and '30s, Martin Luther had written of the spirited plasticity of the language. He had found it to be much like the original Greek from which he had translated the New Testament. High praise indeed. He demonstrated that potential for richness when creating a host of colourful words and expressions. They still have a contemporary ring. In Luther's translations, scapegoat became "sin-ram" (*Sünden-bock*); backbiter became "slander-snout" (*Lästermaul*); and a dispute became "word-squabble" (*Wortgezänk*). Years later, I ventured into the works of Shakespeare in German in the consummate translation by the Romantic-era writers August Wilhelm Schlegel, and Dorothea and Ludwig Tieck. Drawing on a German language that owed much to Luther, they had recreated his plays, I felt, precisely as Shakespeare would have done had German been his mother tongue.

However, each translation is a new creation. Sometimes, the cultural resonances of words are so strong as to render translation impossible. Goethe captured that notion in a scene from his verse-tragedy *Faust*, a magnificent panorama of human endeavour and folly. Here, like Martin Luther before him, the character Dr. Faustus attempts to translate the opening line of St. John's Gospel, "In the beginning was the Word…," by examining a series of possible synonyms for Word (in German, the obvious one would be *Wort*). So far so good. But, of course, both Luther and his literary surrogate were translating from the original Biblical Greek: "In the beginning was the *Logos*." But the word *Logos* didn't refer just to a lexical unit of vocabulary (i.e., a word). In effect, as I learned, it embodied a whole complex of philosophical arguments. It could refer to something that had existed "in the Beginning," before anything else had come into being. It stood for the dynamic principle of creative order and the principle of divine reason. Put simply, it was the Word of God (whatever that meant). Thus, I shared the frustration of Dr. Faustus who tested all the possibilities—in the beginning was Word, or perhaps Mind, or maybe even Power—and rejected the lot in favour of "in the Beginning was the Deed." Through my love of literature, I was discovering the possibilities and ambiguities in intellectual and spiritual life.

AS MY studies advanced, I gradually recognized my parents' ambivalent relationship with higher education. On the one hand they respected it; on the other, they were suspicious of its effects on me. My mother in particular lived in a static world of right and wrong, good and evil, and insiders and outsiders; a world in which one shouldn't presume to enquire too deeply or cross established boundaries. With her homespun wisdom, mother liked to caution me that "curiosity killed the cat," and that I should learn to know my place.

When I had set off to school as a young lad, she had cautioned me
to not ask too many questions and never to bother the teacher. And,
if I did know something, I should never show it, as that would be
presumptuous and boastful. For her, the sin of pride always lurked
near at hand. Perhaps, I've since thought, she just meant for me to
act toward others with probity, dignity, and respect; as a child of
God (in her view), I had special responsibilities. Yet such teachings
risked inhibiting my intellectual growth, and so I pushed back. I
later took the words of Goethe to heart: "Whoever is not inquisitive,
learns nothing" (*Wer nicht neugierig ist, erfährt nichts*). Recognizing
my adolescent waywardness, mother said I was becoming "uppity."
She was right, of course. So, at the end of a summer spent working
as a warehouse labourer prior to entering university, I had made her
a peace offering: a tacky garden gnome to grace her garden. She
painted the smirking ornament with ample dashes of her favourite
colour, chartreuse; planted it by the fishpond; and dubbed it "the
professor." It was her way of ribbing me about where my studious
habits might lead me. (Surprisingly, she seemed rather proud of my
becoming a professorial oddity myself.)

My father, by contrast, was a highly skilled radio technician and
administrator. With minimal formal education, he had advanced
from a navy signalman to a leader in the electronics of air navigation.
In fact, he was proficient in many trades, from plumbing to wood-
work to engine rebuilding. I admired his skill sets, and often wished
I could be like him. For him, books were a practical matter—you
consulted them for technical information when you needed to "do
something." The study of literature and philosophy was all well and
good, but you couldn't really "do" anything with them. Ironically,
he had always encouraged me to pursue education. He insisted I
should never become a tradesman, carrying my tools in a toolbox.
I should carry my tools in my head. Without realizing it, he was a
closet aesthete, harbouring a barely acknowledged fascination with
language and the arts.

I remember his delight in taking me to see the 1950 movie
Cyrano de Bergerac, with José Ferrer in the lead role. Based on
the French writer Edmond Rostand's 1897 verse-play, the movie

dramatizes the swordsman and poet Cyrano's wooing of the beautiful and intellectual Roxane. The original version had been written almost entirely in alexandrines (verse lines with a six-beat iambic metre or rhythm), yet the English movie script captured my father's imagination as much as it did mine. I still hear him whispering his astonishment at the power of language: "Words, words, such wonderful words." I now recognize what he was experiencing. It was that dichotomy between craftsmanship (embodied in Cyrano, the soldier and swordsman) and Cyrano's expressive poetry, shaped by rhetoric and the creative alexandrine; in short, it was the tension between technician and aesthete that wove its way throughout my father's life. He and I were not that far apart at all. Quietly, we were sharing a moment of healing and reconciliation. Years later, in retirement, he studied French in night school. Just before he died, he wrote one of his final letters to me in a fluent French hand.

Throughout those years my mother and I often locked horns in lively discussions about religion. For mother, my relentless questioning of religion was both naive and misguided. This was because, much like Gretchen—the devout young girl in *Faust* who raises the question "what do you think of religion?" while conversing with Faustus—my mother felt that her faith in God could never be a matter of definitions and opinion. Devout and unquestioning, she was devoted to the Church and convinced that there are things we humans are simply not supposed to understand. That had suited me as a youngster, but I soon took my leave of such pieties and ventured forth on my own.

From my presumptuous undergraduate perspective, I considered religion to be little more than an intellectual exercise; a glorious entertainment even. I could just as easily have cited a character in Steinbeck's *The Grapes of Wrath*, which I was beginning to read: "There ain't no sin and there ain't no virtue. There's just stuff people do." Mother doubtless regarded me as a cocky little devil, always trying to upstage her with my new-found learning. Yet, she understood my ferment. "Once He has hold of you," she would say, "He will never let you go." She might have been thinking of Psalm 139:

"Where can I go from your Spirit? / Or where can I flee from your presence? ... / Your right hand shall hold me fast." Yet, whether over tea and scones, or while brewing beer together in the basement, our tragicomical debates usually ended with peals of laughter as one or the other of us claimed a fatal thrust. We were, after all, two caring people, trying to understand each other's point of view. Sometimes our debates went over the top. A cartoon torn from my student newspaper, *The Ubyssey*, became our mantra. It pictured a wiry broncobuster riding a scrawny nag at full speed over a cliff in a power-braked vertical dive. The caption read "Who-a-a-a-a-thar, you sonofabitch." Knowing "God," I later learned, could never involve a creed or a piece of scientific data lodged in the brain. It was a dimension of experience. Only life itself could help me approach the *mysterium tremendum.*

Mine were generous and deeply loving parents. The sadness that sometimes overshadowed us in our shifting relations derived from our living in different worlds, which could seem irreconcilable. Yet in all things, my parents fostered the wisdom of Solomon and the patience of Job.

SERENDIPITY STRUCK again toward the end of my penultimate year at UBC. At least I thought it had. But this was 1958, the year that German neuroscientist Klaus Conrad had developed the concept of apophany: the tendency of human beings to seek meaningful patterns in random information. Be that as it may, the federal government was seeking forty-eight senior students or recent graduates to serve as guides and interpreters for a seven-month posting at the Brussels World Fair of 1958. Candidates had to be comfortable in both official languages, knowledgeable about Canada, and able to welcome the world to the Canadian Pavilion on the nation's behalf. Ultimately, just two candidates were selected from mostly unilingual British Columbia, myself and a third-year history student named Anita Borradaile (more on her later). In March 1958, I set off for my fifth transcontinental train journey from Vancouver to Montreal. My days of travel by colonist car lay five years behind me.

Settling this time into a first-class compartment, with access to the
dome car and a lounge and restaurant, I once more thrilled to my
country's vastness and geographical variety.

After four days of travel, my train pulled into Windsor Station
in Montreal, where I joined the other members of the Canadian
Pavilion team. We were white francophones and anglophones, all
from Southern Canada, a geographical expression that didn't exist
in our day. Our homogeneity of culture and life experience no longer
exists in the multicultural, multilingual, and multicoloured Canada
of today. But there was little time for getting acquainted amidst the
rush of the meet-and-greet and photo ops for the Canadian press
before boarding our train to Saint John, New Brunswick. Here the
twenty-thousand-ton RMS *Empress of France* lay alongside in the
harbour, ready to begin the seven-day crossing that would take us
down the Bay of Fundy, east about Cape Sable, and on across the
Atlantic's rough and tumbling seas to Liverpool, UK. From there we
would spend the night in London before travelling to Dover for the
ferry to Ostende, Belgium, and onward by train to Brussels. In the
days before international commercial air, this was one of the main
routes for overseas travel. The full journey from Vancouver to Brussels took almost two weeks.

The thirty-year-old *Empress of France* had steamed the world's
oceans in peace and war, and was just two years away from the
breaker's yard when we boarded her. She had helped evacuate Sin-
gapore in 1941 and convoyed troops during the Allied invasion of
North Africa in 1942. We could sense that her time had come. As
she flexed and twisted her way through the North Atlantic, we wondered how much longer her rivets could withstand such punishment.
The ship's navigation log had registered high seas and heavy swell
as we passed Cape Sable, Nova Scotia. Worse was to come. As we
edged into the broad Atlantic, the winds hit force 8 on the Beaufort scale. That meant wind speeds of forty knots and waves from
4.5 to 7.6 metres (18 to 25 feet). In the days of tall ship sailing and
hundred-gun warships, we'd have called it "a double-reefed topsail
breeze." Mind you, a breeze in those days was not the soft zephyr

boaters today associate with a summer coastal cruise. A Beaufort scale breeze whips up high, foamy seas and blows twisting masses of spindrift off the crests of ragged, breaking waves. Almost sixty years later, our memories of spindrift on the Atlantic and the Pacific inspired Anita and me to name our co-edited anthology of ocean-themed writings *Spindrift: A Canadian Book of the Sea*. It presents a new mosaic of Canada.

BRUSSELS PROVED a transformative experience for me. Here, we met the world head-on. Forty-four countries had gathered for a five-month celebration of their achievements in science and technology, industry, and the arts. At the centre stood the Atomium, a monument to the atomic age. Composed of nine glistening, aluminum-clad spheres, each measuring 20 metres (65.5 feet) in diameter, it rose like a modern-day Eiffel Tower a hundred metres above the beautifully designed Parc du Heysel. Shaped, so we first thought, like a stylized atom, the impressive structure represented an iron-crystal cell magnified 169 billion times. As the fair's central symbol, it proclaimed the modern world's unbridled faith in scientific progress. This was, after all, 1958. The Second World War lay thirteen years behind us, and the Exposition Universelle et Internationale de Bruxelles, to use its official name, was the first such fair since before the war. It stood as a promise of peace and prosperity. The carillon bells of the Vatican Pavilion playfully heralded as much. Daily, they pealed forth the lilting French folk song "Auprès de ma blonde, il fait bon dormir," suggesting, perhaps unintentionally, that life was as much about the pleasures of the flesh as it was about discoveries of the mind.

Our Canadian pavilion was a windy, chilly place, conceived to celebrate Canada as a vast land of bountiful natural resources. Architecturally, that meant few walls and large, open spaces. Yet it also highlighted two of Canada's high-tech contributions to the fields of cancer treatment and jet propulsion. The cobalt bomb, a teletherapy machine that used gamma rays from the radioisotope cobalt-60 to reach cancer tumours deep inside the body, marked a revolutionary advance in radiotherapy. The Orenda turbojet engine, with its name taken from the Iroquois language and meaning "tribal soul on the right path," had been designed to power Canada's newest fighter jet, the Avro CF-100 Sabre. It outperformed all competitors. Canada built four thousand of the engines in the 1950s. For the pavilion display, a full-scale cutaway of the turbojet engine stood beneath a huge copper map of Canada's natural resources. Together, map and engine seemed to argue for the rightness of our NATO commitment to peace and our readiness to defend our vast territory stretching between three vital oceans. That would have been the thrust of my presentation to the very personable King Baudouin of Belgium when he toured our pavilion one day. Arriving with neither fanfare nor a uniformed coterie, he stepped up to the display where I was working and engaged me in conversation, as relaxed as if we were two neighbours chatting about the latest car on the block. Impressed, I warmed to the Belgian style of monarchy.

Over the seven months of the fair, I visited every participating pavilion. I thrilled to the magnificent art on display in the Czech Pavilion; admired the industrial advancements being made by the once war-crushed Germany; was captivated by Holland's wind-driven energy systems and electronics industry; and was intrigued by the tenuous political and cultural relationships of the Arab-speaking world, in particular, the parlous state of the United Arab Republic. In contrast, Belgium's Congo Village, with its display of "real" Africans living out their daily lives in a grass-hut village, appalled me. It struck me as a shabby fantasy portraying the glory days of Belgian colonialism. (Public reaction eventually closed the Village down.) Yet, despite discordant strains, a holiday spirit reigned over the exhibition site. Beer gardens, cafés, restaurants, concerts, and cultural festivities of every description dotted the fair's 198 hectares (490 acres). At one point, I arranged for my alma mater, the Vancouver Kitsilano Boys Band, to play in the Canadian Pavilion and in other venues in the Expo site.

The bonds among those of us working at Expo 58 ran deep. The members of our Canadian group were forming new friendships and revelling in the stimulating international milieu. Long into the night, we'd gather and socialize over good Belgian beer, in French, English, or a mixture of both. On Easter Sunday (my twenty-second birthday), I joined others on a bus tour to Cologne, Germany, to visit its magnificent Gothic Cathedral, which had miraculously survived the war. After years of studying the culture, I was excited to be on German soil, little knowing that one day the city would hold deep personal meaning for me.

Despite Expo 58's message of hope, the darkness of the Cold War hung over Europe. Cold War was a new concept, formulated by George Orwell in 1945 to describe a geopolitical stand-off when a couple of nuclear-armed superpowers threatened one another with mass extinction. His popular novels *Nineteen Eighty-Four* (1949) and *Animal Farm* (1945), served as chilling reminders of the dark undercurrents in a world threatened by the ambitions of competing superpowers. Certainly, my Quebec roommate and I, both of us with naval commissions, feared we might be called up at any moment.

As it happened, the USA and USSR had built their pavilions next door to one another. Both structures made strong political statements. The Soviets' pavilion, built in the brutalist style, projected a rooted sense of brute power. At its centre, a 4.6-metre (15-foot) concrete pedestal supported an enormous bronze statue of Lenin, the first leader of the USSR following the Russian Revolution in 1917. The statue's presence in the Great Hall proclaimed Lenin's political theory of world revolution, that would replace corrupt regimes with an enlightened "dictatorship of the proletariat." Nearby stood a model of Sputnik, the world's first artificial earth satellite. Launched on 4 October 1957, it was the first of several Soviet advancements that outstripped the USA's programs and effectively launched the space race.

By contrast, the US Pavilion had been designed to show the dynamism, creativity, and vision of democratic societies. Its open cluster of differently sized buildings with facades of metal and white ceramic grille conveyed lightness and accessibility. A Walt Disney-designed "Circarama" formed the centrepiece. This 360-degree circular cinema, boasting eleven film projectors, entertained stand-up audiences with an impressive, if jingoistic, movie tour of the USA under the title "America the Beautiful." Close at hand was an 1,150-seat theatre featuring stage shows, fashion pageants, musical theatre, and concerts of unprecedented artistic variety. One of the resident composers created a stage show about life at Expo 58 and engaged staff from several pavilions to perform in it. I played my trumpet in one of the dance numbers.

BEYOND BRUSSELS, Europe beckoned. With the freedom and energy of unfettered youth, we Canadians thought nothing of hitch-hiking or hopping onto a train or bus for sightseeing trips. We'd frequently travel as couples (observing the social proprieties, of course), and I soon began to accompany Anita Borradaile on brief getaways. On one such trip, we headed to Paris to meet her relatives, and I realized I was becoming drawn into a relationship I had not anticipated. Anita was a striking young woman. She was beautifully bilingual in English and French, steeped in her studies of Art History and Spanish, and an engaging conversationalist. There was such an elegance and poise about her that we called her "La Duchesse." And my Duchess she has remained for going on sixty-five years. She had a mind of her own, and years later would join the faculty of Royal Roads Military College, in Victoria, BC, and publish a fascinating book on her famous father, Osmond Borradaile, *Life Through a Lens: Memoirs of a Cinematographer*.

Paris was wonderful that summer of 1958, especially with my soulmate. We enjoyed generous luncheons offered by her congenial uncles and aunts, and visits to galleries and cafés. Her grandmother proudly squired us around her quartier to show off her Canadian granddaughter to the local shopkeepers. During strolls along the Seine, Anita and I browsed the *bouquinistes* (booksellers' stalls), where I purchased Voltaire's philosophical work *Traité sur la Tolérance* and a French translation of a history of British submarine warfare. Both texts augured for me the beginning of new directions. We returned to Brussels, convinced that our real relationship had gone undetected by her relatives. Unknown to us, however, a letter was already on its way to Anita's mother, Christiane, in Chilliwack, BC, signalling "there is something in the wind"—*il y a anguille sous roche*. Our work contract allowed for a more extended period of vacation leave, and on the spur of the moment, my buddy Paul Chamberland and I embarked on a three-week-long, 4,000-kilometre (2,500-mile) odyssey aboard a beat-up 160cc Vespa. It would be the quintessential trip of a lifetime, one in which the scooter proved itself the most trustworthy machine I have ever known. Packing a devil-may-care attitude—and just enough cash to keep our scooter fuelled and ourselves in cheese, bread, and wine—we set off in the dead of night, eager to maximize our time on the road and beat the traffic out of town. In retrospect, our route was daunting, and not a little risky. It involved two crossings of the Alps, a run down the boot of Italy, and a hard slog from Kotor, near the Albanian border, up the coast of Yugoslavia on an all-dirt road. Despite a couple of rough tumbles, we remained undeterred.

From Brussels, we crossed into France and passed through Metz and Nancy to Lucerne, Switzerland, where a feeling of unbridled freedom gripped us as we climbed up and over the Alps via the 2,106-metre-high (6,860-foot) St. Gotthard Pass. In the Canton of Uri, I recall pausing in Altdorf to view the statue of William Tell—the Swiss freedom-fighter who had led a rebellion against Austrian rule—standing by his young son, Walter. The statue portrays the incident where Tell is forced by a tyrant to shoot an arrow through an apple balanced on his son's head. The scene reminded me of my study of Schiller's 1804 drama *Wilhelm Tell* (which we read in an annotated school edition of 1915), a gripping account of the popular uprising that led to the founding of Western Europe's first democratic state. The statue seemed to affirm Schiller's assertion that "People will speak of Tell the archer for as long as the mountains stand" (*Erzählen wird man von dem Schützen Tell, / Solang' die Berge stehn auf ihrem Grunde*). Our journey through Switzerland would include many more scenes of the adventurous life of William Tell.

Italy was calling us, and we picked up the pace until one bitterly cold night when, forced by exhaustion, we stopped to hunker down for a few hours near a heat vent by a pumping station. Awakened by discomfort, we resumed our journey over the summit and down the precarious, overlapping serpentines of narrow road until our brakes threatened to burn out, at which point we rolled at a breathless pace toward Genoa. Breaking out onto the coastal plain, we felt that all of Italy was ours.

Soon we were en route to Rome, where we spun off to visit the twelfth-century campanile known as the Leaning Tower of Pisa and climbed the 296 steps to the top of the 55-metre-high (180-foot) structure. Along the way, I felt my schoolboy Latin come alive. As we passed by scenes similar to those portrayed in my old Latin textbook, I recalled lines written about the Via Appia Antica: horses carrying grain, soldiers waging war, beautiful women singing, and poets writing song. Next, it was on to the house of the Oblate Fathers in Rome. Serendipity again. During our Atlantic crossing aboard the *Empress of France*, we had met a convivial Oblate Father who was heading to Rome. In an unguarded, but very gracious, moment he had invited us to visit if we were ever passing by. Little did he realize that two of his co-passengers would actually take him up on his offer. Brazen to a fault, Paul and I knocked on the door of the Oblate house late on the evening of our arrival in Rome and found ourselves ushered into the building's warmth, not as the rugged-looking ragamuffins we no doubt resembled, but as welcome guests.

We quickly fell into our hosts' routine of daily prayer and meditation, with time allotted for study, meals, and conversation. Paul himself had once felt called to the priesthood. Still quietly devout, he was delighted to encounter there a fellow francophone school friend from Alberta, who had joined the order and was undertaking a formal course of study. By that time, I had left the Anglican Church, but I had not abandoned my interest in religion. Since my earliest university days, I had been following my own path of spiritual enquiry. Our stopover with the Oblates during our hectic trip gave me much to ponder. I recall one evening meal with clarity. We had joined a large group of priests in a refectory typical of the dining halls in European monasteries and religious houses. The furnishings were spartan, the atmosphere at first glance austere. Yet the warmth of fellowship transformed the space into a community. On this evening, we dined on spaghetti and green salad dressed with balsamic vinaigrette. Bottles of chilled white wine, beads of condensation trickling gently down their sides, stood in rows along the centre of the long wooden tables. After prayers and grace, we ate in silence while one of the priests read aloud from sacred scripture.

The devotional period concluded, we ended our meal in conversation. To my delight, I found myself sitting opposite a recently ordained German priest who had fought in General Erwin Rommel's Afrika Korps during the Battle of Gazala, from May to June, 1942. This was the tank battle in which Rommel, "The Desert Fox"—*der Wüstenfuchs*—had forced the British to a resounding defeat and caused them to lose the vital port of Tobruk. At the time, I was unfamiliar with military history, but we found ourselves engaging in matters of faith that went far beyond the battleground. Both of us were happy to be speaking German. At the end of the meal, we retired to the large rooftop patio, where baskets of black cherries stood against the darkling outline of St. Peter's Basilica and the skyline of Rome. We conversed in pairs, pacing thoughtfully back and forth, much like naval officers on their postprandial strolls on the quarterdeck. Whenever I recall that experience, I'm reminded of Rilke's lines, in which a great cathedral takes shape under the hands of skilled craftsmen. The image is often understood as a metaphor for the path of deepening spiritual awareness. On leaving the worksite at nightfall, the workmen in the poem see the nascent outline of their cathedral emerge: "Just as it grows dark, we let you go: and your coming contours merge in twilight. God, you are great" (*Erst wenn es dunkelt, lassen wir dich los: Und deine kommenden Konturen dämmern. Gott, du bist groß*). On this evening, my own spiritual labours began again, ever so slowly.

Before leaving Rome, we felt called to attend the noon-hour blessing in St. Peter's Square. I can't say I was particularly persuaded of the spiritual efficacy of such an exercise, but I was nonetheless moved to return home with a gift for my Irish Aunt Molly, who had married into our Protestant family. I rather admired her devotion in walking to Mass every morning in Vancouver. On this day, however, I found myself rifling among the trinket stalls in search of a crucifix ripe for a papal blessing. I found it and entered the swirling crowd of the faithful. Never had I been among such a multitude of boisterous Christians. "Papa, Papa!" they cried out as Pius XII appeared in his window overlooking the square. "So, what's the drill, Paul?" I called out to my buddy as I caught sight of the Pope and squeezed forward with the crowd. Caught up in the fervour, I did as Paul instructed and knelt on the cobbles, crucifix in hand, and let the blessing wash over me.

But I couldn't help thinking about this particular pope. As Cardinal Eugenio Pacelli, he had been the papal emissary to Berlin in the 1930s and had been openly critical of the Nazi movement. However, as Pius XII in 1939, he had insisted on papal neutrality and consequently suffered sharp criticism for not having taken the moral high road in the face of rising Nazi evil. But this was June 1958, and he would be dead in four months' time. Clutching the crucifix in my hand, I took comfort in the understanding that not even a flawed priest or pope could disarm a well-intended Holy Spirit. I had learned this from Graham Greene's *The Power and the Glory*, a compelling novel about a deeply flawed though committed "whisky priest," who serves the poor under a Mexican dictatorship where the Church is illegal. I remained skeptical of the Faith. Yet, beneath my skin grew the awareness that I had been touched by something huge, something I would have to investigate further.

From Rome, our journey took us to Monte Cassino, some 143 kilometres (89 miles) southwest of Rome. The Benedictine Monastery of Monte Cassino is a powerful symbol of the Benedictine way of life, and is one of the West's most influential monastic communities. It had commanded the heights since 530 CE. Paul and I wanted to touch that world, however briefly, for in our conversations both en route and in Rome we had explored the Benedictine concepts of *ora et labora*—work and pray, with their emphasis on community, humility, and obedience to the Word of God. Of course, we also knew that Monte Cassino had been the scene of fierce fighting during the Italian Campaign of the Second World War. As Allied forces forced their way northward into the "soft underbelly" of Hitler's Europe, with amphibious landings at Anzio in the east and brutal battles at Ortona in the west, German paratroops had established the Gustav Line of defence right across the boot of Italy. Its axis lay directly on the monastery mount, over 500 steep and rugged metres (1,640 feet) in height. For both topographical and tactical reasons, Monte Cassino lay in the crosshairs of armies and air forces alike. No other breakthrough was possible. It would take bomber raids and hand-to-hand fighting to dig the Germans out.

I pondered these things as our plucky Vespa chugged and strained up the narrow, winding, fog-assailed pathway to the monastery. As we reached the top, the mist shifted, and we laid eyes on a scene that telescoped the past and present. Above the main gate, the word *pax* (peace) was chiselled in stone. Tethered beside it, like an avatar from an ancient world, was a young donkey. The unexpected contrast between Biblical imagery and the contemporary world took our breath away. With startling clarity, we understood the final key to the Benedictine path: first *pax,* then *ora et labora.*

Only thirteen years after its near annihilation, the Monastery of Monte Cassino had reached a remarkable stage of reconstruction. We breathed in the spirit that had dominated the site for almost fifteen hundred years, and could only surmise what *pax* could mean after almost six years of untold savagery. Looking out over the ramparts, we reflected on the terrible costs incurred. Over four thousand Commonwealth soldiers had died in the Battle of Monte Cassino. Allied cemeteries lay like cast-off checker boards on the surrounding hills. The closest was the Polish Cemetery. It held the bodies of over a thousand soldiers of the Polish 2nd Corps, who had participated in the Warsaw Ghetto Uprising of 1943 only to die storming the bombed-out abbey in May 1944, during the third and final assault.

I HAD first learned of Poland's wartime exploits from Tadeusz Halpert-Scanderbeg, my Polish mentor at UBC. He had tutored me privately for four years. I recall seeing the framed letter he had received from King George VI at war's end, thanking him for his outstanding service to the Allied forces. Tadeusz's contributions had indeed been remarkable. In his large home, he had given shelter to downed British airmen before spiriting them to safety through the Polish Underground. He had also billeted SS officers while operating an underground printing press in his cellar. Besides his mother tongue, he was fluent in English, French, and German. When he and his wife finally made their escape from German-occupied Poland, he travelled with falsified papers as an ethnic German, while his wife, who also understood German well, travelled as a person who was deaf and speech-impaired so as not to betray her Polish accent. As I left his office one day, he had turned to me as an afterthought and whispered, "By the way, my dear fellow, do tune in to CBC this evening and you'll hear the latest of my compositions for strings." I did so and was deeply impressed. If only I could be such a man, I thought. His secret badge of the Polish Underground—an anchor (*Kotwica*) showing the capital letter W surmounted by a P—*Polska Wojna*—stood for Fighting Poland. In combatting the evil of the Nazi occupation of Poland he had drawn on his many strengths: intellect, talent, and immense courage.

Tadeusz frequently introduced me to subjects beyond the study of Polish. One day, while discussing semelfactive verbs (words that describe actions that happen once only), he announced that I simply must read George Orwell's satirical novel *Animal Farm*, about the insidious drift of a society from violent revolution to dictatorship. On another day, he urged me to read Sir Philip Gibbs's *No Price for Freedom*, about the Polish resistance to the Nazi occupation. On yet another occasion, he launched me into a study of Czesław Miłosz's *The Captive Mind*, a cogent analysis of an alluring communist future that ultimately seduced intellectuals into spiritual captivity. A gifted intellectual and poet, Miłosz would win the Nobel Prize for Literature in 1980. In retrospect, I realize that had I resisted Tadeusz's engaging tutelage and instead stuck to my regular courses, I would perhaps have obtained higher grades. But I have never regretted the rich political and philosophical education I received by straying from the academic grindstone. As I had long ago scribbled in Polish on a page in Miłosz's book, the old world had died—*stary świat skonał*—and I was setting off in new directions.

PILING BACK onto our Vespa, Paul and I headed further south to the port of Naples, where we manhandled our scooter onto a small, shallow-draft boat and headed across 30 kilometres (18.6 miles) of dazzling blue sea to the island of Ischia. At that time, the island was not the preppy, tourist-infested place it has since become. Unlike the Isle of Capri to the south, Ischia was still a quiet, sun-soaked isle. By chance, we had arrived on 24 June, in time to celebrate the Feast of St. Jean Baptiste. We immediately felt a connection with the island, for la Fête de St. Jean Baptiste is also the national day of the Province of Quebec. Night was falling, warm and sultry, as we chugged in low gear up a narrow road into the hills, while islanders with lit tapers trod alongside us in a hymn-filled procession, filling the shadows with prayerful song. The scene picked up tones from our stay at the Oblate House and resonated with the ebullience of St. Peter's Square. I was yet unaware of the full import of the inner journey I had innocently embarked on during my undergraduate years. But deep within, an understanding was forming along the lines of the *philosophia perennis*, a set of ideas first enunciated by Leibniz in the seventeenth century and articulated by Aldous Huxley in 1945 with his illuminating study of religion, *The Perennial Philosophy*. Encapsulating mysticisms both East and West, Huxley illustrated the metaphysics of a world view in which a divine reality permeates all human minds and lives, and indeed all things. Elements of this philosophy have been my companions through life.

We returned to Naples for the turnoff that would take us to the ruins of the ancient city of Pompeii. The site had been buried under several metres of ash and lava when Mount Vesuvius erupted in 79 CE. For seventeen centuries it had remained largely undisturbed, until 1951 when archeologists began excavating the city in earnest. The unearthing of Pompeii was still a work in progress when we arrived in June 1958 to stroll the empty streets and examine the artifacts. Imagining those final seconds before the fearful explosion that brought an end to an eight-hundred-year-old culture, we could only guess at the helpless horror the populace faced. The sight of a young lad's body encased in lava filled us with conflicting emotions of pity and wonder. Transformed into a statue while fending off the deadly lava, he lay before us in a gesture of petrified disbelief. Are natural disasters evil, we wondered, or simply the way the world works? And how can one account for innocent suffering in any meaningful way? As we drove onward via Foggia to Bari, on the Adriatic coast, we tentatively agreed that natural events are morally neutral. Yet we couldn't avoid the niggling thought that we should blame the Pompeii disaster on something more than superheated gas bubbles thrusting magma through a mountaintop. And how did violent death in a volcanic eruption differ in moral terms from the violent deaths during the Battle of Monte Cassino? How can we be peacemakers instead of warmongers? Indeed, how did these events and passions fit in with the devotions we had experienced on Ischia and in Rome? Our unresolved philosophizing continued as we crossed the lumpy Adriatic Sea by ferry to Dubrovnik, Yugoslavia, and began the 700-kilometre (435-mile) stretch of dirt highway northward, via Split and Rijeka, to Trieste.

As if in partial answer to the questions we had been posing while negotiating the rough road and rocky crags of the scarcely travelled coastal route, we chanced upon a ragged shepherd. Or rather, he was the one who stumbled around a corner with his scrawny herd of goats and bumped into us. If the sight of two scruffy vagabonds startled him, the old shepherd didn't show it. But he was clearly intrigued and watched inquisitively as we unpacked our meagre lunch of bread, cheese, and honey and prepared to take a lazy swig of wine. While the goats milled about us in a miasma of barnyard smells, we gestured to him to join us. The old man especially enjoyed the honey, amply spread on a thick slice of bread so that it oozed between his calloused fingers. He wanted nothing else. His weathered face beamed with pleasure. And so we tarried together. We shared no common language or culture and no common history or vision; just the bare necessities of food and wine. Yet we felt a blessed sense of peace. It struck me at the time that the first step in human understanding and peacemaking is quite simply to break bread.

Stubborn and exhausted, we pressed on along the Adriatic coast, the Vespa straining ever more under the stress of the rugged road. Our journey had thus far shown us the human dimensions of time in a broad sweep of European cultures, natural disasters, and the ravages of violence and war. Now, we would experience geological time. Finding ourselves at the crossroads of Croatia, Italy, and Austria, we were seized by the urge to cross into Slovenia to visit the fabled limestone caverns of the Postojna Cave. The lure of a subterranean world seemed to thrust the detour upon us. On arrival, we were met by the attraction's sole guide, who seemed glad to welcome his only visitors. Together, we entered the magnificent, filigreed galleries of stalactites and stalagmites. The remarkable shapes had been formed by mineral-filled water seeping—drop by inexorable drop—through the ceilings of the vast limestone caverns. As the calcium-rich droplets coursed downward, they twisted themselves into exotic, icicle-shaped stalactites, all while shedding beads of moisture that slipped from their tips, leaving deposits on the ground that slowly built upward as stalagmites.

Awed by the sight, we stood in wonder at the eternal processes that had created these cathedrals of illuminated crystals. They seemed to shimmer around us like symphonies of convoluted form. A thousand years is scarcely enough time for stalactites or stalagmites to reach the size of a cubic inch. The oldest among them were over two million years old. The sensual splendour of it engulfed us. Striking some of the formations with a marimba mallet, the guide evoked an echo chamber of tonal and visual delight. Humbled and uplifted, our senses quite spent by the grandeur, we kick-started our

Vespa and pressed on. In the big picture, it seemed, our lives last but a microsecond. What are human beings that they presume so much importance despite these cosmic dimensions that are everywhere around us?

Under threatening skies, we crossed the Alps via Brenner Pass (altitude 1,370 metres, or 4,495 feet) and drove toward Innsbruck, Austria, where torrential rains hit. For the first time since leaving Rome we were forced to seek out accommodation, for the countryside was awash and neither field nor hedgerow offered any shelter. Desperate for lodging, we tapped on the door of an isolated cottage boasting the inviting sign "*Zimmer frei*" (room available). As I greeted the landlady who opened to us, I realized how roguish and unkempt we must have looked. A couple of weeks without a bath can do that. Suspicious at first, she overcame her reluctance and led us up to a small attic room that seemed the very picture of heaven. After settling in, we were invited to join the family in the cozy farm kitchen, which I found quintessentially Austrian, with its smart, rustic wooden furniture, a *Herrgottsecke* (a traditional shrine in Christian houses) with crucifix by the tall stove, hot coffee, and *Gugelhupf*—a baked sponge cake of French origin. It felt good to be speaking German again and hearing the lilting Italianate German of Austria. This domestic scene of *eine heile Welt*, with its qualities of probity, compassion, and familial warmth, touched us deeply. As we began to share some of our story—of our lives in Canada, student life, Expo 58, the Vespa, and sleeping rough—the relationship became hearty, and at breakfast the next morning we continued the threads of the previous evening's conversations. The family would accept no payment for their hospitality. We were young, they said, and the world lay before us. "Go with God." Sent off with blessings and farewells, we began the final leg of our journey, through Nancy and home to Bruxelles. Months later, when Paul left Europe and returned home to Canada, he drove our battered Vespa to Amsterdam and left her by the side of the road. Our faithful scooter had served us well.

Expo closed in October 1958. A fairy tale had ended. We forty-eight Canadians set off for home or other pursuits with strong convictions about the value of international cooperation. Globalism was our future, and we embraced its spirit. Though we recognized that the next phase of our lives would involve hard work and many tough decisions, we were buoyed by the knowledge that our world offered a wealth of opportunities. After saying our goodbyes to the ones remaining in Europe for work and study, we retraced our steps to London and on to Southampton, where we boarded the 22,000-ton Italian Lines *Homeric* for Montreal. There, our group dispersed further, leaving a mere handful of us to board the CPR transcontinental train westward.

One by one, our friends alighted at one whistle stop after another, thus ending their adventure. I poignantly remember a morning stop in Virden, Manitoba, where our dear friend Lore Bewer, whom our children would come to know as Aunt Lore (*Tante Lore*) Brongers, got off to return to the family farm. Nobody was there to meet her. As she stood on the tiny platform by the weathered red stationhouse, there wasn't another soul in sight. The lonely prairie stretched to the distant horizon; beyond, lay the town, with a population of 2,500. As the transcontinental pulled away, Anita and I waved from the observation lounge. Standing now on the track with her luggage, Lore looked every bit the immigrant she had once been when her family arrived from war-torn Germany to start a new life.

That left just the two of us to continue the journey to the West Coast. By end of May 1959, we were married. In retrospect years later, recalling our time in Brussels, we remarked at how the interview board at the Department of Trade and Commerce had gotten it right in choosing us to work at the Fair. Our marriage seemed to have been "government approved." Indeed, it continues to thrive, long after the great symbol of Expo 58—the Atomium—had lost its sheen.

5

PASSPORT PERSON

The passport is a human being's noblest part.
BERTOLT BRECHT, *Refugee Conversations*

OTTAWA IN the spring of 1959 struck us as a down-at-heel, parochial excuse for a capital city. Wartime office buildings still prevailed, the roads lay in need of repair after a harsh winter, and the city itself breathed the angst of a cramped bureaucracy. Somewhat reminiscent of a Franz Kafka novel, Ottawa evinced an aura of doorkeepers, bureaucrats, secretaries, and clerks. Everyone, it seemed, was known by an alphanumeric; they might be an AO2 or an EO3 or any other combination of designators. Neither Anita nor I had ever lived in a society in which shoptalk and the classification of people into categories of labour was the norm. Yet the Public Service of Canada proved to be an excellent employer, womb to tomb. I had recently passed my Foreign Service examinations and had been accepted into the Department of Citizenship and Immigration. After a week-long road trip from the West Coast with my bride in our tiny forty-horsepower Austin—long before we had a Trans-Canada Highway—I was ready to join the club.

Stepping into the Woods Building, a relic from the Second World War, I became a bureaucrat. (I was an FSO1, Foreign Service Officer, Grade 1.) The training program for my new profession was both excellent and expensive—excellent for me and expensive for the government. It included a thorough schooling in the theory and application of the Immigration Act and Regulations, and of the various administrative manuals by which the government service managed its business. Preliminary short-term postings in the high-volume border crossings of Fort Erie and Malton Airport trained us in border inspections, while assignments in Toronto and Montreal engaged us in settling new immigrants into the job market. It also entailed a year of work and travel by road and rail on an exceptionally well-planned industrial and commercial tour of Canada.

My awareness of immigration had begun in the 1940s while growing up among the Italian and Sudeten German families in our Vancouver neighbourhood. As a youngster, I was glad to gain new playmates and learn about different languages and customs. Our Anglo parents and neighbours, by contrast, saw nothing but unwanted social change. Even at that young age, I was beginning to question the rightness of British colonial culture. But I lacked the vocabulary to express my new inclinations. In time, popular concepts like "melting pot" and "cultural mosaic" began to colour my language. The impacts of immigration on our closed neighbourhood marked the beginning of my venture into multiculturalism. Of course, migration has shaped human history since time immemorial. Driven by politics and economics, war, hunger, and pestilence, our species has never hesitated to seek a better life. Migration had built our country as we knew it. I found the idea of migration enriching and exciting. The best immigration policies, I soon realized, addressed the issues of mass migration with justice and compassion. I wanted to be part of this vital dimension of nation-building.

Our training room in the Woods Building was a hive of activity. Eight of us sat at separate desks, each with a Dictaphone machine. File clerks scurried about bringing us "grocery carts" of variously sized case files on which to hone our skills. Thin files suggested fresh cases, thick ones invariably turned out to be thorny cases as yet unresolved. We trainees were unlikely to resolve them either; yet our task was to study them and prepare an official response. Once we had adjudicated the cases, we'd dictate our letters into the recording machine; clerks would then take the files and recordings to a typing pool of some twenty typists. Copy clerks would return their baskets of completed files to our training supervisor who would examine our responses. Good letters he would sign and mail; others gave him cause for rebuke, or at least a demand to rewrite.

With his tight-fitting suit and tie, bifocal spectacles, and humourless demeanour, the training supervisor struck me as a cross between Dickens's pre-Christmas Ebenezer Scrooge and the fawning Uriah Heep. One day, I discovered in a weighty personnel manual that employees were eligible to apply for paid study leave to upgrade their qualifications. When I brought this to the attention of ol' Scrooge, he puffed himself up and announced: "We pride ourselves on never having approved a single application." From his narrow perspective, the notion of staff development meant little more than indoctrinating us in clerical expertise. He had no notion of a big picture, in which human beings weighed values and took calculated risks. Such attitudes in the Public Service did not augur well for my long-term adaptation to bureaucratic life. Eventually, I would resign from the Public Service and return to academe. But that was much later. For now, the work was good and so were the travel and pay.

My training posting to the most European of all Canadian cities, Quebec City, offered stirring variety. It was from here that our team of immigration officers worked the immigrant ships arriving from Europe: Greek Line's *Arkadia,* Home Line's *Homeric,* the CPR vessels *Empress of France* and a new *Empress of Britain,* and the Europe-Canada Line's *Seven Seas.* In the days before commercial air travel had become the norm, these ships and many others transported thousands of new Canadians along centuries-old routes into the Canadian heartland. Quebec, with its state-of-the-art Immigration Hall, served as a major port of entry. Working in relays, we immigration officers would cross the St. Lawrence to catch the train at Lévis for the four-hour trip to Rimouski, then head to the wooden clapboard auberge where we would spend the night before boarding one of the incoming ships. From the pilot station at Pointe-au-Père Lighthouse, we would rendezvous with one of the many inbound immigrant ships and return with it upriver to Quebec City. Along the way, I conducted immigration interviews, examined documents, and stamped passports. When the formalities were over, I always rejoiced in welcoming the new arrivals to Canada. On reaching Quebec, I would repeat the whole circuit: Lévis, Rimouski, Pointe-au-Père, immigrant ship. For the old hands at this game, this was the pattern of a lifetime career. For me it was but a relatively short, colourful part of becoming an immigration visa officer.

I will never forget the impressive marine activity of the St. Lawrence and the beauty of the old seigneuries and the passing villages, with their historic churches and lighthouses and intriguing place names like Kamouraska, Phare du Pot à L'Eau-de-Vie, Rivière du Loup, and Trois Pistoles, each attesting to the vitality of a resilient people. The region was full of surprises. I think of the old wooden auberge at which we overnighted while awaiting our ships. Among its regular clientele were muscle-bound denizens of the local professional wrestling circuit. Vicious enemies they might have been in the ring—with monikers like "Assassin" (Joe Tomasso) and "The Teuton Terror" (Guy Larose)—but these Quebec grapplers were pals at the bar. We joined a strange and transient society of hunks, hulks, and border bureaucrats. Following breakfast the next morning, we would banter about life on the road, the fight circus, immigration, and local affairs. Then we once again took the pilot boat onto the river to meet yet another liner, inbound with hundreds of immigrants.

MY FIRST overseas posting took us to London, England. In those days you travelled by ship and train. Our trans-Atlantic crossing aboard the Home Line's *Homeric* would mark my seventh passage down the St. Lawrence via the pilot station at Pointe-au-Père and the Strait of Belle Isle. Again, it felt haunted by the wreck of the *Empress of Ireland*. With its close link to the Kitsilano Boys Band, the marine catastrophe of 1914 would always overshadow my river journeys. Now, the eighteen-thousand-ton *Homeric* became for me yet another important marker buoy. Anita and I sailed among the 1,100 cabin-class passengers. The adventure of being young marrieds on a great journey could not have been better. The meals, always served with Italian wine, were excellent. And the music! Concerts every afternoon in the Palm Court and dancing every evening to the music of a versatile, contemporary Italian band. Dancing the cha-cha-cha was all the rage, and the band played all the songs that were at the top of the charts. The refrain "Volaré, oh-oh / Cantaré, oh-oh-oh-oh" rang out through the disco, giving wings to our unfolding dreams. Still in our twenties, we had the world on a string.

London received us with flair: a fine, all-expenses-paid hotel in the City, congenial colleagues in the busy immigration office in Green Street, and time to find an apartment. The search through central London for a place to live was rather fun, and we quickly found a fashionable furnished flat at 1 Addison Gardens. The front door was in the upscale Victorian district of Kensington, while the back of the building was in downscale Shepherd's Bush. A colourful twenty-minute bus ride took me each morning to Marble Arch and my office in an old converted Georgian house. Here I shared an open space with several other immigration counsellors. Canadian immigration law of the time favoured recruiting from the UK in order to preserve as far as possible the country's traditional demographics. The Immigration Act prioritized British and French applicants, followed by Northern Europeans, then Southern Europeans, and finally, a restricted number of "others."

It was our task to interview prospective immigrants to assess their suitability for the Canadian job market. We called it "processing." Once they had met our civil and health requirements, they were on their way. Our role involved evaluating their work experience, education, and training, as well as their family circumstances. Supported by government analyses of the "absorptive capacity" of the Canadian economy and its ability to absorb new workers and their families, we counselled our applicants on the most suitable locations in which they might settle. We helped with Assisted Passage Loans for those who could not afford the cost of passage. Whatever the decisions made in our various overseas offices, we depended upon the competent support the immigrants would receive from our settlement and employment offices throughout

Canada. Canada relied on the just decisions of immigration officers in our embassies and legations throughout the world, and upon the sympathetic and compassionate backup of immigration officers at home. In many respects, the organization of the Department of Citizenship and Immigration during the 1950s and 1960s marked the halcyon days of managing the movement of new people into our land, be they immigrants, refugees, or the dispossessed. In doing so, we knew we were changing the face of Canada. In stark contrast, I reflect on the bureaucratic boondoggle of current refugee movements from Syria and Afghanistan, where applicants can wait up to three years before landing on Canadian soil.

In the 1960s, we found the interviewing process to be a tactical challenge. It demanded our utmost in congeniality, civility, and finesse. We became savvy at singling out the tricksters: those trying to escape an unhappy marriage by claiming to be single, then rushing off with dreams of becoming a cowboy in one of the Western provinces; or those wanting to sneak away silently from bad debts. We uncovered many variations on these themes. One day, a new officer got the balance wrong. While interviewing a young couple who were planning to immigrate to Canada following their wedding, he dutifully listed for them the documents required to complete their file: certificates of birth, schooling, citizenship, and so forth. In a loud voice, he concluded with the following instruction: "And finally, you must bring in your proof of consummation of marriage." Hard to say who in that open office blushed the most, the startled officers or the mortified bride.

For our part, life as a bachelor couple offered every opportunity for theatre, movies, galleries, and museums. We took special pleasure in the National Portrait Gallery, the National Maritime Museum at Greenwich, and famous theatres in the West End. London simply pulsed with rich and lively pursuits: markets in Portobello Road, historic sites, antique shops, and book shops. Who could not be happy here? A short train journey to Stratford-upon-Avon introduced us to the finest drama in the country. On one long weekend we took in six Shakespeare plays: *The Taming of the Shrew, Twelfth Night, Romeo and Juliet, Troilus and Cressida, The Merry Wives of Windsor,* and *Hamlet.* On another occasion we set off to my father's hometown of Smethwick (Birmingham), to visit my old uncle, Arthur Cole, at his cookie-tin address of #7 Primrose Hill. I had not seen him since 1958 when my father and I had flown over from Brussels. This time, we enjoyed the deep pleasure of assuring him that we were not passing visitors; we actually lived here.

Later came a spell at debt collection, in a Pickwickian office I shared with two colleagues. The three of us had been tasked with chasing up immigrants who had defaulted on their Assisted Passage Loans and returned home to the UK. At the time, our government advanced the cost of passage in order to entice workers to make the leap into Canadian prosperity. Many took the money and tried their luck in Canada only to return home to Old Blighty disgruntled and broke. The thickness of each file suggested how many letters had been written in a vain attempt to get our money back. Our missives successively cautioned, threatened, sympathized, berated, shamed, wheedled, needled, and ultimately blew a desperate smokescreen by assuring that we would "take appropriate action" if they didn't comply. None of us had the slightest idea just what that "appropriate action" might be. Eventually, we found out.

One day, our supervisor decided to send a "Mr. Muscle" out knocking on doors to make collections. The man chosen for the job was jovial, adventuresome, and ambitious, though by no means the sharpest knife in the drawer. Initially, we tried to dissuade him from his potentially dangerous mission. We had good reason to urge caution. We knew from occasional replies telling us where to stick our "f... ing country" that debt jumpers could get angry. Besides, the impoverished working-class districts of Portsmouth, Liverpool, and Manchester could be rough. Yet our valiant collector sallied forth with a sense of derring-do and self-worth and a healthy travel advance tucked in his pocket. Of course, he came back with nothing except happy memories of swapping tales in the workmen's pubs, and the occasional promise from one delinquent or another that he might once again try his hand at immigration—provided he could again get an interest-free government loan.

I HAD long been hoping for a posting to a German-speaking country. When the break came, I was sent on temporary assignment to Vienna. A quick phone call to Anita, and we were off for a fascinating twelve-hour train journey. We would be staying in the upscale Hotel am Stephansdom, across from the thirteenth-century St. Stephen's Cathedral (*Stephansdom*), the tallest cathedral in Europe, beloved of Mozart and Beethoven. At that time, the city and environs still felt the presence of the postwar Russian occupation. Our one-man visa office in Vienna had at the time been processing a huge backlog of applicants, particularly a special cohort of Yugoslav TB refugees requiring interview and documentation. In addition, the constant flow of Austrian applicants for short-term visitor and business visas also required interviews and processing. The office needed immediate backup. I enjoyed the interviews, especially when they were successful. It was never easy to advise an applicant in a face-to-face interview that we couldn't issue them a visa.

I recall in particular an elderly woman who had hoped to attend her daughter's wedding in Toronto. Her chest X-ray had revealed scar tissue on her lungs—a not uncommon indication in Europe. And there was the rub. Where a European physician would invariably find the scars old and benign, a Canadian physician following the policy of Health Canada would find them "possibly" malignant. Thus, the applicant fell into a prohibited class. Forbidden from discussing her medical results—if only because they were beyond my professional competence—I could do nothing more than offer my regrets and advise her to consult her personal physician. Helpless, though moved, all I could do was witness her tears.

Apart from such downers, I appreciated the independence that came with having my own office and secretary, the freedom to make my own decisions, and access to challenging cases such as I would rarely, if ever, encounter in the UK. And, of course, I was now working in a variant of German with unique roots in the Austro-Hungarian Empire. German being a pluricentric language, its standard forms had arisen in different geographical and cultural centres like Saxony, Prussia, Bavaria, and Switzerland. Here in Austria, I experienced different linguistic terms in law, administration, and even cooking. Thus, where the German rendered "potato" as *Kartoffel*, the Austrian said *Erdapfel* (earth apple). Horseradish was *Meerrettich* (sea radish) in German and *Kren* in Austrian, a word from the Serbo-Croatian. While the German word for pancakes was *Pfannkuchen*, Austrians drew on the Romanian and wrote *Palatschinken*. With my passion for languages, my work as a visa officer on the European continent provided an unexpected linguistic dimension I hadn't found in the UK. I found Austrian culture endlessly fascinating, from the *Hofburg* Imperial Palace, seat of the Habsburg Empire, to the Baroque ambiance of the Spanish Riding School, to its wealth of art galleries and museums. I especially enjoyed the suburb of *Grinzing,* with its distinctive Viennese wines. I much later discovered that in 1914 Austria had boasted the sixth largest war fleet in the world: the Imperial and Royal Navy (*Kaiserliche und Königliche Marine*). Its submarine operations in the Adriatic during the First World War ultimately became a focus for my subsequent research into German submarine warfare.

Of course, I knew that my posting in Vienna could not last. But it was satisfying to feel more embedded in the culture than I would have been as a passing tourist. This came home to me in mid-February 1961 when strolling to work from my hotel among the press of morning crowds. I enjoyed my habitual route through the pedestrian spaces of the Old Town, and the feeling of being one among the office workers and tradespeople hastening along in the flow. Somehow it felt all about belonging. But one morning I felt something deeper. Shortly before eight o'clock—records show it to have been precisely 07:48—the streets fell quiet. Our world began to grow dark. It felt apprehensive and haunting. A total eclipse of the sun was turning morning into evening. It cast the cathedral behind me into a brooding blackness. The air hung heavy. All movement in the crowd ceased in eerie silence. We paused as if by instinct—the German word for pause is *innehalten,* suggesting a quiet inwardness. The suspended moment felt somehow portentous and out of joint. Moments later, the morning sun passed out from behind the shadow of the moon. And Vienna picked up its daily life once again.

In one sense, we had experienced no more than an astrophysical phenomenon, although a vivid one. In quite another sense, we experienced a heightened awareness of the interrelationships between the individual and the crowd, darkness and light, and the self-preoccupied throng against a beckoning cathedral. As I walked away, I recalled the nineteenth-century Viennese novelist Franz Grillparzer's tragic novella *Der Arme Spielmann* (*The Poor Street Musician*). The book opens with a crowd at a popular folk festival. People from all walks of life in the story forget themselves for a time and feel part of an organic whole. At such times, the narrator explains, "every folk festival is a soul-fest, a pilgrimage, a meditation." Such was my experience of the solar eclipse over St. Stephen's Cathedral.

I regretted leaving Vienna. My life there had been deeply satisfying. Yet I returned to London with heightened anticipation of my next posting: this time, to Cologne, Germany. This was the very move I had been seeking. With precious little to pack other than our suitcases and a portable record player, it was an easy move. Our sense of flexibility and freedom could at times be quite overwhelming. Our route from London to Dover and on to Brussels via channel ferry and train was already familiar to us. The new stretch lay by rail onward to Cologne, where we were met by new colleagues at the visa office. We would be staying in the Hotel am Dom, right across from the magnificent Gothic cathedral, a treasured landmark. The war had destroyed some 80 percent of the city. Miraculously, the grand cathedral had survived virtually unscathed. The Allies claimed they had never wanted to harm it; locals said they had aimed at it—and missed. Happily, such conflicting views never became grist to the postwar reconciliation mill.

Our first order of business after my settling into work was to find a more permanent place to live. In surprisingly short order, we took an apartment that was being vacated by a Canadian doctor who was returning home. Situated less than a half block from the Rhine River, a short walk took us to the cathedral and shops, and just a few minutes' drive to the visa office. It proved ideal. Living in Germany was for me sheer pleasure. Anita was happy too. Being settled was comforting, for our first child was on the way.

The Cologne office was a large operation, and in many respects much more complex than the London one. The difference lay not so much in the fact that British applicants fell under the preferred class of section 20(a) of the Immigration Act and Regulations, and therefore did not require a visa for Canada, but rather in two critical aspects of the regulations governing the processing of immigrants from Germany. Not only did German citizens fall under 20(b)—a notch lower than the British—but for the period from 1939 to 1945 they had been our enemies. Close screening was therefore of the essence. A half-dozen Mounties took care of security screening; while four Canadian physicians conducted medical examinations. We visa officers then drew all the data together during what were called "civil interviews" before issuing visas to the successful applicants. Assisting us through these steps were a number of locally hired translators, typists, and file clerks. Not requiring a translator, I found interviewing and counselling particularly satisfying. I could engage with Germans in a more natural and personal manner. It was actually fun.

In Cologne, the Rhine pulsed with life just a few steps from our door. We never tired of walking along its paved embankments and watching the deep-laden barges thrusting against the powerful current in one direction and coasting with the flow in the other. Water-borne traders running between Amsterdam and Basel linked up with river traffic on the River Main. From our home, a short stroll took us to the partially rebuilt city centre surrounding the magnificent cathedral, which had begun construction seven hundred years earlier, in 1248, over the remains of a Roman temple. Over 630 years would pass before its soaring Gothic towers proclaimed its completion in 1880. Stepping into this medieval place of worship was both uplifting and humbling. I always experienced it as a symphony of architectural form and divine presence, a sanctuary from the hurly-burly of the shops and the bustling main railway station across the crowded square.

THE VISA office in Cologne served as my base of operations for work in Hamburg, Stuttgart, and Berlin. I enjoyed working independently. In Berlin, I witnessed the East Germans building the infamous Berlin Wall in August 1961; in Stuttgart, I enjoyed the almost patrician quietness of a provincial town. By contrast, the high-paced and colourful port city of Hamburg, with its theatres, museums, and concert halls, and its seedy entertainment quarter, St. Pauli and *Grosse Freiheitstrasse,* was lively. These regional offices, where I worked alone with locally hired office staff, reflected the spirit of their locales. Where the Stuttgart office lay squirrelled away in a rather drab-but-decent downtown shopping zone, the Hamburg office stood in a down-at-heel, red-brick mercantile building on Admiralty Street (*Admiralitätstraße).* One of the few buildings to have survived the war, it projected a salt-stained image of ships, sailors, and shantymen. On the other hand, my quarters in the sedate Hotel am Alster gave me access to all the upmarket sights and sounds of a multifaceted, exciting society.

Like all the major centres I visited throughout Germany, Hamburg still showed the deep scars of war. The docklands had been savaged in 1943, when the Allies had launched their devastating bombing attacks dubbed "Operation Gomorrah." The name betrayed a sense of righteous revenge and had been drawn from Scripture: "The Lord rained on Sodom and Gomorrah sulphur and fire from the Lord out of heaven..." These ferocious reprisals against Germany caused the greatest man-made firestorm in history. With fifty-knot winds twisting from all directions, they created a tornado of phosphorus-fed fire almost five hundred metres high. These horrors struck me each time I saw the tall spire of the *Nikolaikirche* (St. Nicholas Church) rising alone among the ruins. I was reminded of Hans Erich Nossack's 1948 publication entitled *Der Untergang*

(*The End*), which covered the attack during the last eight days of July 1943. Reprinted with photographs in 1981, it documented the appalling destruction that killed over 42,000 civilians. *Der Untergang* dispensed with the binary values of good and evil. It offered instead a penetrating personal reflection on the emotional, physical, and psychological impact of total annihilation. These physical scars found their counterpart in the post-traumatic disorders of the surviving victims.

Canada, by contrast, was offering a fresh start in a new country that claimed no such history. Canada needed immigrants and actively sought them. This meant we were competing with Germany for the same trades and professions it needed to feed its burgeoning *Wirtschaftswunder* (economic miracle) of full employment. Were we to advertise openly, we would have to seek the approval of the German Labour Office for every successful candidate. So, we did an end run into open-ended public relations. We cultivated interest in immigrating by hosting cultural talks and engagements throughout the country under the rubric of "Canada: The Land and its People."

This advertising strategy had been in full swing when I arrived in Cologne. It promised Germans new beginnings and open spaces. Under the direction of my German-speaking Mennonite colleague, Otto Thiessen, it was proving successful in reaching even the smallest towns. I soon left my visa desk to become his partner. As immigrants still travelled by ship, Otto twinned with the Greek Lines, while I linked up with Home Lines and its agent, the irrepressible Austrian Günther Reibhorn. Günther and I remained lifelong friends. Together we worked out a remarkably effective promotional campaign, beginning in the southern city of Lindau, on Lake Constance (*Bodensee*), and ending months later in Flensburg, near the Danish border. Our three-pronged plan of attack consisted of a press conference in one town, then an illustrated public lecture in another, followed by a press conference in another before backtracking to the first to give the advertised public lecture. Leapfrogging our way from south to north and east to west, we criss-crossed the Federal Republic of Germany in what we jocularly called our mutual educational journey—*unsere gemeinsame Bildungsreise*.

THE IDEA of a *Bildungsreise* reaches back to the seventeenth-century tradition of the grand tour once undertaken by wealthy young British gentlemen to imbibe the classical culture of antiquity. It was a rite of passage, often undertaken with a tutor. The months-long, cross-Europe journeys ended in Italy. By the eighteenth century, the European gentry also were doing it. The notion of education through travel had its precursors in the medieval practice of wandering scholars setting off to sing their troubadour songs, think their thoughts, and broaden their narrow lives. So, too, Günther and I explored Western Germany. Armed with an annotated Shell road atlas, we held the key to all the cultural landmarks, from castles to war graves and prehistoric archeological sites to the blatantly contemporary. Our professional and personal interests meshed. My battered Shell atlas remains a memento of that journey of discovery.

As we travelled, both Günther and I read voraciously; our discussions flowed in many directions, sometimes between extremes. The poetry and letters of Rainer Maria Rilke (which I had first encountered as an undergraduate) engaged us in reflections on language, love, and mysticism. Documentaries on the Second World War led us into explorations of human conflict and suffering. One day, we wandered into a record shop and fell into conversation with the proprietor, a veteran of the campaign in Poland. He recommended a remarkable recording entitled *Letzte Briefe aus Stalingrad* (*Last Letters from Stalingrad*). Based on a sixty-eight-page anthology published in 1950, and recorded by Deutsche Grammophon in 1961 with actor Hansjörg Felmy, the letters triggered reflections on victimhood, fate, exploitation, and misplaced allegiance to a criminal political regime.

As a teenage Wehrmacht soldier, Günther had fought in the defence of Vienna against Soviet forces. For Günther and the proprietor of the record shop, the Stalingrad letters struck raw nerves. Widely held as authentic, the letters document the harrowing last days of the German Sixth Army at Stalingrad. Encircled and trapped by no fewer than seven Soviet armies, the Germans faced annihilation. Unmoved by the loss of a quarter million soldiers, Hitler insisted that Field Marshal Friedrich Paulus fight to the end. High Command in Berlin permitted each man to write one last letter home. The last aircraft out of the combat zone would fly the letters to Berlin for delivery. I could only imagine that dreadful choice: with just one final letter permitted as a last personal witness, a last solemn act before annihilation, to whom would I write? What would I say? These soul-searching human documents remain among the most illuminating and sobering I have ever encountered.

The letters never reached their destination. In a cynical ruse designed to assess the morale of the soldiers in the field, staff in Army Headquarters removed the addressees and signatures and sorted the letters according to tendency and mood. The consensus condemned the Nazi regime. Propaganda Minister Joseph Goebbels found the damning results "intolerable for the German people" (*untragbar für das deutsche Volk*) and relegated them to the cellars for disposal. He might as well have called the results "un-German" (*undeutsch*), a term describing anything that ran counter to Nazi ideology.

I have often wondered what the effects might have been had those letters been delivered to their intended recipients. One soldier, a former concert pianist, wrote to his family that he had lost his fingers in the minus-forty-degrees winter. Another wrote to his wife, whom he had once deceived, begging her forgiveness. Yet another wrote to his father, a senior Wehrmacht officer. Beginning his letter in the official tone appropriate to a junior writing to his senior, he sharply criticized the flawed army leadership that had destroyed a nation. Switching moods and style, he then spoke as a loving son to a distraught father, assuring him of his abiding love. He would do his duty to the bitter end, he wrote, and bade his father farewell. Yet another confessed to his pastor-father that he had lost his faith: "There is no God, Father. At least, not in Stalingrad." In the end, Field Marshal Paulus surrendered in order to save the 91,000 soldiers who remained out of the 300,000 who had engaged in battle against the Soviets. Five years later, only five thousand would return home from captivity. I subsequently met one of the survivors, author Willy Kramp, who had written of his five years as a prisoner of war in the Soviet Union. We maintained a close relationship until his death. Ironically, Paulus appeared in the Nuremburg War Crimes Trials as a witness for the prosecution.

It took Kramp fifteen years after his release from Soviet prison to clarify his thoughts and begin speaking publicly about his experience. His memoir of those years, *Brüder und Knechte* (*Brothers and Slaves*), speaks of men who faced mortal dangers and decisions, yet somehow managed to sustain a vestige of their humanity. A member of the Confessing Church (an anti-fascist movement within the German Protestant Church), many members of whom had participated in the assassination attempt on Hitler's life, he described himself as an opponent of the Hitler regime. Yet he felt just as guilty as those who had succumbed to Nazism, either through blindness, weakness, or ambition. Kramp wrote: "My generation has been deeply wounded by the recognition of how small a step it is to become guilty" for all that happened. During our visits in the 1970s, we spoke frequently about this and often addressed the lead question, which Kramp raises in his memoir: "Who are we Germans?" Coming to terms with one's identity takes a long time. But as Kramp explains in his book *Die Welt des Gesprächs* (*The World of Dialogue*), it is through words that "people share their worlds, and thereby interpret, clarify, and reconcile a piece of their Being."

Sharing one's stories could also turn lowbrow, as was often the case when, while travelling throughout Germany, I would meet with German acquaintances for a beer after work in one town or another. In such situations, "whisper jokes" from the Nazi period frequently bubbled to the surface. In the 1930s and '40s, you risked imprisonment or worse for speaking against the regime. But Germans did so anyway in their intimate circles. These jokes reveal much about the angst and malaise that prevailed in the general population in those days. A collection of these jokes was first published in 1963, as a serious contribution to what Germans called "coming to terms with the past."

Take the story from the early days when Nazis were rounding up "asocials"—Jews, gypsies, homosexuals, and communists among them—under the guise of ethical law. One day, the story goes, a group of rabbits appeared at the Belgian border, seeking asylum. "Why are you here?" asked the border guards. "We are political refugees," they replied, adding "The Gestapo wants to arrest all giraffes as enemies of the state." "But you are not giraffes," said the nonplussed border guard. "You are rabbits." "*We* know that. But just try telling it to the Gestapo." Others pilloried Hitler himself. "Who is the world's best electrician?" asked another wag. Answer: "Hitler. He switched off Russia, wired Italy in parallel, isolated England, put the whole world in high tension, and has not yet had a short circuit." Or, closer to the bone: "Many members of the Nazi party have bladder disease. They'd like to slip away, but can't manage it."

Indeed, a wealth of whisper jokes involving Jews suggests that the average citizen might have had a good idea of what was going on in Germany. In one of them, a New York Jew visits a relative who had managed to escape from Nazi Germany. He finds his relative surrounded by pictures of Hitler. When asked to explain himself, the refugee replies, "They're an antidote against homesickness."

Meanwhile, the dramatist Bertolt Brecht had been unleashing sharp social criticism of Germany's past since the end of the First World War. The German stage featured him throughout my time in Germany. A communist, internationalist, and provocateur, Brecht was the poster child of Germany's burgeoning theatre. I read him as a weather gauge of the new postwar Germany. While we were still living in London, Anita had given me a copy of Martin Esslin's critical study *Brecht: A Choice of Evils*. The first major study of Brecht in the English language, it remains among the best, even sixty years later. Ever adept, Esslin had described Brecht's approach as "a philosophy of enlightened self-interest based on the conviction that survival—and success—is more important than the striking of heroic attitudes." To that end, Brecht employed what he called his "alienation effect." This V-effect (from *Verfremdungseffect)* aimed at alienating his audiences from any emotional engagement in the dramatic action they witnessed. He called on audiences to think critically and to make judgements.

Brecht's life was a study in contrasts. Haunted by his childhood experience of the First World War, he was almost expelled from school for having written an essay attacking the prevalent notion of Horace that it was "sweet and fitting" to die for one's country. Both the Germans and the British had propagandized the classical saying *dulce et decorum est pro patria mori*. Like the British poet Wilfred Owen and others, Brecht had been among the first in Germany to debunk the lie as cheap propaganda (*Zweckpropaganda*). He saw it as a ruse justifying the carnage on the Western Front. Appalled by the rise and dominance of Nazism in the 1930s, Brecht chose exile in the USA for the duration of the Second World War. Drawn by the artistic creativity of Hollywood, he nonetheless endured harassment during the McCarthy era for his alleged un-American activities. A committed communist, he returned to Germany at war's end to settle in East Berlin under the Communists, where he created his own theatre—*Theater am Schiffbauerdamm*. His themes pilloried Nazi racial theory and the role of greed in promoting poverty and war. He railed against profiteering in wartime and warned against the threat of social engineering and political and capitalist opportunism. He argued for freedom and justice. I saw many of Brecht's plays and began collecting both West German and East German editions of his collected works. The fact that East German editions were not permitted in the West made them all the more valuable.

On a brisk and frosty day in January 1962, I walked into a small bookshop in Speyer, on the left bank of the Rhine River, where I discovered Ernst von Salomon's autobiographical novel *Der Fragebogen* (*The Questionnaire*). First published in 1951, it was a runaway bestseller that had been recently reprinted. This was another of the many social and political documents, like those of Brecht, that bore directly upon my work as a visa officer. Our embassy staff resorted to questionnaires not only for our civil interviews of prospective immigrants to Canada, but also as a means for assessing their criminal and political backgrounds. I found the task of compressing a person's lifetime experience into an official application form a rather problematic exercise. Ultimately, we interviewers had to winkle out any missing details. In the case of von Salomon's *Der Fragebo-gen,* however, questionnaires had been a tool of the postwar Military Government of Germany in its nationwide process of de-nazification and re-education. Established by the Allied powers on the collapse of Nazi Germany, the Allies' process aimed at stripping Nazi ideology from every facet and fibre of German and Austrian society. They would do it initially with a bilingual German-English questionnaire posing 130 questions. Ernst von Salomon found the procedure inadequate and responded with his 668-page autobiographical novel.

Ironic, sardonic, ascerbic, and frequently cynical, von Salomon's novel excoriated the bureaucratic attempt to categorize people according to the West's scale of values. In doing so, his very subjective persiflage ranged through German history from 1917 to the end of the war in 1945 and the subsequent occupation. This was precisely the period with which I had been wrestling. The book articulated many of the arguments I had heard throughout my working tour. I had had many conversations, for instance, with Franz Martischewsky, a travel agent and war veteran, about the major themes of the day: war guilt, nationalism, a divided Germany, and the challenge it faced in coming to terms with its immediate past. The latter notion had a newly minted technical term: *Vergangen-heitsbewältigung.* It was the kind of blockbuster word that humorist Mark Twain once said would make you choke if you tried to swallow it. In conversations with Franz, I had frequently cited Germany's intellectual and artistic traditions, highlighting the artistic worlds of the classical writers Goethe and Schiller. Franz's final letter to me recalled our conversations and signed off with profound regret: "The Germany you love is dead"—*das Deutschland, das Sie lieben ist tot.* He was right, of course, and I had known it all along.

Günther and I ended our grand tour on a melancholy day in Flensburg, at the very top of Germany. We had spent a long time on the road together. We had explored the country's geographical and cultural contours. We had visited sites from the Neolithic Stone Age and Bronze Age pile dwellings at Unteruhldingen on Lake Constance (*Bodensee*) in the south, to the Viking Museum Haithabu on the outskirts of Schleswig in the north. We had viewed outstanding Roman ruins along the Rhine, and the sites of prehistoric bog corpses (*Moorleichen*) in the northern peat moors. We had met with business leaders, scholars, and veterans, and the media. In all this diversity, the energy and innovativeness of Germany's economic miracle had impressed us. We had also become equally impressed by the number of Germans hankering for new horizons far from a burdensome past.

We had even experienced a performance of Brecht's *Refugee Conversations* (*Flüchtlingsgespräche*) in Munich, starring the famous political cabarettist Werner Fink in the lead role. A survivor of one of Nazi Germany's first concentration camps—Esterwegen, near the Dutch border—Fink had gone on to a stellar career in political theatre. The biting satire and verbal jousting of his performance in Munich still resonates today, over sixty years later, in a world coping with the tragedy of mass migrations and the failure of bureaucrats to deal with them justly. "The passport is a human being's noblest part" (*Der Paß ist der edelste Teil eines Menschen*), Brecht had written. A year later, novelist Erich Maria Remarque underscored the point in his *Die Nacht von Lissabon* (*The Night in Lisbon*) about refugees escaping Nazi Germany: "A human being is nothing anymore; a valid passport is everything." Without it, the faceless migrant would perish.

My travels through Germany had brought this point home to me repeatedly. Late one evening, I pulled off the main highway to explore a quiet country road that ran along the no man's land bordering East Germany's frontier with the West. My sense of illicit adventure increased as heavy snow began to cover the forest road. Catching sight of an armed West German border patrol approaching on foot, I stopped the car and got out to meet them. At first suspicious, they soon fell into easy conversation after confirming my identity as a member of the Canadian Embassy. An East German minefield lay in cleared land between the two Germanies, defended by a jagged line of barbed wire fencing and watchtowers running along either side from Lübeck in the north to the juncture of Austria and Czechoslovakia. The so-called firebreak, or forest aisle (*die*

Schneise), had become a household word in border towns. Successful escapees into the West were rare. Many had lost their lives in the attempt. Occasional explosions punctuated the night air during my stroll with the border patrol. Another foiled escape? we wondered. Someone lying wounded in the snow? Or perhaps nothing more than some unfortunate rabbit or deer triggering a mine. As I climbed back into my car and pushed off through the snow, I felt a shiver of relief that I was free to determine my own life without the fear of violent retaliation. I had a Canadian passport and a valid German ID. Brecht had gotten it right. The passport is indeed a noble body part. And besides, as the political cabarettist had spoofed, it takes far more skill to produce a passport than to produce a human being.

DURING OUR travels, Anita and I had always shared our reflections about the human condition. We continue to do so. When holidays came around, we would pack up our camping gear and books and head to the south of France to relax and explore. Juan-les-Pins on the French Riviera always beckoned. Monet and Picasso loved the place too. It was a wonderful location at which to enjoy simply being. Or, as one might say philosophically, to enjoy Being with a capital B. We felt a wholesomeness camping by sunny seas or driving along the Corniche, the coastal cliffside roads linking the elegant villas of the rich and famous in places like Monaco, Nice, Monte Carlo, and a favourite spot of ours, St. Jean-Cap-Ferrat. The trips gave us time to think about our values and how we wanted to live, and for our reflections to coalesce. Thoughts of returning to academe had long been percolating. Though the theme of migration as a reflection of the human condition remained important to us, a lifetime career stamping passports did not. Our government's immigration policies showed no signs of veering from their essentially colonial view of Canadian society. While I could see my world becoming more cosmopolitan, Canada's immigration service insisted upon dragging its tail. If I could have worked as a cultural attaché, as I had essentially been doing in Germany, perhaps I might have stayed. But "culture" remained the work of the Department of External Affairs, and many years would pass before our three foreign services—External Affairs, Immigration, and Trade and Commerce—would combine into one. Besides, Canada and the academic life were calling us back. Almost twenty years would pass before we engaged with refugees again, this time as the co-sponsors on the receiving end in Canada. Refugees from Laos were fleeing the violence spilling over from the Vietnam War and from Cambodia. After a risky night-crossing of the Mekong River in fear for their lives, they found temporary refuge in camps in Thailand. In 1980, we received a family of five who would become our friends for life. For the moment, however, all this was beyond our envisioning.

Now, in 1962, we found ourselves facing the equivalent of what submarine commanders call their "Perisher," the final critical test for command which puts one's whole future at stake. It meant you either passed or you didn't. The French aptly called this naval exam the "Risque-Tout," for everything would indeed be at risk. We decided to go for it and made a radical decision that changed our lives. In August that year, we boarded the train from Cologne to Cuxhaven with baby Pauline, buggy, and baggage. Once again, the good ship *Homeric* ferried us across the sea to Montreal and a migrant's train journey to Winnipeg. This marked my eighth and final Atlantic crossing by ship. Once again, the ship's band played its signature tune, "Volaré, oh-oh / Cantaré, oh-oh-oh-oh." We would indeed be singing and flying. Our future passages to Europe would be by air.

6

WINDS OF
CHANGE

Deeper and deeper into the well of his life he went:
a rainbow, a gravestone, a slant of morning light.
CAROL SHIELDS, *The Stone Diaries*

A BLISTERING August assailed us when we arrived in Winnipeg from our home in Germany. Baked by the merciless sun, we felt heat waves rising from the parched ground. From horizon to unlimited horizon, the sky stretched to bursting point and threatened to crack. We had never experienced a prairie summer. This steaming cauldron, touted as the "land of ten thousand lakes," was to be our new home as I returned to university life. Nor did the onset of a brilliant autumn give any hint of the biting deep freezes of the winter to follow. Yet in time, we came to experience what licence plates proclaimed: "Friendly Manitoba." Our journey to Winnipeg, and our subsequent life on the prairies, bore echoes of an immigrant experience. We had given up a secure life in exchange for a new venture. We were on our own, though in our own country. We depended upon our own energies and ingenuities. We faced a common challenge and had made up our minds to succeed.

Little could we have imagined that one day the lieutenant-governor of the province would present us with an oil painting by R.G. Pollock in recognition of our services to his office. It depicted the fishing boats of Gimli, idle and boarded up on the hard at Lake Winnipeg due to environmental pollution. The obvious motifs were boats, a lake, and inland seafaring. Even more compelling for me was the painting's vortex of a summer sky evoking the hush before a storm. *Fishing Boats at Gimli* has for years symbolized what we experienced in those years: challenge, uplift, sorrow, survival, and ultimate success. Much was on our side. The academic world in Canada bristled with opportunities. Full-time tenure-track positions were opening everywhere in the 1960s in a burgeoning market of academic institutions, even for those with bachelor's and master's degrees. Based on my undergraduate degree and overseas experience, I was about to settle into a lectureship with St. John's Anglican College, one of four faith-based colleges of the University of Manitoba. In but a few years time you would require a PhD and a list of publications in order to get your nose in the warm. Our strategic return to Canada had struck at precisely the right time.

In all our endeavours I had always been mindful of the calculated risks we took. Even now, just thinking about them gives me the cold shivers. Our own families must have questioned our sanity in having left the security of a government job for the insecurity of academic life. I recall that sunny Sunday morning in Cologne when we said goodbye to the foreign service and strolled along the Rhine from our apartment to the Main Station, pushing our pram with baby Pauline. Our move, in the expression of psychiatrist and Holocaust survivor Victor E. Frankl, had been triggered by my "existential frustration" with bureaucracy. Our journey from Cologne to Winnipeg marked the beginning of a fresh start with new horizons. It would not be our final migration.

Shortly after our arrival in Winnipeg, a Russian bear of a man knocked at our door. It was the ever-jovial Mennonite scholar Jack Thiessen—a future colleague. "Come along with me," he beckoned. "I've got something to show you." We left town and drove into the open spaces of southern Manitoba until he pulled off onto a narrow road and stopped by a farmer's field. "Now just look at that!" He sounded like a connoisseur of art who had just discovered a lost Renoir. I gazed into the direction he was pointing and saw ... nothing. Nothing, that is, except a broad horizon and big sky framing infinite miles of rolling prairie. Captivated by what he called the

"Russian steppes" of Canada, he contemplated the land much as I had always contemplated the sea. This was Mennonite country. Generations of Jack's forebears had experienced the land this way, both at home in the Russian village of Chortitza and here, where their migrant journeys had led them. I delved into this history. When I chanced upon Mennonite writer Arnold Dyck's self-published novel of 1944, *Verloren in der Steppe* (*Lost in the Steppes*), I discovered a gem. A minor writer in the broad scheme of things, Dyck yet spoke for the Mennonite experience. "In such moments," he had written in his German mother tongue, "the man of the steppes grows silent; he forgets the world of everyday, the burden of being bound to earth falls away, and his eyes and soul reach for the stars." For many Mennonites, this tie to the land was the emotional equivalent of prayer, much as the sea had always been for me. As twilight fell, I experienced an unexpected and grateful kinship. My friendship with Jack would deepen over the years.

Dyck's work *Verloren in der Steppe* was a novel of cultural crisis. Unwittingly, perhaps, he had chosen the form of the "novel of education" (*Bildungsroman*), long-since established in European literature. The genre explores the synergies involved in human development: physical, cultural, spiritual, and intellectual. True to his Mennonite roots, Dyck's novel uncovered two conflicting understandings of what education was all about. Some Mennonites saw education as alienation—a threat to the integrity of the social and moral order; others saw it as a means for outreach and self-fulfilment. At one point in his outward journey, Arnold Dyck's young protagonist experiences the outspread reaches of steppe and sky: "Even Hans' sensitive soul strives into the heavens to fetch from the stars his happiness—and unrest!" The homespun novel helped me understand my students, both at St. John's and later at United College, most of whom came from Mennonite traditions.

That first Winnipeg Christmas found us in the grip of a sub-zero, snowbound winter. Gusting winds were piling heavy drifts along roads, walks, and into doorways when another memorable knock called us to the door. There stood a smiling, larger-than-life Jack

Thiessen again, fur cap and greatcoat covered in glinting flakes, his arms laden with gifts. His casual spontaneity transformed our experience of a strange city into a homecoming. He had drawn us into his community. The Mennonite world that Jack represented became part of our life. We quickly came to appreciate its principles of generosity, community, and pacifism. We recognized that the key to their ethics of social action was rooted in the Beatitudes enunciated by Jesus in the Sermon on the Mount (Matthew 5:1–12): "Blessed are those who hunger and thirst for what is right, ... Blessed are the merciful, ... Blessed are the peacemakers." Such are the ethics of a people seeking to create a just society, a concept that Pierre Elliott Trudeau would trumpet in April 1968. That winter of 1962, I read my way deeper into the Mennonite world via works like Rudy Wiebe's *Peace Shall Destroy Many*. Forty years later I would draw upon the wisdom of the Mennonite Central Committee when developing my concepts of restorative justice. Despite criticism of Mennonites being a backward-looking and closed community, liberal sectors of their pacifist tradition offer a vision of a compassionate future. Progressive Mennonites have shown that the road to justice, forgiveness, and reconciliation follows a spiritual path. But what that dynamic might mean in the post-religious age into which I was happy to grow would only evolve in my mind many years later.

While at St. John's College, I picked up a copy of Bede Griffiths's remarkable autobiography *The Golden String*, which had been recommended to me by my friend, the medievalist scholar Joan Greatrex. For Joan, the book had been a stepping stone to her embracing Catholicism. What intrigued me about Griffiths was his detailed description of the intellectual and spiritual influences in his life. The wisdom of the West had led him to recognize what he called the "divine order in the universe" and had turned him from atheism to life as a Benedictine monk. Both Anita and I felt drawn to his view that to be Christian meant acknowledging our responsibility for others. Bede Griffiths had rooted the notion in the Benedictine principle of *ora et labora*—work and pray. Persuaded that we must view our existence and our purpose through lenses other than our own,

Griffiths later established in India a monastery for Christian-Hindu dialogue. My later studies in eighteenth-century German rational-ism would confirm for me Gotthold Ephraim Lessing's principle that what really matters lies not in *finding* truth but in establish-ing a *relationship* to it. Such concepts led me to a re-evaluation of religious understandings, or what my friend, the theologian John J. Thatamanil, today calls "theology without walls." This theology points to nothing less than the possibility of interreligious wisdom. In 2001, these ideas would find expression in my "Spiritual Roots of Restorative Justice" project, an international, interfaith research initiative that I directed in the Centre for Studies in Religion and Society at the University of Victoria. This approach has remarkable practical consequences. The life of the late Sister Elaine MacInnes is a salient case in point. A Catholic nun and Zen Buddhist master, she worked with prison inmates in Japan, the UK, and Canada.

But I wasn't there yet. It was now 1966, and Anita's birthday gift of Nikos Kazantzakis's controversial novel *The Last Tempta-tion of Christ* gripped me. Deeply rooted in the macho culture of Crete, Kazantzakis had repudiated Friedrich Nietzsche's scorn of Christianity as weak and effete. Instead, he had stood Nietzsche's *Antichrist* on its head and drawn upon the vitalism of Henri Bergson's *élan vital*. In many ways, the gritty novel was a testament to the spirit prevailing in the 1960s. A gutsy grand slam of a book, it wove narrative threads of the Gospel into a troubling, if not tortured, portrait of a profoundly human Jesus. The Roman Catholic Church condemned the book and the Greek Orthodox Church excommu-nicated the author. If Kazantzakis's Zorba in *Zorba the Greek* was an irrepressible bon vivant bristling with unbridled yet compassionate machismo, then his Jesus in *The Last Temptation* blends the roles of revolutionary and prophet.

This flesh and blood social-justice Jesus appealed to me, with his susceptibility to the temptations of which human flesh is capable. He shadowed me for years. As the fictionalized Jesus confides to the Apostle Paul in the novel: "I too set out to save the world. Isn't that what being young means—to want to save the world?" This was the zeitgeist of the 1960s. You can just hear the throbbing guitars with their plaintive and sharp-edged songs of protest.

But I was in career mode, with responsibilities for my wife and now four lovely children. Thus, I remained in the mainstream, though the six of us did engage in protest marches in front of the US consulate against the Vietnam War. Our sympathies were moving to the Left. In 1965, I left St. John's Anglican College and joined Jack Thiessen—a Mennonite Zorba of gentler temperament—in the German Department of United College in downtown Winnipeg. This was two years before it became the University of Winnipeg. A collegial and burgeoning college, it served a cosmopolitan range of students and offered a wealth of teaching opportunities in my own discipline. I now had a master's degree, and found here scope for a career with which St. John's could not begin to compete. As it turned out, most of my students were Mennonite and spoke Low German, or were first- or second-generation Germans. I found the scope of the curriculum and the keenness of the students challenging and enriching. A significant cohort of mature students—a special category of adults who had never completed high school—brought maturity of judgement, life experience, and purpose into the mix. I empathized with them in the difficult adjustments that a late return to school often implied.

Living in the 1960s, we felt we were standing at the dawn of a new age. We were walking a tightrope between the extremes of peace and violence, between protesters against the violence of Vietnam, pumping slogans like "make love, not war" and "hell no, we won't go!" and those who argued that citizens had a civic duty to take up arms against a foe, however immoral the cause. Many Canadians at the time were against the Vietnam War, but argued that the wave of American draft dodgers seeking refuge in Canada should go home and fight the Vietnamese. Civic duty trumped ethics. The Cuban Missile Crisis of 1962 had forced us to face imminent nuclear disaster. The beginnings of the Civil Rights Movement and the women's and gay rights movements in the USA were spilling over into Canada, accelerated by the young and photogenic

President Kennedy, whose grassroots social policies contrasted with the seething pressures of social unrest in the States. Trudeaumania took hold of Canada. We witnessed the rise of the counterculture, in the form of outlandish hippies, Jesus Freaks, and Flower Power, together with protest songs and sit-ins. Even the popular music of the day was countercultural. It was a rebellious blend of folk, blues, and country, all of which peaked in psychedelic rock. The electric guitar dominated the music scene, twanging and squealing its way piteously through the airwaves. As traditional jazz musicians would say about the new popular music, "the lower the talent, the higher the decibels."

Even the new age of jazz itself—from bebop to avant-garde—competed with rock music in intensity and volume. Straining at the upper limits of their range, trumpets and saxophones plied their howling, cacophonous rant against the social order. Squeezing their tortured riffs and arpeggios through sweat-soaked passages, proponents of the new idioms confused yelling with singing, and instrumental screeching with accomplished musicianship. It was all a chaos of sound and fury that, to my mind at least, signified nothing but the ugliness of the pop music scene. And yet at the end of the era, hope seemed to flourish: astronauts broke away from our troubled world and landed on the moon. It was 20 July 1969. If we had never thought of our place in the universe before, we had to start thinking about it now. Our rabbit-eared TVs brought it all into our homes: "That's one small step for a man, one giant leap for mankind."

Other ferments were also in the air—intellectual ferments. At the University of Winnipeg where I was teaching, these were fostered as much by the creative intermixing of disciplines working alongside one another—historians, theologians, literary scholars, scientists, anthropologists, and linguists—as by what many called "the winds of change." One of these great gusts of air had found its way to Winnipeg as quickly as it had Berlin and London. Known as Vatican II, the Second Vatican Council (1962–65) had quite unexpectedly thrown open the doors of the Catholic Church to the contemporary world. Announced by Pope John XXIII in January 1959, it urged dialogue with the contemporary world, a "recomposition" of the faithful, and a reformulating and updating of the Faith. They called it *aggiornamento*, and even the secular world picked it up.

The Protestant world responded in kind. Academic and popular books rolled off the presses. We discussed them as current events. Bishop John A.T. Robinson's *Honest to God*, published in 1963, rattled the cages of conservative Christianity by arguing that modern, secular people had long since rejected the notion of a God "up there in Heaven" as an outdated, simplistic view. Certainly, I had done so in my early teens. Taking up the cause of existential theology, Robinson had argued with Paul Tillich that God was instead the "ground of being." Robinson endorsed Dietrich Bonhoeffer's concept of religionless Christianity, popularizing the term "situational ethics." Ethics, he urged, are not etched in stone by religious fiat or Biblical law but are subject to the complex circumstances in which they occur.

Two years later, Robinson's *The New Reformation?* once again tackled the antiquarian Church of England, and Anglicanism at large. "Those who change history most," he argued, "are not those who supply a new set of answers, but those who allow a new set of questions." The book underwent four printings in a single year. Hard-hitting, lucid, insightful, and exhilarating, Robinson's ideas challenged Christians to take atheism seriously. In doing so, he summarized atheism's key objections to religious belief: God, as traditionally conceived, is intellectually superfluous, emotionally dispensable, and morally intolerable. His approach to contemporary thought led to his being dubbed "the atheist bishop." That same year, the American theologian Harvey Cox sold over a million copies of *The Secular City*. He argued, among other things, that God was just as alive in the non-religious secular world as within the confines of religious institutions. To be relevant, therefore, the Church should be at the forefront of change.

Leading Roman Catholic thinkers spoke likewise. Indeed, Hans Küng, in Tübingen, was leading the charge. By 1987 he envisaged "new shores" for the third millennium. This meant embracing world religions, not, as in the past, for conquest or conversion, but as sources for insight and wisdom. Reformative voices like these percolated throughout the university. Judaism, too, found itself tested by Martin Buber, whose popularized concept of "life in dialogue" (*dialogisches Leben*) opened religious thought to multifaith encounter through the medium of "authentic" relationships.

These threads wove their way throughout my life. Many lapsed Christians, myself included, joined progressive parishes that had begun practising the new principles of modernization: contemporary language and liturgy, updated theology, and active community-building. We moved into the Anglican parish of St. Luke's, where we experienced the openness of a welcoming and forward-looking faith community that understood—as the sciences long since had done—the creative power of doubt. We celebrated a great day at St. Luke's when Anita and our four young children were baptized together.

BY 1967 we were on the road again like nomads. The University of Winnipeg granted me a leave of absence to attend Queen's University to complete my studies toward a PhD. In Kingston, Ontario, we rented a house on campus, sight unseen. No safety net, no job security, no tenure, and no guaranteed salary. Anita transformed the old cottage into a very happy home. With its small garden and long, covered veranda, our small student shack introduced us to the joys of spartan living. Of course, our children accepted our change of lifestyle with a sense of adventure. I found their absolute trust in the enterprise uplifting and humbling.

Living as we did in student housing, the children made their mark on campus life. During Freshman Week they joined in the parade of freshmen (and women), dancing and singing past our door in a carefree imitation of hazing antics, as though they themselves belonged to the incoming class. They became known as "the four little elves." One day, a fellow graduate-student, Robert Common (later a noted BC educator), hosted them to a costumed "Hobbit Tea Party," where he presented them with an inscribed copy of Tolkien's *The Hobbit*. Our children's joyful transition to life at Queen's eased the stress of my preparing for my PhD exams. So much hung in the balance, and I couldn't let my family down. But they were always there for me, and Anita kept a steady hand on the tiller of the good ship *Enterprise*.

Sometimes, one or the other of the children would accompany me partway on my walk to the Arts Building or the library, or be bold enough to meet me at some close point on my return home at the end of the day. And during the warmth of spring and summer, Anita would stroll with them through the lovely campus, stopping under the window of my second-floor office in the Arts Building, where their chirpy voices would sing out to me "Papa, Papa," and bring me to the window ledge for a chat. Our family joined the cathedral parish of St. George's, which widened our social network and enhanced our lives enormously. Yet, we were also struck by how old-fashioned, compared to Winnipeg, the Kingston parish was, both theologically and liturgically.

In Kingston, Anita had joined the Elizabeth Fry Society and was making regular visits to the Kingston Prison for Women in support of women's rehabilitation. I've always been struck by words attributed to Elizabeth Fry (1780–1845), the founder of the justice charity that bears her name: "When thee builds a prison, thee had better build with the thought ever in thy mind that thee and thy children may occupy the cells." We lived but a few minutes' drive from the prison. From time to time, Anita would bring an inmate home for a brief visit or a Christmas tea by the fireside. On other occasions, the children and I would accompany her to the prison gym for a family-day tea with inmates. In this way, as in so many others, my soulmate influenced my life, for through her I found myself becoming increasingly attracted to issues of criminal justice.

My research director (*Doktorvater*) at Queen's was the eminent Germanist Hans Eichner. Ever the seeker, he was a consummate scholar. With his deep Jewish roots, he exuded an almost rabbinical exactitude and thoughtfulness, along with a quizzical wit. He epitomized the very best in intellect, ethics, and humanity. He had escaped the Nazi occupation of Austria in 1938, a country that, in his understated expression, "had behaved very badly" during the war. Crossing France and Germany into Belgium, he had taken the migrant route to England, where he found himself declared an enemy alien and shipped off to Australia. Ironically, he returned to England to obtain his doctorate in German at the University of London in 1949, and immigrated to Queen's two years later. Not until his early poetry was published posthumously in 2021 did a wider circle of former students come to appreciate what he had experienced in the 1930s and '40s. While some readers saw his poems solely as technical experiments with language, an attentive reader will gain from them intimate insights into autobiographical elements of love, loss, and longing.

"There are paths," Eichner had written in his native German about the refugee journey. But "who knows where they lead?" In evocative language, he captured their experience: while one traveller was "buoyed along by yearning" and found "a signpost at every turn," another wandered onward, "afflicted with dreams," leaning precariously on his staff and wondering which paths might come next. For those who themselves have undertaken such journeys, Eichner's poetic judgements are both personal and generic. Life is precarious, particularly in matters of the heart, where relationships can be transient and easily broken: "Snow lies on the grave of my love / A willow laments in silence." Or, in another poem: "There is no day that doesn't end."

Obviously, I knew nothing of Eichner's past when I arrived at Queen's. I encountered an astute and meticulous thinker and a demanding yet generous-minded mentor who did all he could to facilitate my entry into fields in which he had been expert for many years: German aesthetics and philosophy and the history of modern literature. The more we came to know one another—and especially after I had graduated and was no longer under his tutelage—the more we became congenial friends. As my own primary interest lay in literature as a social document, I set my research sights on popular culture in the eighteenth-century age of rationalism. This was not as arcane as it might at first seem, for an examination of the rise of popular culture during the Age of Reason was at the time an innovative approach to history. (I eventually applied the techniques to writing the popular history of the German submarine, a literary history examining the role of fiction and memoir in promoting and memorializing war.) Squirrelled away among the library stacks at Queen's, I read voraciously. Of course, I also attended seminars and wrote exams in a range of areas including medieval literature, Reformation and Baroque, and the modern novel. I also taught a German course. This period of rigorous academic study was followed by the inevitable, but mercifully forgettable, oral comprehensive exam.

At the end of my studies in Kingston, we traded our Morris beater for a newer Chevelle station wagon to transport us all back to Winnipeg, where we managed a down payment on a house in River Heights and settled in for the long haul. I returned to the University of Winnipeg and resumed teaching full time while I tidied up and successfully defended my thesis.

Looking back on those days over sixty years ago, I cannot help but think of young people today, who have similar dreams and aspirations but are frustrated by lack of opportunity at every turn. Here I was, a graduate student with five dependents, able to upgrade to a better car to drive myself and my family back to Winnipeg, and make a down payment on a comfortable home in leafy, upmarket River Heights. A tenure-track appointment awaited me. Was this serendipity, chance, grace? It certainly wasn't personal wealth, for we were living like church mice. Opportunity and national economics had certainly conspired. If ever there were a lotus land—and a lotus time—in which to be young and adventuresome, this was it. I received my PhD from Queen's in 1971.

My parents never knew of this final accolade. Innocent victims in a horrific traffic accident, they had been killed on the Trans-Canada Highway around noon on 01 May 1964, just outside Swift Current, Saskatchewan. They had been driving from White Rock, BC, to Winnipeg to help us renovate our new house when an oncoming drunk driver attempted to overtake a hay wagon and drove into them head-on. The crash had been random and violent. I still imagine my parents' final seconds: the searing shock and paralysis of horror in the face of unavoidable death, and the excruciating moment of extinction. I had never experienced such grief before: soul-tearing, guilty, regretful, buffeted by disbelief.

Only years later, when I became involved in the hospice movement, would I acquire the concepts and vocabulary to express what a good death means. It involves being comfortable and at peace with family, friends, and God, however one conceives that notion. It involves having time to recollect, and being able to seek a safe space for death. Violent death precludes that. In the case of my parents' death, closure would remain elusive for the rest of our lives.

MY MEMBERSHIP in Winnipeg's naval division catapulted me into service as honorary aide-de-camp to two successive lieutenant-governors of the Province of Manitoba: Richard S. Bowles and Jack McKeag. This dimension enriched our life in Winnipeg. It was Jack McKeag who gave us the painting *Fishing Boats at Gimli*. Richard Bowles had presented us with silver candlesticks emblazoned with the coat of arms of Government House and an engraved silver fruit bowl. My association with Government House from 1968 to 1971 introduced us to dimensions of Manitoba life that I had never anticipated. For here I encountered not only the cultural and social diversity of the province, but also its ethnic and political synergies. I came to understand its history and to share its aspirations. Government House proved to be the magnetic hub through which all these elements flowed. It was here where I met leaders in the multicultural and multifaith communities and, while serving as an aide, dined with provincial politicians and cabinet members. Here I met Governor-General Roland Michener and members of the British Royal Family, including the Queen and Prince Philip and two of their children. It was also from here that I accompanied Prime Minister Pierre Trudeau and his federal cabinet on a historic train journey from Winnipeg to Fort Garry, where they conducted the first-ever meeting of a federal cabinet to be held outside of Ottawa. My role as ADC frequently called upon Anita and me to accompany the viceregal couple to regions and towns beyond Winnipeg. We quickly learned to expect the unexpected. Arriving for dinner with the citizens of Steinbach one time, we were greeted by the local pastor and a bagpipe-playing Mennonite in kilts. Between them, Government House and the University of Winnipeg staked out one of the most diverse and rewarding territories I had ever experienced.

MY PROFESSIONAL life at the University of Winnipeg was rich and varied. The discipline of German studies was in high demand, my students were motivated and keen, and I appreciated my many colleagues. Yet, we longed to return to the BC coast. That was the ultimate goal we had formulated for ourselves when holidaying years earlier in the south of France: leave the foreign service, get the necessary doctorate, and teach German on the West Coast. Of course, in the intervening years I had not only been teaching and acquiring that degree. I had also been networking within the Canadian Association of University Teachers of German, of which I would later serve as president. We could have made a very happy life for ourselves in Manitoba, until serendipity struck again, followed by decisions. In the midst of a lively children's birthday party at home, I received a phone call from Beattie MacLean, head of the Department of German at the University of Victoria, inviting me to join his department. When we eventually broke the news to our children that we would be moving to Victoria, they all burst into tears. We had forgotten that a move to the West Coast had always been *our* dream, not theirs. BC was *our* home. Manitoba was *theirs*.

So here I was again (with Anita's help), giving up my tenure in Winnipeg and breaking all the bonds in order to drive with four children to Victoria to begin once more earning my spurs in a new professional and cultural environment. The University of Victoria would be my professional home for thirty years. In the fullness of time, I would gain tenure, be promoted to full professor, earn the Queen's Jubilee Medal, and be elected a fellow of the Royal Society of Canada.

We arrived in Victoria in July 1971. Our children had crossed the prairies with us by car, seen their first mountains when we transited the Rockies and Coastal Range, and sailed "right across the ocean," as they put it, in just an hour and a half by ferry to Vancouver Island. I checked into my new department on campus, only to be told by Beattie MacLean that he didn't want to see me until September; everybody else was "off and away." In contrast to the University of Winnipeg, this seemed a very sleepy department indeed. This first point of contact reminded me of my arrival in Winnipeg years earlier, when I encountered a young, disgruntled Manitoban who had just returned from teaching in the lotus land known as British Columbia. Ever the aesthete, he complained of "those folks out West who spend more time thinking about sailing than they do about poetry." For him, boating offered so little for the mind. I could not help retorting, "Grab ahold of life, lad. Just let the skill sets of sailing sizzle up your sinews and tingle in your head. Poetic insights will tumble out all on their own."

But for the moment I had to forgo such pleasures as sailing in order to prepare my courses and find a home for my family. We had made the jump to the Coast; there would be no turning back. At the end of each day, we held our family conference and assured our children that we would indeed find a home and that the "best one of all" was just waiting for us to discover. And finally, we found it: a small house in South Oak Bay. It stood but a couple of minutes from the beach at Shoal Bay, had a garden with fruit trees, and was within walking distance of the children's new school. I will never forget their infectious excitement as they skipped around the garden. Here, they would grow up, dream their dreams, make their music, and find their refuge for many years to come. Our new lives had begun. Bright and enterprising, our children exuded boundless energy and purpose. I still hear them practising their music after breakfast, Pauline on piano, Michèle on clarinet, David on cello (later on trumpet), and Norman on trumpet. Together we formed a homespun band to perform our own Christmas pageant. Our family life was very focused—perhaps too much so. But we brought our children up to exercise their independence.

THE UNIVERSITY of Victoria was just eight years old when I joined its faculty. Founded in 1963, it still bore the rough edges and insecurities of its transition to a full university after sixty years as a two-year-diploma-granting college. Its senior teachers, now professors, were adapting with some discomfort to the notion of an institution dedicated not only to teaching but to increasing knowledge through research and publishing. The majority of its senior scholars had researched or published very little. Protected by a tacit grandfather clause, they held the incoming cohort of scholars to a standard they themselves had not been required to meet. I recall a meeting of the Faculty of Arts and Science when an abrasive young contrarian proposed that all faculty members post their list of publications in the library. Amidst the harrumphing and ruffling of feathers that ensued, the old guard successfully argued that posting a list of publications would be an invasion of privacy. But the academic culture was changing, and UVic would become a major university.

What struck me most about the mood on campus during those early years was the lack of collegiality that seemed to lurk beneath the surface. I felt I had exchanged an established academic community in Winnipeg for a gladsome band on Vancouver Island that had not yet found its way. Newcomers quickly gained the impression of a house divided into two opposing camps: the fact-finders and the wisdom-seekers. Thus, some in the sciences saw themselves as pursuing *scientia* (knowledge)—the creation of new knowledge based on demonstrable facts that could push back the boundaries of what we know. Other scholars, in the humanities, saw themselves in pursuit of *sapientia* (wisdom)—the creation of new knowledge based on long-term philosophical reflection. Here, it was not a question of pushing back boundaries so much as deepening our understandings.

We risked succumbing to what Jacques Barzun's 1964 tour de force *Science: The Glorious Entertainment* had called the "culture of research and factuality." It all came down to how you evaluated people and their academic achievement. The so-called exact sciences, to borrow an expression from Goethe, could verify a person's research achievement by counting their scholarly articles, many of them multi-authored. They could turn to the citation index, which revealed the frequency with which articles and researchers had been cited. By contrast, researchers in the humanities worked largely alone, over long periods of time. Clearly, these two approaches—science and humanities—had different rates of "research production." This led to different rates of salary and promotion. Unfortunately, the university applied the measurement standards of *scientia* to all disciplines. This positivist approach lay at the root of some cynicism in the early days of the new university. As one of my colleagues observed, we would just have to go along with "playing the little game." Some humanists felt they couldn't compete. At least two colleagues in the faculty, it was said, had given up in disgust and devoted a year's research-leave to building sailboats as a way to escape it all. In reality, the false distinction between objective and subjective research hid a deeper truth. For ultimately, all of us were pursuing existential questions. We all wanted to know who we are and how we fit into our expanding universe. *Scientia* and *sapientia* actually converge, but along different paths.

MY BEST memories of academe revolve around the bright, self-motivated, and sympathetic students with whom I was privileged to engage. They formed the heart of my teaching experience and my concept of mentorship. Developing their skills of self-discipline and self-expression, weighing new ideas and perspectives, they were seeking their place in the world. They entered wholeheartedly into the great give-and-take of exploring German culture. I enjoyed their company. Together we tackled the sonnets and word-puzzles of Baroque poetry, with its musings about love, politics, war, and religion. We argued over Luther's world view, which saw Christendom as a universal mindset as dominant then as the capitalist world view is today. We debated the rationalist ideas of the Enlightenment, with their insistence on tolerance, the human family, and the rights of the erring conscience. We explored Romanticism and the philosophies of idealism. We wrestled with the philosopher Immanuel Kant and the poet-mathematician Friedrich von Hardenberg. Both had asserted that big ideas like truth and justice can never be fully experienced nor adequately defined. The Ineffable, such poets and thinkers argued, is not a fact that can be measured. In mathematical terms, such concepts are "irrational magnitudes," similar to the fraction $^{22}/_{7}$ used in calculating the area of a circle. If you divide twenty-two into seven (the numerical equivalent of the symbol π, pi) you get a series of numbers that run on into infinity. They never end. As Kant would have it, an idea is the concept of a perfection that does *not yet* occur in experience. By analogy, ideas like justice and truth constitute values toward which we are always moving. We might yet get there. Our seminars had fun with this one.

Nothing could be more relevant to contemporary living than the history of ideas as expressed in works of the creative imagination. Two of my graduate-level courses, "The Luther Bible in German Literature" and "Envisioning our World," embraced an omnibus approach to the examination of science, faith, and philosophy in the thought of German writers.

On other occasions, and with a whole term before us, my undergraduates and I pondered Goethe's classical character Faust. As the tragedy opened, we found him lamenting having studied the academic disciplines of his day—"philosophy, medicine, law, and unfortunately even theology"—and yet remaining as ignorant as he had been before he had started. (He actually called himself "*dumm.*") Faust famously confessed that, despite his master's and doctoral degrees—and despite being smarter than anybody else at the university—he had been "leading students about by the nose" for years. Finally, he confessed, "we can't know anything at all." And as if that were not depressing enough, he was flat broke. Students, too, knew what it meant to have big dreams and no money.

But what was the point of all this striving, some asked, if it led nowhere? Certainly, Faust himself desired to gain an ultimate understanding of what life—the "big show"—was all about. In effect, all the courses I taught in German literary history addressed these issues. Each did so in its own idiom and style and its unique themes and vocabulary. Rich fare indeed, but easily managed in small portions. This excitement of shared discovery is what gave my teaching its unity and purpose. Forty to fifty years later, I occasionally see some of these former students. Professors are among them, as well as engineers and artists, teachers and musicians, military officers and pastors. I am glad to have walked with them during a formative part of their journey.

Surprisingly, the rationale for teaching languages at university had changed little since my days as an undergraduate in the 1950s. Indeed, they had changed little since the end of the nineteenth century. Universities had always regarded language studies as a means for studying cultures, not as a means for producing speakers of foreign languages. Speaking the target language was a by-product, not an aim. For decades, that meant ascribing to the concept of a literary canon. Coined from the Greek word for measuring rod (*kanón*), the canon was a category of knowledge that scholars considered normative and that competent students "should know." This approach allowed us to define the scope of the courses we taught: the Age of Reason, or the Modern Age, for example. A canon allowed us to build a rational curriculum from beginner to advanced, producing well-rounded undergraduates in their chosen discipline. Our program led naturally to graduate studies in the field. Proud as we were of our curriculum, we realized with some regret that social forces and student expectations were overtaking us.

In time universities began dropping the two-year language requirement, triggering the demise of language departments as we had known them. As secondary schools also ceased teaching foreign languages in any depth, the majority of our students arrived with no knowledge of a language other than English. Indeed, because of serious gaps in their grasp of their mother tongue, the university introduced remedial English into the general curriculum. When marking my students' essays, I found myself having to spend too much time correcting their woefully inadequate English. The scholarly study of language and literature attracted significantly fewer students, though it sometimes appealed to those looking to improve their practical communicative skills, or "beer German," as we disparagingly called it. That is an honourable goal, but not for university-level studies.

Soon, even the concept of a literary canon and the value of the humanities came under attack. Declining registrations forced the more traditional among us to recognize that we lived in a quantitative culture where everything was measured and monetized. Holding to a canon, some argued, promoted a conservative, reactionary, and elitist world view that didn't respond to the interests of the students who comprised the so-called market. Others challenged the concept of a classic and argued about the impossibility of judging which works are representative of an epoch or movement. What does it matter what one reads? taunted a colleague who threw up his hands in despair. It seemed the principle of critical judgement, once considered central to a university education, could not help in deciding the matter. The tenor of meetings at all levels became politicized. Colleagues resorted to buzzwords like "equality" and "freedom of choice" to argue against our insisting upon prerequisite courses. To do away with elitism, everyone should have access to any courses they wished. For fear of losing provincial government grants, our administration reminded us we should not lose any of our customers. Navigating through this uncharted territory sapped our creative energy. Of course, there were times when we would have preferred to stop debating and simply kick ass instead. But that was campus life in the 1970s and '80s—an open-ended and even sociable place despite itself.

But with an eye to the pool of potential students, we soon realized that we were out of date. We had to change if we were to survive as a department, and that meant making difficult choices about how to capture our share of "the market." Thus, we turned to duplicating other disciplines by offering translations of German literature, which were already being successfully taught by the Department of English, and German history and culture, already cornered by Political Science and History. In short, our long-held discipline known in

Germany as *Germanistik* was gradually unravelling and redefining itself out of existence. It did so under duress.

A case in point is the teaching of language itself. Germanic studies at the University of Victoria found itself facing a quite different generation of students than the one for which we had prepared and been hired. Had we responded to the declining numbers of registrants realistically, we might have taken instruction in the "communicative approach" to language learning. Had we done so as a group, we might have qualified ourselves to do the job well.

Role models were available. Royal Roads Military College, where Anita was head of the Department of Official Languages, offered a fully functional model of the communicative approach. Fluently bilingual in French and English, she led a team that taught officer-cadets in both official languages. What she explained to me was a breath of fresh air. The communicative approach is learner-centred rather than subject-centred. It trains learners how to communicate real meaning within the social or professional contexts within which they work. This made eminent good sense in Anita's military context, where officers had to be able to deal with their subordinates in both official languages. Their communication was real in the sense that their jobs defined the context. Thus, the conversations for which they were being trained were both interactive and contextual.

But we at a civilian university could never know for which professional context, apart from backpacking, we were to prepare our students. Besides, our language teachers didn't retool. Even worse, they tried instead to adapt the new method (which they didn't understand) to the old textbooks (to which the method didn't apply). In time, tech-savvy Internet language schools like the Berlin-based firm Babbel have outstripped the capacity of universities to deliver multilingual courses to international customers. Drawing on sound business models, these firms respond to the needs and interests of customers—and are able to make money at it. Indeed, Babbel responded to the Russian invasion of Ukraine in 2022 by offering free online Polish instruction to Ukrainian refugees arriving in Poland.

As it turned out, other language departments across the country were also having to throw themselves life rings in similarly troubled waters, as they sought marketability and relevance. From my vantage point today, I observe my successors in Germanic studies in Canada coping with a declining market and trying to escape from what they call the canonical pressures of the past. Having lost their focus, they are clutching at straws by attempting thematic links with gender studies, conflict studies, Indigenous studies, Black studies, and post-colonialism. By trying to be trendy, they are selling themselves short.

This collapse of a richly endowed academic tradition is foreshadowed in Luigi Pirandello's absurdist drama *Six Characters in Search of an Author*. Written and premiered in Italy in 1921, the play was at first scorned for its lack of focus. Yet its popularity grew internationally until the boom year of 1963, which saw over five hundred successful performances. By that time, critics had been promoting the sentiments of the Theatre of the Absurd, a term popularized in the 1950s. The naturalist conventions of theatre, they argued, were long since passé; ultimately, our world was meaningless. Certainly, in Pirandello's concluding lines, a character known only as "the director" wonders aloud whether the madcap mix of plots and players had been real, and indeed, whether the whole production had not been an utter waste of time. In his famous preface to the work in 1925, Pirandello had written of his aimless characters that "their play does not manage to get presented—precisely because the author they seek is missing." Clearly, as far as Germanic studies were concerned, I had had the best years in the profession that anyone in my generation could have enjoyed. At the very least, we thought we knew what we professed.

MANY SEA changes have marked my life. Sailing along with the current under steady winds in one direction, I often met cross-currents and winds that gave me advantages in another. Throughout my professional years, my journeys to Germany continued. It was essential for me to remain current with Germany's life and culture. Through a variety of travel and research grants, I managed to spend time there at least once a year, reserving a desk at one institute or another from which I could take full advantage of a German Rail pass and recharge my batteries. To remain current, I needed to escape the monolingual Englishness of Victoria, which felt far removed from the cultural and historical centres that really interested me. I have often thought that, had I made Germany my home after retirement, I would probably have chosen Munich or Hamburg, cities where I have always felt particularly happy. Throughout my teaching career, the museums, theatres, libraries, and archives of Germany have nourished my intellectual and spiritual life.

Of course, I frequently visited Berlin. Here I felt the pulse of international power politics and sensed the beat of one of the most liberal and free-wheeling cities in the country. Berlin offered history and modernity, art and technology. Its wartime associations still hung in the air, and bullet-scarred buildings attested to past violence. It was here in 1961 that I had watched the hideous Berlin Wall being built and felt the Cold War closing in. Many times, I passed through Checkpoint Charlie into East Berlin to walk among the tank traps, under the eyes of armed patrols, and down to *Unter den Linden* (Berlin's historic boulevard) and the *Staatsbibliothek zu Berlin* (the State Library). Until 1989, the Eastern Zone still exuded the aura of a John Le Carré spy novel. Always suspicious of the State Police, one of the librarians in East Berlin would usher me into his private office, a place, he explained, "where we won't be overheard," and where we could chat freely about literature and life. I enjoyed these covert meetings. Returning through the checkpoint, I was not supposed to carry any contraband and was, of course, always searched. When asked on one occasion whether I was taking anything with me out of the country, I took boyish delight in opening my case for the border guard, who pounced on some volumes of Marx and Engels. He waved me through with a smile. Both the guard and I were pleased— though for quite different reasons. Where I was enjoying exporting East German artifacts, he thought he had found a convert.

Once I spent three months of a bitter winter in West Berlin, living in student digs and studying in the modern *Staatsbibliothek*. Like many West Berliners, I tried to ignore the wall. Yet the throb of regular patrols by military helicopters reminded me of the political reality in which I was living. Later, I spent some six weeks in Munich as a guest of the German Academic Exchange, in a special training course on contemporary affairs. Housed in the comfortable *Katholische Akademie* in downtown Munich, I steeped myself in the summer course that brought together poets, musicians, journalists, and political commentators, and offered lectures and seminars on current events. The academy hosted us at concerts and theatre performances and at important historical sites. The impressive program engaged us in a wealth of contemporary German culture.

For the most part, however, I explored and worked on my own. Each of my visits offered up nuggets of gold for my teaching. Of course, I had many friends throughout the country with whom I could fine tune my understandings. I felt upbeat journeying from Schleswig-Holstein in the north; along the Rhine, Mosel, and Main Rivers to Goslar, in the Harz Mountains of Lower Saxony; and—after the wall had fallen—to Weimar and Dresden in the East. The small Swabian town of Marbach am Neckar, the birthplace of Friedrich Schiller, provided the archival resources of the Schiller Museum, with its wonderful collection of documents on contemporary writers. A daily stroll after lunch, past the house where he was born, conjured up his genius. It could also evoke Goethe, with whom Schiller had a rather difficult professional relationship, although together they were major figures in what became known as Weimar Classicism. Then, too, the Franconian town of Rothenburg ob der Tauber, with its medieval buildings and cobblestone streets, drew me into reflections on war and criminal justice. Besieged during the Thirty Years' War (1618-48) and stricken with bubonic plague in 1634, this well-preserved "ideal German town," as the Nazis called it, clarified my images of early German history. The town's *Kriminalmuseum*, a disturbing chamber of horrors, lent impetus to my later studies of modern justice issues.

One way or another, my sojourns in towns and sites from Cologne and Speyer (with their impressive Roman ruins) to the rococo *Wieskirche* (church in the meadow) near Munich, and from the North Frisian island of Sylt to the southern university town of Freiburg in the wine-growing district of Baden, all shaped my appreciation of Germany's diversity. Later, when I had shifted my research focus to naval history, other locations became my stamping ground: the Federal and Military Archives in Freiburg, the Library of Contemporary History in Stuttgart, and the U-Boat Archive in Altenbruch, near Cuxhaven, Lower Saxony. In all of them I felt at home. History, Schiller had asserted in his inaugural lecture of 1789, was a "fertile and broadly comprehensive area" that embraced the whole moral world (*in ihrem Kreise liegt die ganze moralische Welt*). The word *moralische*, in Schiller's usage, meant not only moral, but "receptive to ideas." In both senses, the field of history included everything I had been studying up to now.

GRADUALLY—AND LONG before these changes had happened—I had begun easing myself out of the German department through engagement in historical research. By the mid-1980s, I had published the first of my prize-winning books, *U-Boats against Canada: German Submarines in Canadian Waters* (1985), followed by two translated editions in German. These were followed by *Tin-Pots and Pirate Ships: Canadian Naval Forces and German Sea Raiders 1880-1918*, in 1991, which I wrote with my good friend Roger Sarty; *Count Not the Dead: The Popular Image of the German Submarine*, in 1995; and *A Nation's Navy: In Quest of Canadian Naval Identity*, in 1996, a volume of studies by scholars and naval officers that I led and edited. This new "directional thrust" (*Richtungsstoß*), to borrow an expression from the eighteenth-century German philosopher and playwright Lessing, gave me a new lease on academic life. But greater change was yet to come.

UNKNOWN TO me at the time, the former "boy bishop" of the Roman Catholic Church, Bishop Remi De Roo, had envisioned the creation of a research centre at UVic for the study of religion and science. In 1962, at the age of thirty-eight, he had been the youngest bishop to attend Vatican II in Rome, the council that had opened his church to the world. For Bishop De Roo, who remained Bishop of Victoria for thirty-seven years, the event had been a personal epiphany, a guiding light for his lifelong ministry. Part of that ministry was his dream of a research centre. Two generous parishioners, Allen and Loreen Vandekerkhove, had come to him with a million dollars burning a hole in their pockets, and asked him: "Bishop, do you have any ideas?" He most definitely did. Thus began his lengthy project of negotiating with the university, parlaying a parcel of Diocese-owned land bordering the campus, and drawing in two of his friends, the Rev. Bill Howie, a skipper-pastor in the seagoing mission of the United Church of Canada; and the Rt. Rev. Ronald Shepherd, bishop of the Victoria-based Anglican Diocese of British Columbia. Early on, Bishop Shepherd invited me to represent him in the negotiations, thus bringing me into close association with Remi.

My engagement with others in founding the Centre for Studies in Religion and Society (CSRS) was a matter of intellectual and spiritual kinship. It had begun innocently enough after our arrival in Victoria in 1971, as we gradually discerned the profile of our new community. One man in particular stood out among the colourful characters: Roman Catholic Bishop Remi De Roo. We first encountered him in the francophone parish of St. Jean Baptiste, near our home, and later read much about him. He was a bishop for the people. Always pushing against the patriarchal closed world of Rome and Catholicism, he was both a maverick and an innovator. The Vatican's Second Ecumenical Council in Rome made him especially proud to be a Catholic, for it aimed at modernizing every aspect of the Church's world view. The Council proposed opening windows onto the world, taking down barriers, empowering the laity—and listening to the voices of other religions. For the rest of his life, Remi saw himself as a pilgrim of Vatican II. A gifted and open-minded thinker, he always sought out new avenues for engaging his faith in fundamental issues of human existence. Faith, he wrote in his memoir *Chronicles of a Vatican II Bishop*, is a matter of relationships, not of rules and doctrine. He liked to discuss liberation theology. As formulated by its founder Gustavo Gutiérrez, a Dominican priest in Latin America, this was a "new spirituality" focused on social justice. Liberation theology proclaimed a permanent cultural revolution. It was about liberating the poor and oppressed. Worried by its Marxist flavour, Pope Paul II pushed back. But for Remi, the issues were clear: faith is about relationships, not doctrine; peace is the fruit of justice and love. The work of all people of good will was to live the Beatitudes that Jesus taught—peacemaking, justice, and mercy among them. As he wrote in his memoir, "Trusting in the Spirit, let each one of us reach out to our neighbour in a creative dialogue..." He eventually realized this vision in the Centre for Studies in Religion and Society.

I WAS a young child when I first heard the stirring words of Psalm 137: "Those who go down to the sea in ships, who do business on great waters, they see the works of the Lord, and His wonders in the deep." I had meditated on the cosmos when conducting celestial navigation across the Pacific, and when contemplating the arc of the heavens beyond the loom of cities in the magnificent Great Lakes. Later, eco-theology became a source of inspiration. In the words of an old expression, I had come to understand faith traditions as a vehicle for the cure of souls. They were social, communal, and pastoral in nature. I had drawn upon the solace offered by people of faith in times of profound sorrow, and—like Remi—embraced the Beatitudes in the Gospel according to Matthew. I sought the spiritual roots of justice. At its best, religion was for me a creative dimension of journeying through life. At its most compassionate, it offered a moral measure for human interaction and the stewardship of creation.

I felt drawn to a theology that embraced new knowledge and new relationships. Remi had understood that a university as secular as Victoria's would never consider establishing a purely Catholic institution. Religion, many argued, had no business on the campus of a modern university. Not even as an object of academic enquiry. By arguing this way, they revealed a basic fear: a centre of religion might step out of line, seek converts, and proselytize. In thinking thus, they failed to acknowledge the groundbreaking role played by religious communities over the centuries in establishing centres of education and research. They disregarded the roots of their own institution, as revealed by the twin mottos on the University of Victoria's coat of arms: "Let there be light," written in Hebrew, from the Creation scene in the Book of Genesis; and, in Latin, "A multitude of the wise is the health of the world," from the Apocrypha's Wisdom of Solomon (6:24). Strikingly, the university's president, Howard Petch, was a proponent of the centre and helped to guide it with Remi through the rocks and reefs.

I recall a particularly intense meeting of our working committee, chaired by Howard Petch, when we discussed the draft of the founding document. Remi began his presentation by quietly announcing that he had spent the early morning in prayer. An embarrassed silence ensued. Then, as we began in earnest, Remi conceded many points of contention, particularly where the document used terms referring to the founding faith traditions or to the important role of religion in human society. We at last agreed to the bare bones of Remi's vision. The centre would concern itself with the academic study of religion in relation to science and the other academic disciplines, as well as to human experience. It would concentrate solely on research, but offer no courses. Privately funded, it would be fully integrated into the university but would be answerable to the Vice-President Research.

As we drove home together after the meeting, Remi and I rehashed what had taken place. I suggested that he had come perilously close to throwing out the baby with the bathwater, and that, in his place, I would have been less gracious. To which he replied: "If the Holy Spirit wants the centre to happen, it will happen. If not, then I'll take my money elsewhere." In retrospect, it seems that the Holy Spirit did want the centre to happen. I know that's how Remi saw it. He would never have agreed that this convergence of friends and opportunities was a matter of chance. In his unassuming way, he saw it as grace.

What had started as an ecumenical venture ended as a multifaith institute. Remi's inspiration through Vatican II had become reality. Many years later, over coffee at the centre, a small group of us gathered around Remi as he recounted his visit to Rome in March 2013 for the installation of Pope Francis. Now in his nineties, he had been sitting wheelchair-bound in St. Peter's Square when he saw the new pope moving among the crowd. Remi stretched out his hand bearing his Episcopal ring and called out to the Pope in Italian: "I'm a Bishop of Vatican II." In Remi's words, Francis came to him, knelt, and kissed the ring. Having told his story, Remi removed his heavy ring and passed it around our circle. This was one of the most moving coffee hours in the centre's long process of development.

The word "process" provides a key not only to understanding the centre; the word also applies to theology. I have felt close to "process theology," which sees God not as the omnipotent, omniscient, and omnipresent curmudgeon of old, but as One who exercises relational and persuasive power. This spiritual force, as I understood it, works through all people, urging them to develop their powers in growing toward compassion and justice. The process recognizes suffering as part of the action. Process theology, as I had found, draws on a broad range of thinkers, from the mathematician and philosopher Alfred North Whitehead (whom I first read as an undergraduate) to the Jesuit priest and paleontologist Pierre Teilhard de Chardin (whom I first discovered in graduate school). As Teilhard wrote in his *Le Milieu Divin: An Essay on the Interior Life* (1957), it is a matter of perceiving "the ocean of forces to which we are subjected and in which our growth is, as it were, steeped." Its exemplars include Jesus, Mahatma Gandhi, and Martin Luther King Jr.

The Centre for Studies in Religion and Society opened in 1991 with great promise. Led from its earliest years by scholars of vision and energy, it became a dynamic institution. I had been on the selection committee that chose its founding director, Harold Coward, a well-established scholar of Hinduism who was also a United Church minister. I likewise served on the committee that chose his successor, the Mennonite scholar of philosophy and ethics Conrad Brunk.

The three of us became close friends and associates, and I replaced both of them as acting director when they took their research leaves. When setting out and fine tuning the centre's founding principles, we recognized, of course, the role of religion in shaping human experience and reality. We understood religion as central to social dialogue and societal cohesion. We realized as well that we wanted to be measured by the highest academic standards. We aimed high and succeeded. Equally important, we fostered the highest level of collegiality and cooperation.

The centre's atmosphere has always struck me as a model for how university departments should always operate. We discussed, debated, and conversed right across our academic ranks. Our style was collegial and congenial. We engaged in team research projects in which we critiqued each other's papers. We shared potluck luncheons and dinners, and once a year we closed the shop right down so that we could picnic together in what we called the "sailing seminar." Pastor-skipper Bill Howie hosted us aboard his large motor launch; I hosted aboard my sailing yacht, and others joined in with a variety of watercraft. Always a grand catch-as-catch-can occasion, we could count on at least one of us falling overboard. With an eye to my experience at both Queen's and the University of Winnipeg, my joining the centre was a homecoming. My work there took me out of Germanics for long periods of time leading up to my retirement. This new phase mobilized all the values I had been teaching in the humanities and engaged them in socially useful issues. In the words of Canadian philosopher and political commentator George Grant, "moral commitment is too precious not to be put into the service of reality." I was beginning to exercise my own version of liberation theology.

CLEARING OUT my office in Germanic Studies after thirty years of teaching was an exercise in nostalgia. I liked to think that by retiring I was making room for a younger generation to move in and make a career just as I had done. But the university was changing and offered young academics little room or hope for long-term meaningful employment. From my earliest days I had enjoyed academe in its best years. The bold expansion of universities and colleges had given us opportunities, options, and an expectation of tenure. It made us feel like the inheritors, as well as the creators, of a grand tradition.

As I packed the last books and papers, I could not help but think of the students I had taught and who had sought me out. Many of them I would have served well; others, perhaps, less so. As I culled amidst the last traces of my career, I could almost touch figures from the past who appeared at my door like the "flickering phantoms" whom Goethe had invoked in his prologue to *Faust*. Some greeted me with smiles and stories of their victories; others chided me for having fallen short and let them down. Yet others gave me a hug and introduced me to their children. Wistful memories haunted the end-of-term hallways, where I now stood alone among texts and lectures that I would no longer use. In a flash, I recalled myself as an undergraduate at UBC, testing the waters of academe, unsure of myself, and perhaps a little overawed by the idea of the omniscient "professor" who sat among his learned tomes, puffing on a pipe in sedate seclusion. Goethe had gotten it right in the scene where his fictional student, Wagner, enters the study of the jaded Professor Faust. With all the passion and zeal of youth, Wagner wants to grasp knowledge of the whole world in one fell swoop. "I want to know it all," he blurts out. On hearing the words "to know" (*erkennen*), Professor Faust gives a wistful and sympathetic shrug and dismisses young Wagner with an indulgent sigh.

I've always wanted to believe that I was not an avatar of Friedrich Schiller's academic drudge, the "bread scholar" (*der Brotgelehrte*), whom he evoked in his 1789 inaugural lecture as Professor of History and Philosophy at the University of Jena. The bread scholar did his teaching job in exchange for earning a wage. I liked to think of myself instead as an example of what he called the "philosophical mind" (*der philosophische Kopf*), one who is drawn, like a calling, to profess life's deeper values and the joy of discovery. History will be the judge. If it even remembers. Shutting the door behind me, I slipped along the corridor and dropped my keys onto the secretary's desk. She was a temporary secretary and didn't know who I was. Perhaps that made my leave-taking easier. As I walked down the empty hallway, lines from *The Lord of the Rings* caught up with me: "The Road goes ever on and on / Out from the door where it began. / Now far ahead the Road has gone. / Let others follow, if they can!" By this time, my book *The Spiritual Roots of Restorative Justice* had appeared. New fields beckoned, and I found myself marching to a new drummer.

7

PASSAGES

When the squall comes running down the bay,
Its waves like hounds on slanting leashes of rain...
Pull well... Your aim is another helping of life.
MILTON ACORN, "The Squall"

FIRST CAME the distant, salty tang of the beach. Then the crunch underfoot of shells and pebbles. And finally, the broad, windswept vista of a wild seashore. Here at the edge, we have always read the sea by the tides, and watched it suck at the shores during ebb and flood, covering and uncovering—in its diurnal and semi-diurnal cycle—the fragile forms that cling to the intertidal zone.

The Victoria seashore was as exhilarating for our youngsters as it had been for me in the 1940s. For them, the summer of 1971 marked a new age of discovery as they clambered along the shores of Oak Bay or paddled on logs in Smuggler's Cove. Along the glistening, rocky shores, the glaucus-winged gull and the black oystercatcher stalked their prey like squires surveying their estates. Off in the surf, red-breasted mergansers, their tousled top feathers blowing in the breeze, dived and dashed in an effortless hunt for herring. Crabs scurried furtively from one rocky pool to another, while anemones and mussels lay exposed in the receding waters. Tough-rooted seagrasses, their leafy fronds undulating lazily, rode out the sea's rhythms. Clinging to exposed rock faces, barnacles and starfish braved the surge and spray.

I still hear them —Pauline, David, Michèle, and Norman—calling out gleefully to one another as together they pounced upon one fascinating find after another: shells, crabs, anemones, coloured stones, and the tidal detritus, which ofttimes came to us from as far away as Japan. Once, David and Norman cast a bottle into the sea bearing a note claiming they were castaways on a desert isle—and giving their ages and address in Victoria, BC. Months later, a beachcomber on the Oregon coast came across the bottle and returned their note by mail, a graphic lesson in tidal forces. Skipping joyfully in the primordial soup, they encountered things wet, wiggly, and wonderful, and slippery, slimy, and slabby. Such abundance seemed to confirm that all life had indeed come from the sea. Childhood was a blessed time.

Our return home to the Pacific Coast had brought us back to my roots. Like so many others, I too had explored this world of wonders that our children were now discovering. I had made my own first discoveries as a young child, hopping along the rocky shore near Clover Point in search of treasure, teasing anemones and crabs, and squishing the slippery bulbs of the bull kelp. Sometimes, while slopping barefooted along the shores of Vancouver's Spanish Banks and Locarno Beach at low water, I felt I could walk forever, right out to the ships anchored a couple of miles offshore. Later, as a twelve-year-old, during a dawn fishing expedition with my father and my Uncle Cecil off the shores of Campbell River, I thrilled at pulling in salmon or scooping up Dungeness crabs. The sea was bursting with life; yet, once our hooks and nets drew in their trophies, I realized I had destroyed something precious.

Thus, on returning to the coast, I found myself picking up traces I had left so many years earlier. Beachcombing or sailing, I rediscovered the world of oceanic life: digging for butter clams and "gooey duck," chancing upon stranded moon jellyfish, and drifting softly under sail among pods of orcas as they migrated north. Island time meant sea time, whether sailing my own boat or going to sea regularly with the naval reserve. Kenneth Grahame's *The Wind in the Willows*, a favourite with our children, had gotten it right: "There is *nothing*—absolutely nothing—half so much worth doing as simply messing about in boats." That philosophy resonated with much of BC's laid-back culture that influenced the children's teenage years.

Over the years, drawing upon the legacy of the BC coast, our family set out in a variety of boats and discovered new ways of looking at the sea—and each other. While researching for my book *God's Little Ships: A History of the Columbia Coast Mission*, I came across a telling entry in the journal of the mission's founder, John Antle. Journeying in 1904 with his ten-year-old son, the maverick skipper-pastor confessed to having survived a near-calamitous attempt to navigate the powerful whirlpools of the Yuculta Rapids in his 4.9-metre (16-foot) homemade boat. "Verily, there is a Providence, who takes care of children and fools," he wrote. My own experience suggests you shouldn't count on it. "We never make mistakes," confessed another chastened survivor. "But we do have exhilarating educational experiences." Later, our own zest for such experiences coloured our sea adventures and misadventures together.

Perhaps no one relates to the sea as it actually is, but rather as they view it through a personal lens. One facet might be memory, another culture, and yet another the immediacy of visceral experience. That is what is meant by having a romantic and Conradian relationship to the sea. Reading the sea has always been a craft practised by sailors, artists, and literary buffs. A sailor does so to gauge its movements and moods, and to survive. Others look for its meanings and myths, and yet others seek both delight and instruction.

I recall skippering a small naval vessel under conditions that caused me to reflect on our relationship to the impinging forces of these waters. Natural phenomena can be impressive enough in themselves. But it's the way we perceive them that shapes our mindset and attitudes. Viewed from the deck on that particular day, the seascape overawed us. A blistering gale, sweeping out of the west, lashed the faces of the watchmen on the open bridge of the six-hundred-ton ship. Curling around a headland out of Juan de Fuca Strait in angry stallions of rolling waves, and whipping into Admiralty Inlet and Haro, the seas hinted at worse to come. The barometer had been holding steady when we began the crossing, but had been dropping for the past couple hours. Gale-force winds were on the way. Already, spindrift was forming in long, swirling streaks along the backs of rolling waves. The seventh, custom said, was always the biggest, a rogue wave that could bring our eight-knot advance to a dead stop. Such was the lore. So we perceived and so we believed.

The biting, blinding cold stung our eyes and dug into our bones, slicing to the marrow. The sea showed an angry, hostile face, as though plotting a cunning act of defiance against sailors who had set forth expecting a quiet passage. Inexorably, the powerful current was thrusting us onto a distant lee shore where breakers were bursting and crashing onto obdurate rock. Everywhere we looked, we inferred the sea's nasty, evil intent. Those implacable physical forces that engulfed us sparked a range of emotions, from anxiety to awe.

Of course, the sea remained morally neutral in all this. No matter what human emotions we projected upon it. Standing on the exposed bridge deck, we could not escape the impression that the sea was consciously working against us as an expression of its anger, spite, menace, and a malignant desire to control. In response, we bent every effort to punch our way through all that opposed us. Confronted by a sea that had long ago turned a tumultuous white, we had to thrust our way around the point. Our ship bucked, wallowed, heaved herself upward, and slammed into deep troughs with a shuddering impact. Driven by a deepening Pacific low of impressive intensity, these waves held us in their grip.

Our planned change of course would place these forces on our quarter, thus pushing us forward instead of assaulting us head-on. Perceiving a pattern in the tangled onslaught of green and white water, we poised on the keen edge of a decision—"hard a' port," to bring her about. Slowly, we eked two more knots out of our shuddering ship. Painfully, in aching, agonizing steps of the compass, her head came around. As we crested a wave, scudding down its back into the trough and rising again to another mane-shaking peak of spray and spume, we turned our stern to the sea. We then ran free with the wind, leaving wave and weather astern.

The shift in sensation was dramatic. It was still the same angry sea as before. But once we had turned our back upon it—its effect on us had changed. And with this change came a marked alteration, not only in *its* mood but in ours. The symphony of sea played on, but now in a different key. The shift in our perception was like a rapid modulation from a minor key to a major one. We now experienced an upbeat romp. The cruel sea had suddenly become a cheeky, boisterous element; a riotous, taunting, laughing tumult of pushing, shoving, serpentining water that was carrying us away from the eye of the storm. And we, too, began to laugh along with it. Teasing and taunting the once angry sea, we careened and slithered toward calmer waters and a still distant safe haven.

Many years and many voyages later I encountered seas of equally memorable character when delivering a small sailing yacht from Vancouver to Victoria. The voyage was a perfect example of the serendipity of uplifting surprises. I had calculated the passage under power in order to catch the last of the ebb through Active Pass. Stormy weather had foiled that hope, and we found ourselves stemming the beginning of the flood as we rounded Gossip Shoals and headed into the pass. Working the vessel doggedly through the back eddies of the pass, we clawed our way through, barely eking out a speed over the ground of one knot. Of course, that was all we needed to escape the grip of the current against us, but we could never be sure that the eddies would remain in our favour. And then a most astonishing sight caught us by surprise: a "raft" of six or seven Steller's sea lions—each weighing up to a ton—following in our wake. They were pushing through the flood dolphin-fashion, their huge brown forms muscling against the crests. I had often observed sea lions basking lazily on rocks, but never before had I seen them thrusting effortlessly in powerful, visceral rhythms through an icy sea.

Afterward, I reflected on the sea as the setting for rites of passage. The themes are timeless: steadfastness and mastery, survival and isolation, loneliness and restoration, hope and despair, awe and dread. Romanticism lies at the core of this musing—but a romanticism touched by flashes of realism and conviction.

Had these journeys been anything more than just a wild adventure? Why does anyone want to go to sea? The answers to questions about seafaring are many and complex. We forsake the sanctuary of home to earn a living, to voyage because we have to get somewhere, or simply to seek adventure. Whatever our motivation, the sea is an environment filled with protean life; a world that fascinates and forms all those who encounter it. Indeed, it evokes reflection on the meaning of human endeavour.

As our children grew into seafaring and took turns rag-hauling or playing captain at the tiller, they gained nautical and interpersonal skills, while I honed my family-centred, small-boat skippering talents. It was all part of bonding that added zest to family ties. Our jaunty vessel *Titatoo* often took the six of us picnicking and gunkholing among the islets known as Chatham Islands. But that still left all the water between Chatham and Oak Bay for us to roust about in, amidst the twisting currents and wayward winds. Pauline, our eldest, was a vivacious and happy sailing buddy. Slicing through the waters on a twenty-degree heel, our feet hooked firmly beneath the toe-straps, we would perch on the sides and lean backward over the sea, our bottoms skimming over the surface. Our exhilarated shouts echoed over the bay as we scudded along in perfect harmony in the bracing tumult.

Pauline's siblings reiterated the jubilant shouts whenever they took to the sea with me. In time, each of them could handle the boat well. On the day in July 1976 when we sold *Titatoo*, Norman and I put her through her paces for the prospective new owners who had come aboard for sea trials. The boisterous sea proved tricky under the rising breeze as young Norman took the tiller and sent her skimming over the waves. It was a zestful sail. In the words of Harold Horwood's *Tomorrow Will Be Sunday*, it made each one of us feel "like a buccaneer of a younger day, coasting down through the glittering Spanish Main, seeking the isles that lie under the wind." Our passengers nervously declined all offers to take the tiller themselves. But they did buy the boat.

That same month, we brought our next boat, the Crown 23 *Patmos*, from Tsehum Harbour to Oak Bay. Our notes in the log for the next decade reveal happy times; some visceral and demanding, others relaxed and lackadaisical. "Very blowy ride, very exhilarating," wrote one of our children. "Blustering gusts" and "very exciting," wrote another. Some of us took mini-cruises to the Gulf Islands. Crowded into the cozy cabin that first autumn, the boys and I logged a typical pause after a day of sailing. As we lay at anchor among the Chatham Islands— the sole visitors at that time of year—we experienced a deep sense of peace. "Star-filled sky, calm air, darkness, and the sweet aroma of Chatham's growth and decay," our log records, followed by "Later, sat by the fire ashore with snacks and conversations. We knew we were making memories."

We laid hold of life at every opportunity. One day, *Marabel* called. The 41.5-metre (136-foot), twin-diesel wooden minesweeper had been recently purchased from the War Assets Corporation by my friend and naval colleague Claude Lacerte. In the midst of converting her into a floating sport-fishing lodge, he had committed to hosting his first guests among the magnificent fjords of the Great Bear Rainforest, some 563 kilometres (350 miles) from Victoria. He was short-handed, so I offered to navigate *Marabel* to his planned anchorage at Rivers Inlet provided I could bring my family along for the ride. As it turned out, Claude left the running of the ship completely to me while he and two crew members beavered below-decks on some last-minute adjustments to cabinetry and machinery before the opening day. Time was of the essence. This would be "big-ship time," as our children called it, for they found themselves working as real sailors, both as quartermasters at the wheel (they could box the compass) and as lookouts. They spelled each other off at each position throughout the day. I couldn't have handled the job without them. Thus, we worked our way up the coast at fifteen knots, keeping a seaman's eye on the navigation while steeping ourselves in the mystique of coastal life. I admired the children's can-do approach and the speed with which they learned. Each evening, we tied up or anchored for the night so that everyone could get a good sleep. By the time we dropped our hook in Rivers Inlet, we had become a well-knit ship's company and felt at home. When I had first come here in the early 1950s as a young sailor aboard Union Steamships,

SS *Cardena*, the shoreline had been dotted with canneries. They were long-since gone; their docks decayed. The breathtaking natural world had reclaimed the scene for itself. Scarcely had we anchored and rigged the floating docks alongside when a Beaver seaplane arrived with the guests. Our two crewmen were still sweeping up sawdust and making the beds as the guests came aboard, and we six Hadleys climbed into the Beaver. A storm front was moving in, and we couldn't delay.

Clouds hung low over the fjord, and rain began to sting our windscreen as the pilot completed his checks and gunned the engine. We lifted off in a belly-wrenching slalom into low-lying clouds and turbulent air, accelerating around steep-sided forests and surging to clifftops before side-slipping down to sea level, beneath the murk, and scudding back up again. Anxiety marked our children's faces, while we adults tried to lend an air of normality to the ordeal. They saw right through us. One daredevil act followed another in the bush pilot's dash to home base. The tortuous flight seemed to last an eternity until at last we dropped through thinning cloud and touched down in the dreary, rain-soaked harbour of Prince Rupert. Shaky-legged yet spunky, David spoke for us all when he exclaimed, "I've never been so glad to get to such an ugly place."

Eventually, it would be the boys who took to the sea long-term. The three of us spent the better part of one summer cruising the Gulf Islands and beyond in *Patmos*. I had christened her after a favourite German poem by the Romantic poet Friedrich Hölderlin. Its virtually untranslatable opening lines proclaim that a saving grace is always at hand whenever danger lurks. Be that as it may, we frequently tested Hölderlin's concept of the interrelationship of sacredness with danger and rescue during our ventures into BC's challenging coastal waters. On one passage in particular, my boys and I had departed our anchorage in Bachelor Bay, in West Vancouver, after having visited their maternal grandparents. We weighed anchor by mid-afternoon in order to catch the thermal outflow winds blowing out of Howe Sound, and set course for Thrasher Rock on the opposite side of the Strait of Georgia.

We enjoyed a brilliant passage, fixing our positions on the paper charts we had prepared, with bearings derived from our hand-held magnetic compass. About halfway across, our course left the influence of the thermal winds and entered the northwesterlies flowing down the sixty-four-kilometre (forty-mile) fetch of the Strait. Ready to reef sails, we worked hard amidst rollicking swells and boisterous winds. Our Hölderlin principle—"wherever danger lies, the saving power grows to meet it,"—came into play as the winds almost overpowered us, and sent us bounding across the crests of white waves. With mounting exhilaration, we turned to reef our mainsail, for we were beginning to sail too fast for the sea conditions. Suddenly, sea water began squirting through gaps in the daggerboard of the dinghy we had been towing astern, slowly turning it into a sea anchor that slowed us down. Held back from cresting over the wave tops, we sliced our way across the Strait, taking turns at the tiller. Taking the helm under such trying conditions took skill and endurance. I was proud of my lads as they intuitively handled *Patmos* with an eye to every contingency. When we finally anchored in safe haven in Silva Bay, we collapsed with fatigue to the bottom of the boat and slept the sleep of the just. Stamina, teamwork, and sea sense had given us a wonderfully memorable passage. The lesson of the day? Spiritual forces help—provided you've done your homework.

I HAD always felt a tension between vocation and avocation. My research into the history of German submarine warfare kept calling me back to Germany. Frequently, this meant spending the precious summer weeks on my own in various archives in Germany, while *Patmos* lay bobbing at the end of a rope in Oak Bay. Surely it made better sense to sell her and save the expense of ownership. Yet, home again, it took only one day on the water to remind me that selling would be folly. My log entry for 17 April 1983—"Sea birds screeching over the waters, the surge of white-topped waves"— reminds me of those days. "Glad the boat's still here, despite the fact that I have had so little time. I long for the [submarine] project to be done so that life can take a more measured pace, with much more sea time." Then follows the notation "A magnificent wind, hard and steady." Six months later, I expressed similar thoughts about time, money, and values: "Almost sold *Patmos* today, but she's too much a part of my life, and I love the sea in all her moods. Took her out in the chop and spray." She would enrich our lives for another six years of family picnics, spray-soaked thrashes, sun-filled doldrums, and a voyage to Desolation Sound. By this time, the boys were skippering our boat on their own, taking solo trips or heading off with friends.

But I still felt a tug between work abroad and boating at home. As a note in the log for 10 August 1987 reads, "Cheerio, *Patmos*. We're off to Berlin, Athens, and Salzburg. I miss you already!" By the end of August 1989, Anita and I wanted a larger vessel and bit the bullet. "The thought of selling *Patmos* and moving up is really bittersweet," I noted in her log. "She's truly a lovely little vessel ... a wonderful sea boat." And then, the final entry for 3 October 1989: "*Patmos* sold after over thirteen years of fine service and golden happy times. The end of an era." While the sea had been a passing fancy for the girls, it deepened its grip on both boys. David sailed the South Pacific and French Polynesia with Claude Lacerte in his barquentine, *Belle Blonde*, before joining the coast guard and going on to study medicine and become an emergency physician. Years later, he competed in the famous Victoria-Maui race and the Van Isle 360, the six-hundred-mile, fourteen-day international sailing race around Vancouver Island. Norman, an active naval reservist, earned his naval watchkeeping certificate—the revered WK—aboard a destroyer before leaving to set course for successful careers in international rugby and international finance. Both lads had served in the Canadian Coast Guard. Both had formed deep relationships with the ocean. They could say, with the seventy-five-year-old East Coast schooner skipper Captain Andy Publicover, "I never could have lived away from the salt water or the salt air, because the sea runs in my blood."

We purchased our Ericson 32 *Peregrine* in November 1989. The children, now in their twenties, had launched themselves, leaving us oldies to fend for ourselves. In the 1990s, Anita and I retraced the voyages of explorers and the pastor-skippers of the Columbia Coast

Mission through the northern reaches of the Discovery Islands and up through the Yuculta Rapids ("the Yoo-cla-taws"), with their treacherous whirlpools and surges. We continued on through the daunting Dent Rapids and Green Point Rapids and the exhilarating Hole-in-the-Wall. Dangerous eddies, whirlpools, and overfalls marked the routes, along with tales of death and disaster. Famous channels and inlets like Cordero, Nodales, and Okisolo evoked tales of local Indigenous settlements and of the earliest European explorers. The Arran Rapids, with its floods and ebbs reaching heights of ten to eleven knots, reminded us of the eighteenth-century Spaniards and English who had marvelled at the sheer power of these waters racing through narrow passes and gorges. We ourselves had recourse to tide tables and charts, but two hundred years earlier, explorers—and later the settlers—could not know what they were getting into until in the midst of it. Our hands-on experience of sailing this section of the coast was as valuable for us as sleuthing in archives. In the summer of 2022, we once again explored these waters. They had lost none of their attraction.

One of our summer cruises took us to the former mission station in Whaletown, on Cortes Island. There we met Reverend Rollo Boas. As we swapped sea stories, Boas recounted his 1944 job interview for the position of skipper-pastor. A native of Montreal, where the interview took place, he had no experience whatsoever with boats. Nor had he even glimpsed the BC coast. The whole nautical business was *terra incognita*. He was, however, an attractive candidate. His strong social conscience, and his marriage to a nurse who shared his faith, sealed the deal. At the end of the interview, the recruiter casually remarked, "If you can assure me that you can get along with the gas engine, you've got the job."

With a cavalier indifference to nautical realities, the recruiter shrugged aside every practical consideration: "You can soon learn about the sea and about boating and the coast," he assured Boas. With the bliss of ignorance, Boas set off with his wife and two young daughters aboard the mission ship *Rendezvous*. In all seasons, and through some of the most hazardous waters on the BC coast, he skippered his vessel from 1944 to 1954. He taught himself how to become a mariner while on the job. His story, though bold, was not unusual. At sea, life is always a calculated risk. Especially, of course, when the whole purpose of the venture is to experience the untamed power of nature at full tilt.

Pumped up with that very expectation, I once pulled into the floats at the village of Egmont, about half a mile from the famed Skookumchuck rapids. My son David, who was coxswain of the coast guard station at Pender Harbour that summer, had invited me to join him for an exciting passage. The twin 150-horsepower outboards on the stern of the Canadian Coast Guard's rescue inflatable were purring comfortably when I arrived. Under David's command, three trainees and I embarked on a venture in high-speed rescue techniques. Over the years, as records claim, some sixteen persons had drowned in these waters. We had timed our entry into Skookumchuck Narrows to coincide with the height of the ebb. Thirteen knots of furious water were against us. Hunkered down in our survival suits, and well-briefed, we affirmed our readiness to go. Easing our boat away from the float, David slowly opened to full throttle, and we blasted off. Almost immediately we were twisting and turning among whirlpools as wide as 10 metres (32.5 feet) across, ducking and running like a ball-carrying rugby player breaking free from a ruck. Bucking body-slams and boisterous water, our skillfully skippered boat slithered and slashed through the tumult. Then, with firm hands on the wheel and throttle, David ordered an old life jacket be tossed into the gaping vortex that opened each side of us, and his crew leapt to their rescue routine. Not just once, but again and again. Repeated recoveries of the surrogate body soon fine tuned the bracing exercise.

Riding astride the midship seat behind my son, and gazing into the swirling abyss, I could not help but recall my first impressions of Edgar Allan Poe's gripping story "A Descent into the Maelstrom," which I had first read as a schoolboy. Poe's hallucinatory imaginings remain a fine example of the literary sublime. Yet they didn't match the adrenaline-charged reality of our blistering passage through the

Skookumchuck with David. Preoccupied by the sheer physical joy of the ride and the demands of training, we negotiated powerful forces that concentrated both mind and muscle. Buoyed by my pride in David's skillful seamanship, I leaned into our boat's leaping gyrations. Our slalom return with the fading ebb to the calm waters of Egmont left us to reflect on the audacity of what we had done.

Educational experiences come in many shades. On emerging from Hole-in-the-Wall aboard our sloop *Peregrine* on one occasion, Anita and I decided to skirt northward around Stuart Island and poke our noses into Bute Inlet. The route northward beyond Desolation Sound shows little sign of human habitation, and the winding fjords are prone to gale-force winds that thrust their way through narrow passages rimmed by steep, high mountains. Safe havens are few. In summer, you can expect calm days and quiet nights, though you must always be prepared for wind shifts and powerful thermals. For thousands of years, these waters have been home to the Kwakwaka'wakw Peoples. I myself had first ventured into this challenging network of rockbound fjords as a teenage crewman with Union Steamships. Years later, I had patrolled here as a junior officer aboard HMCS *Fortune* and skippered HMCS *Porte Quebec* through the region. I had always found it bracing. Especially in a small boat.

On this particular day, Bute Inlet felt particularly inviting. Ahead of us lay some seventy-five kilometres (forty-seven miles) of deepsea canal, no wider than a couple of miles, running between high mountains. The canal ran right up to the end of the gut at the mouth of the Homathko River. The inlet's remoteness stirs in the traveller an uncanny wilderness feeling. I had often spoken about Bute with my good friend Bill Wolferstan, whose cruising guides to BC waters have extolled the region for its haunting isolation and beauty. The mood it casts had disturbed Captain Vancouver in the 1790s. He called the whole region Desolation Sound. Now, two hundred years later, that eerie quality drew us into the silent, scenic wonder.

Drawn ever onward through Bute Inlet's milky waters, we found ourselves softly impelled by a warm and gentle quartering breeze. Under light press of sail, we ghosted ever deeper up the fjord, the only sail as far as the eye could see. We felt suspended in a dream-like time warp that might have lasted forever. Lines learned in youth from Coleridge's "The Rime of the Ancient Mariner" came to mind: "All in a hot and copper sky, / The bloody Sun, at noon, / Right up above the mast did stand, / No bigger than the Moon." Knowing where we were was one thing. Knowing where we were going to be, and when, and precisely under what conditions was quite another.

For the mariner, navigation is all about anticipation. The signs were all around us: ripples reshaping themselves into wavelets; wavelets into striations; striations into foamy swirls. Despite the pre-dominantly placid waters, we felt suspended in a state of deepening unease and overwhelmed by the steep topography of the Cosmos Heights that lay to port. And still, not another sail or sign of hab-itation in sight. Nothing but us, our ship, the wilderness, and our imaginations. We felt sadness for the pioneer women of Bute who had struggled to make a home here, in desperate isolation. We, by contrast, knew we could leave whenever we wished, and could relish the seductive bliss of the wild beauty around us.

As evening fell, we managed to perch our anchor upon a narrow ledge within a bear's leap of the densely wooded shore. We laid out our cable along the ridge and poured ourselves a sundowner. Just a few feet from that ledge the shore dropped precipitously beyond the range of our echo sounder. Technically, that meant no bottom at two hundred feet. That was typical of the region. A profound peace set-tled over an early mountain-top sunset, its rays barely touching the top of our mast. Hundreds of feet below the peaks, tucked right up to the shoreline in a manner no seamanship manual would approve, we settled down for a quiet, though watchful, night.

And then it began. A whistling in the rigging, a shuddering of the mast, a slapping of waves against the hull. In the small hours, our sloop had begun to shift position over the narrow ledge. Sensitive to her every movement, we arose, dressed quickly, snatched up our life jackets and a thermos of tea, and cleared for a hasty departure. While I weighed anchor with my old "handraulic" winch, grinding away as I knelt on the foredeck, Anita turned over the diesel and prepared for departure. "Anchor aweigh!" I shouted from the foredeck, and she bore off into deeper water under the most resplendent, star-filled sky we have ever experienced. Wisps of cloud scudded across the face of the moon, which cast its silvery light across the inlet. As soon as we were clear of shore and shoal, we hunkered down at the helm over mugs of tea, switched off the diesel, and sailed off under jib with a quartering nor'westerly wind. The swishing of water along our hull and the occasional snapping sound of our headsail punctuated the silence. Gybing our way southward, with only the moonlit shores to guide us, we talked quietly for hours, sharing the night watch until the break of dawn. The experience, in the language of Karen Armstrong, was "a spirituality of silence and unknowing." A prayerful night, in other words, though not in any sense of petition or intercession. Rather, it was life fully in tune with the silent symphonies of wisdom and experience. Like poetry in motion.

FROM MY youngest days, I have indulged my armchair appetite for ocean passages by steeping myself in deep-sea lore. I've been a voracious reader, of fiction and non-fiction alike. Now in my senior years, I've found myself rereading Francis Chichester's *Gipsy Moth Circles the World*, if only to persuade myself that I should never allow age to discourage me from living fully. As a sixty-five-year-old, Chichester had sailed his 16.5-metre (54-foot) yawl solo around the world via Cape Horn. An accomplished yachtsman and ocean racer, Chichester had established many sailing records; he understood the virtues of meticulous planning and took the challenges in stride despite his age. "I don't think I can escape ageing," he once wrote, "but why beef about it? Our only purpose in life, if we are able to say such a thing, is to put up the best performance we can—in anything, and only in doing so lies satisfaction in living." Chichester's relationship to the sea was frequently awe-filled and existential. Even prayerful. As his wife's epilogue to the book attests, "the spiritual side of any venture is of immense importance ... far more so than the material side." Responsible as she was for all the logistics of her husband's voyage, her watchwords were pray, plan, and be prepared.

So often, the physical achievements of senior citizens impress me. In September 2019, seventy-six-year-old Jeanne Socrates became the oldest person to sail solo non-stop around the world. Setting off from Victoria, BC, in her Swedish-built 11.6-metre (38-foot) *Nereida*, she would spend 339 days at sea alone. In July 2020, sixty-two-year-old Bert terHart fulfilled a similar dream, returning to Victoria after a 267-day non-stop voyage around the world in his thirteen-metre (forty-three-foot) Ontario-built sloop. He relied solely on celestial navigation, using a sextant, nautical almanacs, and charts. Now, as I write this in June 2022, eighty-three-year-old Kenichi Horie has become the oldest person to sail alone non-stop across the Pacific Ocean. It took him 69 days in his 5.8-metre (19-foot) sloop. Such nautical adventures constitute a great escape, either away from, or into, a self-fulfilling prophecy.

These seniors clearly have the same emotional relationship to the sea as my forebears in the naval reserve, which I joined in 1954. The navy's extraordinary expansion from two thousand personnel in 1939 to ninety thousand in 1945 had meant that young civilians unfamiliar with the ways of the sea, and who perhaps had never seen it before, became professional seamen in astonishingly short order. They had to, in order to survive. For thousands of volunteers in the naval reserve, wartime service became a rite of passage. Ultimately, their legacy permeated the mindsets of those like me who joined the Navy in the 1950s.

In Hugh Garner's historical novel *Storm Below*, one such recruit sets off to sea in 1943 aboard a Flower-class corvette, on his first tour of convoy duty across the Atlantic. During the voyage, he contemplates the "dark, dreadful loneliness of the sea." As a landlubber drawn into the vortex of war, he finds the sea "an alien thing armed with a multitude of claws ready to pull them beneath it with scarcely a ripple or trace." Indeed, it is both "beautiful and terrifying, and gigantic and insatiable; a desert of water over which men travel through necessity." We postwar recruits had read the book as a foretaste of what might lie ahead.

By contrast, the multifaceted lens through which naval captain Alan Easton contemplated the sea drew upon his intimate experience with deep-sea navigation in wartime, as well as upon his reflections on the nature of war, suffering, and loss. Easton was an unusual naval reservist. He had joined the Merchant Marine in 1916 at the age of fourteen, and the Canadian Navy in 1939. By the end of the war in 1945 he had been commanding warships for over four years and had sunk three German submarines. His memoir *50 North: An Atlantic Battleground* is a classic. His reflections reveal a profound relationship with both the horror of war—and the overwhelming beauty of the sea. "The sea itself filled my thoughts as I gazed down at the dark water from the lee wing of the bridge," he wrote. "I marveled at its phosphorescence and at the strange fascination a phosphorescent sea always held for me. Brilliant like boiling silver on ebony, a million drops of shining metal falling from the bow wave. The sea could be beautiful. It was that night." At such times, being alone on the bridge at night was among the finest experiences.

Perhaps it is this tension between inspiration and apprehension that moved poet and naval officer George Whalley to speak of "the inscrutable sea." Later a professor of English literature at Queen's University, his wartime poetry explores both the human condition and the intriguing—though unforgiving—oceanic world. What drew me to Whalley's work in later years were not only his powers of observation and expression, but a similar life pattern. Both of us had been seagoing naval officers; both of us became professors of literature (he at Queen's and I in Victoria); and both of us had served as commanding officers of a naval reserve division while fully engaged as university teachers.

Like George Whalley, I switched hats easily. In the spring of 1973, the German training vessel *Deutschland* called in at Pedder Bay, just outside the Esquimalt Naval Base. I was to serve as her liaison officer during her stay in Canadian waters. I looked forward to working with my NATO counterparts in blue. On the day of our first meeting, my launch sped out of Esquimalt Harbour with a bone in her teeth. With me was the German military attaché from Ottawa, a combat veteran of the 1940s air war, complete with a *Schmiß*—the old-fashioned duelling scar that cut across his cheek and marked him as having once been a youthful firebrand. I, however, was feeling rather less than nautical, for under Canada's new regulations for the Unified Armed Services, I was dressed in green, now the common colour worn by army, navy and air force alike. We Canadian sailors had balked at unification, though most of us were pleased that the "Royal" had been dropped from the navy's name. The adjective had identified us since 1910 as a colonial outfit. Dropping the Royal was one of the most important acts in the navy's otherwise flawed process of modernization. Officially, we were now the Sea Element of the Canadian Armed Forces. However, for many of us still serving, we had become the Canadian Navy / La Marine Canadienne. We took pride in the name. Though we valued our origins in Britain's Royal Navy, we no longer saw ourselves as a subset of the British. National identity aside, it was glorious to be among ships and hastening across a sparkling sea in brilliant sunshine. As we pulled alongside the *Deutschland*, our hosts lowered a long rope ladder and we clambered aboard. Pipes twittered, the side party snapped to attention, and salutes greeted us with all the flair of an ancient naval tradition that Canadians still observed.

I felt immediately at home on the bridge with the captain, as we slipped our moorings and edged out of Pedder Bay en route to Vancouver. It was good for the soul to find myself once again in a German-speaking milieu. Conversation moved easily amidst our technical concerns, and I found space to point out local features such as the old fortress of Fort Rodd Hill. Designed at the end of the nineteenth century to fend off up to a half dozen enemy light cruisers, its Mark VI "disappearing guns" had been installed in 1897. They could rise up from their position, fire one shot every two minutes, and then quickly drop out of sight to reload. In the midst of my storytelling, the skipper asked with a chuckle how Canadians would have responded had his heavily-gunned *Deutschland* arrived on scene in the early 1940s. "That would have been good timing, sir," I quipped. "The government didn't update them until 1944." Typical watchkeeping banter between shipmates.

Our ceremonial entry into Vancouver Harbour started with a bang. Protocol called for our exchanging gun salutes with Canadian Army gunners on Prospect Point, once we had passed beneath the Lion's Gate Bridge. Timing was of the essence. Onlookers had gathered along the seawall, and a line of bumper-to-bumper rush hour traffic was crawling its way across the bridge. Just as I was about to caution that we hold off until our guns had passed the span, the ship fired her first round directly underneath it. The pressure wave reverberated with dramatic force, jolting the startled car passengers on the bridge above. Scarcely had the smoke and echo subsided than our second round fired. I wondered what my late parents would have said of my entering Vancouver Harbour on a German warship. And with such bravado.

SINCE THOSE days, Anita and I have undertaken many voyages under sail in local waters. Our routes to and from points in Desolation Sound and the Broughton Archipelago tended to converge at Welcome Pass. Between Merry Island (where my parents had lived with the wireless service) and Vancouver Island lay the Strait of Georgia, with its sixty-four-kilometre (forty-mile) fetch of wind and current running from northwest to southeast. Sometimes placid and contemplative, these waters can also be wild and unforgiving. Each passage tossed us a different experience that could range from monastic, sun-drenched calm to riotously favourable winds and seas, to scenes of sheer wave-beaten, sea-slopped struggle. Whatever came our way, it reminded us of the reflections of our friend Silver Donald Cameron, a Nova Scotian writer, boat builder, and yachtsman. "Voyaging is one of the great metaphors for life itself," he wrote, "life stripped of its fever and fret, focused on ultimate concerns." He offered a unique perspective on the sea: "The mysterious, tragic quality of the sea echoes the unknowable reaches of the human situation, of our relation to chance and destiny, glory and disaster. In his view, "sailing requires a powerful development of crucial human qualities: courage, determination, ingenuity, cooperation, honesty, competence."

Returning home from northern waters at the end of August 1991 in our sloop *Peregrine*, we paused at anchor in Secret Cove. We had spent the better part of a glorious summer in Desolation Sound tracking down the Columbia Coast Mission story. With a glass of cheer in hand, I hunkered down in the cabin to pour over my charts and plan our westward crossing of the Strait of Georgia. These were the days before electronic chart plotters, so I depended upon paper charts and magnetic compasses. This meant drawing onto the chart a series of bearing lines from prominent coastal features such as headlands and lighthouses; I drew them to intersect the line marking my planned course. The resultant lattice work of bearings helped me fix our boat's position during the crossing so that at any point I could take a spur-of-the-moment sight with my hand-held compass and construe from it our position and the distance-to-go. There would be no need to calculate the difference between the magnetic reading of the hand-bearing compass and the true reading of the chart, as I had already made those calculations. But, of course, I would need to know the difference between true and magnetic bearings. In sailors' terms, variation and deviation are the variables. I taught my young sons David and Norman how to convert from one to the other and they found it a breeze. To transpose from true (T) on the chart to what's on your compass (C), you apply the Variation (the earth's magnetism) and the Deviation (your boat's magnetism). To remember the sequence, just remember the initial letters of the naughty mnemonic Tender Virgins Make Dull Companions. It always triggered a smirk.

Wisps of mist and drifting swirls of thick fog obscured our anchorage as I tidied up our passage plan. As the fog slipped into our cove and gripped it, I knew that this was to be no leisurely sail home. In short order, the atmospheric conditions were worsening. Entries in our log reveal what we were up against: "27 August. Gale during the night and morning. Merry Island reports south-east 30 with five-foot seas. Spend day in port." On our VHF radio I heard other boats saying they were doing the same. And later that evening: "Storm-force winds forecast." That meant fifty knots of wind. In the night a couple of boats began dragging their anchor and flashed up their engines. The air became unstable, then quiet. By six the next morning, with calm seas, we weighed anchor in a heavy downpour and headed under motor to position ourselves relative to our departure point in Welcome Pass. Then a freshening breeze kicked up, and we were off with drum-taut sails in a handsome blow, fully under control and happy as the sea was blue.

But as we edged out into the strait, the high winds of the previous night had dropped, leaving lumpy seas. By the time we were halfway across, the fog had closed down visibility. We were on our own in the murk. Up to that point, we had been on track by dead reckoning. Now, however, we were dependent upon listening intently for the fog signal of Entrance Island Light. Though woozy from the motion, we were safe. I could not help but recall the wisdom of my uncle, Skipper Llew, so many years earlier: "If ye ever does get caught ... a well-found boat will never let ye down. Trust yer sea sense, 'n she'll get yer through."

Anita has a special memory of that passage, in which physical reality assumed a spiritual dimension. We were running blind. Vancouver Island lay hidden in thick mists. Both of us strained to hear the fog signal of Entrance Island Light. We knew that once we heard it, we would bear off in a southerly direction toward Thrasher Rock Light and then feel our way into the shelter of Silva Bay. So we listened—focused and discerning—tensing ourselves to pick up the first sounds of the warning horn. We checked and rechecked our dead reckoning against what we could infer. We trusted our navigation and our perceptions, and watched and listened for other vessels in the illusory shadows of heavy mist. By now, we ought to have heard the fog signal. After all, it stood on a lighthouse built on solid rock, and our vectors of course and speed had brought us within hearing. Fact and inference vied with one another. We became apprehensive.

And then she heard it. The low, attenuated diaphone groans of Entrance Island—*whooo-ah, whooo-ah*. It was unmistakable—and exhilarating. It struck Anita as a voice calling us home. Though we stood a little off dead reckoning, we now confirmed where we were. As Gabriola Island emerged from the mist, we bore off toward Thrasher Rock and safe haven. Perceived through Anita's lens, that navigational adventure had turned our journey into a pilgrimage, a life journey in which the pilgrims, having done their spiritual homework, trust in—and listen for— the voice of insight and deep consolation. Like the pilgrims in Chaucer's *Canterbury Tales* over seven hundred years earlier, we were glad to have put this journey safely behind us: "At nyght was come into that hostelrye / Wel nyne and twenty in a compaignye, / O sondry folk, by aventure yfall / In felaweshipe, and pilgrymes were they alle..."

ONCE WE ourselves had "come into that hostelrye" at anchor, and poured ourselves a wee dram, I spread out a large nautical chart on the table to examine the big picture of our summer's journeys. I had large-area–small-scale charts to examine a wide geographical area in minute detail; this was one of them, and it was excellent for long-distance passage planning. Likewise, my collection of small-area–large-scale charts zoomed in on local areas for close-up navigation. Taken together, they offered bird's eye and wave-top views of the marine worlds. Such charts for many years remained the standard for detailed marine navigation. But by the 1940s a new technology had begun providing quite a different perspective and feel for the coast: flight.

I recalled flights in the 1940s with my father in Tiger Moths, Cessnas, and Fleet Canucks. By 1947, we could stroll across the airport to inspect the Stranraer "flying boat" of Jim Spilsbury's fledgling Queen Charlotte Airlines, which was beginning to service the outports of the BC coast. Jim Spilsbury was a friend among my father's coterie, and I rather prided myself in being able to bask in his reflected glory. His Stranraer, known variously as "the flying birdcage" or the "flying Meccano set," was an ungainly looking craft. Built for coastal reconnaissance and anti-submarine patrols, the biplane had two 16.7-metre (55-foot) wings affixed one over the other. With two propeller engines suspended midship beneath the uppermost wing, and its long fuselage suspended beneath the lower, it would trundle from the hangar to its launch ramp at the Fraser River. Squatting in the river while the pilot ran through his checks, the plane would suddenly thrust into motion with a roar of its engines, belching blue smoke and surging downriver for its flight upcoast at a cruising speed of 265.5 kilometres (165 miles) an hour.

As I had learned when flying with my father in two-seaters, over-flying the BC coast for the first time changes one's approach to the sea; it alters what living "at the edge," between ocean and shore, actually looks like. Jim Spilsbury had spoken of feeling momentarily jolted by vertigo on his first flight, as the changing patterns and perspectives unfolded before him. For me as well, flying had awakened a sudden and quite unexpected feeling of immediate discovery. In a single moment, a pilot could oversee broad areas that would have cost a mariner days or even weeks of arduous voyaging. Where a sailor once struggled for hours, tacking and gybing, heaving on ropes, and turning winches for each mile gained, an aircraft pilot could overfly an unfolding panorama and tick off each mile of his flight plan as little more than a transient detail in the grand scheme of things.

After all these years I am still gripped by the euphoria of my first flights over BC coastal waters. From the perspective of my mature years, I sense the impact of flying even more strongly than I did as a child. Spilsbury had spoken of discovering, through the airplane's window, "the new coast," something at once "less mysterious, less forbidding, less grand" than in the days when he depended upon boats. In that sense, at least, flight had demythologized the coast. Yet, in another sense, it hadn't. For, as I have so often found, discovering what has already been discovered, and making it one's own through direct experience, is a vital creative process that repeats itself from generation to generation. The call of the sea will surely always be with us.

Yet, the inevitable tension between landlubber and seafarer, between earning a living and letting my yacht take her head, kept me in check. The entry in my log for 13 December 1994 captures the tone: "Today I completed my manuscript *God's Little Ships* after three months of steady slogging on sabbatical. The period of intense work is delightfully over, for which reason I played hooky this afternoon in order to enjoy sunlight and a crisp breeze. I'm not at all convinced that I want to write another book—it requires too much sustained concentration, with little respite for the immense pleasure of this afternoon's brief outing, 'simply messing about in boats.'"

On the upbeat to New Year's Eve, I set out in a low chop in nippy temperatures and a biting northeasterly wind of twenty knots. Clear skies, I noted in my log, afforded "extraordinary views of the surrounding mountains"—Mount Baker in the east and the whole Olympic range to the south. Ever pensive, I wrote in my log: "Sailed solo round the buoy to mark the end of another year. A mellow feeling about home and boat has come over me in recent days. This is really such a fine place to live—at my stage of life. Off to Germany next week, leaving all that is best. Ah, why do we continue to strive when we have already reached the goal—peace." Entries in the log the following year differed little. On New Year's Eve 1995, the year in which another of my books on German submarines appeared, Anita and I set out for a "tea sail," with coffee and cakes, in light winds. As the log reveals, we reflected on all that had transpired that year. As the log attests for 31 December 1995, "We have suffered great storms with crashing seas at this harbour, yet the coast has continued to cast its spell."

BUT WHEN the blood no longer courses, the oceanic world takes on a darker hue. You can speak, with the prophet Zechariah, of "an ocean of troubles," or "the sea of distress." Such was our mood when we learned of our son Norman's untimely death in 2016. He had died by his own hand in Tokyo, in the land he had come to love. He was alone, ill, suffering from pain, and despairing of a cure. Over a couple of hundred mourners from home and abroad attended his funeral at Christ Church Cathedral, in Victoria. Our eulogies captured the many facets of his diverse life: international rugby legend, international financier, son and father, and many stops in between. He was as charming and congenial in a blue pinstripe suit as he was rugged and powerful in old jeans and a T-shirt. But did we ever really know him? However familiar we may be with someone—however deeply or intimately we might share life with that person—we always come up against an inner sanctuary, an inner space that we can never entirely penetrate. For my part, I will always cherish his companionship as we thrilled to wind and sea while handling small boats, his gifted trumpet playing, and his service in the Canadian Coast Guard and as a young officer in the Royal Canadian Navy. And now, as we say in naval parlance, he had slipped his cable. He was crossing the bar between the river and ocean of life, and we were saying farewell. Alfred Lord Tennyson's poem "Crossing the Bar," which Norman had loved, expressed Norman's sentiments well: "Twilight and evening bell, / And after that the dark! / And may there be no sadness of farewell / when I embark."

We awaited good weather to commit his ashes to the sea, as he had wished. Weather, tides, and currents soon conspired to accord us an unusually quiet passage off Fiddle Reef Light. On the appointed day, David hosted the family aboard his 12.2-metre (40-foot) blue-water sloop *Patience*. By this time, our raw grief had begun to ease, slowly mellowing into a deep ache of love and regret. In a mood of reverential celebration, we headed outbound in brilliant sunshine for the final passage of our *bon mâtelot*. In a devotional act celebrating his life, each member of the family in turn took the funeral urn into their hands and sprinkled his ashes onto a silken sea. In my imagination, I followed his ashes in their descent through shafts of sunlit waters that he had once sailed. As we cast white and red roses over Norman's subsiding ashes—the colours of Canada's World Cup Rugby team, for which Norman had played to such acclaim in 1991— we knew we would never read the sea quite the same way again.

STRANGE SYMMETRIES converge in life to create unusual patterns and associations. Thus, the image of Norman's ashes slipping through shafts of sunlit waters recalled one of my childhood experiences.

I had been lying on the swimming docks off Kitsilano Beach in Vancouver, contemplating the shafts of sunlight receding into the golden gloom below the floats. The summer sun slanting into the silted shoal waters seemed to radiate into what, to my mind, was deep water indeed. I was no swimmer and felt threatened. Yet I experienced a certain frisson at what it might be like to dive down to the bottom, following the yellow shafts of light through layers of blue, golden brown, dark green, and down into what must ultimately be blackness. I could never have imagined that I would one day hold my own son's ashes in the palm of my hand. Nor watch them slip away into the deepening green of silent waters.

Yet, the sea beneath the surface was indeed alive, as I learned as a youngster when I first read Jules Verne's *Twenty Thousand Leagues under the Sea*. His book marked my first venture into science fiction, and I was hooked. I loved Verne's descriptions of fish, coral, and mollusks; narwhals and monsters; and multi-armed kraken and octopi. He wrote of creatures with fantastical names I couldn't pronounce: *choryphenes*, *hologymnoses*, and *cephalopods* among them. Seeing hope and redemption in the sea, Captain Nemo had built his extraordinary submarine in order to escape the land, its institutions, and its people. "The sea is everything," Nemo said. Covering most of the earth's surface, it was to him "the embodiment of a supernatural and wonderful existence. It is nothing but love and emotion; it is the 'Living Infinite...'" He saw the sea as an element in which wars could never take place. "Upon its surface men can still exercise unjust laws, fight, tear one another to pieces," he explained. "But at thirty feet below its level... their power disappears." The fictional narrator summed it up. Humanity, he said, was "called upon not only to contemplate the works of the Creator in the midst of the liquid element, but to penetrate the awful mysteries of the ocean." The word "awful," in the usage of his day, meant awe inspiring. All of this was the very stuff of a young reader's fantasy. Yet Verne had anticipated a kind of eco-theology embraced by environmentalists today. Writing in the late nineteenth century, he was over a hundred years ahead of the time when the notion would have any currency at all.

In 1991, I had had my first Captain Nemo experience when I went to sea aboard the Canadian submarine HMCS *Okanagan* for naval exercises in the Atlantic. The opportunity marked the peak of my long process of development as a naval officer, seafarer, and author of submarine histories. At this time, I was chairman of the Canadian defence minister's academic advisory board on military colleges. Many old friends were now senior officers, including the maritime commander in Halifax, Vice-Admiral Bob George, who once asked me whether I had ever gone to sea in a submarine. I had certainly experienced them alongside, I replied, both in Canada and in Germany. But I had never lived beneath the waves. "I think it's about time," he replied. One day, his staff officer phoned me from Halifax to offer a billet as guest officer in *Okanagan* if I could meet the submarine in Saint John, New Brunswick, for exercises at sea and eventual return to Halifax. Serendipity again, for I had just called a meeting of the minister's advisory board in Halifax around that time and could make the dates work. A slight change of itinerary took me to Fundy shores to join a remarkable group of sailors.

I was with the officer-of-the-watch on the fin as we proceeded outbound down the Bay of Fundy into increasingly lumpy and uncomfortable seas. I was at the periscope when we commenced our dynamic descent, watching the sea flow over the bow, along the deck, and up the fin as we slipped slowly below the waves. We had entered the mysterious element of Verne's visionary writing. He had gotten many things right in his vision of the future. Yet, unlike the *Nautilus* and Captain Nemo, we were not on a mission "to contemplate the works of the Creator in the midst of the liquid element." Research submersibles might do so, but HMCS *Okanagan* was a diesel-electric hunter-killer submarine. And to carry out that function, we were now on patrol. Steeped in the Cold War culture of the time, Canada's preparedness for combat had to be constantly honed.

As I came to realize when researching the Battle of the Atlantic, the seabed in the area of our patrol was a graveyard for victims of previous wars. Nemo and his crew would have found ample evidence of undersea warfare among the twentieth-century wreckage.

He would have regarded the scars as signs of evil, a betrayal of the very nature of the Creator. The decaying hulks offered ample evidence, too, that the sea was now readily accessible to mankind and his inventions. Some of the inventions Nemo would have regarded as quite infernal. I had come aboard with blueprints of the German submarines that had wreaked such havoc, and gave presentations to off-watch crew about wartime submarines and their tactical success.

Yet in all this, my voyage aboard HMCS *Okanagan* as guest officer resonated with my recollection of the sublime dimensions of Verne's science fiction. For as it turns out, the silent world of Jules Verne and later of Jacques-Yves Cousteau is not silent at all. It is filled with ambient noise of different frequency levels, character, and tonality. Some of the noise travels great distances. During one middle watch— the so-called graveyard shift from midnight to four o'clock AM—I recall passing the time with a very skilled sonarman listening to the inexhaustible sounds of the surrounding sea life: the snapping and crackling of shrimp; the moaning, clicking, and whistling of whales and dolphins; the dull growling and groaning of the longhorn sculpin; the pulsed, low-frequency vocalizing of the red grouper; and the "squeaking door hinges" of the spiny lobster. The sonarman claimed to know all of them and shared the lore with me. Amidst this natural cacophony, we also heard intrusive anthropogenic noise—the man-made sounds of ships and submarines. The distant whoosh of an unknown passing nuclear sub reminded us that we were not alone, and never would be.

I recall our return from the depths. I stood at the periscope as we surfaced off Chebucto Head, Nova Scotia. A strong swell was running. I swept the horizon and caught snapshots of sparkling waves in glorious sunshine as coastal traffic passed our line of approach: an aging coastal oiler from another era and a fishing schooner from the 1940s. The sight reminded me of home on the Canadian West Coast, and small boats with taut sails carrying me and my family on nautical adventures.

Every passage begins at the edge of something. Whether it's an ocean passage, a musical passage, or a rite of passage, one crosses a threshold from known to unknown. Perhaps, as I now see it, that threshold is memory; it's a path that follows shafts of sunlight down the curve of time. I had crossed the threshold of memory while voyaging on HMCS *Okanagan* and had come to know the sea in its many dimensions. Had I been a younger man, I might have chosen a submarine profession. But that was not the case, and a happy surface sailor I remain.

TOP "In the Gap." Lifeboat, flying the blue ensign in my honour, bringing the little bundle of me home to Pachena Point in 1936 after disembarking from the SS *Princess Maquinna* offshore.

BOTTOM, LEFT "Just take another step." Learning to Walk in 1939 with mother (right) and aunt Elsie Lowe (left) at the BC Steamships Terminal in Victoria, BC.

BOTTOM, RIGHT "Just an ordinary Canadian family." With my parents and sister Elizabeth Joan at our new Vancouver home, 1940.

OPPOSITE, TOP, LEFT "Brakes set … throttle set, contact!" Preflight checks in the pilot's seat awaiting Dad, 1948.

OPPOSITE, TOP, RIGHT Fishing with Dad, 1948. My first catch: "… but do I really have to clean it myself?"

OPPOSITE, BOTTOM "All aboard, lads, you're off to England." Enroute from Vancouver on the 1953 UK concert tour. Ronald Wood (right).

ABOVE Departure from Quebec City aboard SS *Samaria* on my second concert tour, 1953. Centre "Mr. D." I am front row, third from right.

P.A.-REUTER PHOTO

THEATRE ROYAL

PORTSMOUTH

Chairman & Han. Dir. : E. H. SPERRING   **IN THE HEART OF THE CITY** Manager : C. A. PAICE

IN CONJUNCTION WITH MOSS' EMPIRES, Ltd.   BOX OFFICE OPEN 10 a.m. to 8 p.m.

TELEPHONE 73228

6.15   Commencing **MONDAY, JULY 6th**   **8.30**
TWICE NIGHTLY

THE MOST FAMOUS BOYS BAND IN THE WORLD

THE

FOUR MEN
ONE SONG

ELSIE & DORIS WATERS

VANCOUVER BOYS BAND

RADIO REVELLERS

Conductor - ARTHUR W. DELAMONT

FROM

SOUSA TO BOOGIE WOOGIE

**RADIO'S
GERT AND DAISY**

EDDIE REINDEER

THE
WISE
CRACKPOT

RONNIE

HIMSELF
AND
OTHERS

LESLIE

SEATON & O'DELL

DANCE TEAM

TRIBE BROS. LTD., London & St. Albans

ABOVE "On Stage Tonight," 1953.

OPPOSITE, TOP, LEFT "Look sharp, feel sharp, be sharp." UBC undergraduates in 1955. My friend Kenneth Dye (left) served as Auditor General of Canada from 1981 to 1991.

OPPOSITE, TOP, RIGHT With Anita at Expo 58, Brussels, Belgium. We are riding the Vespa that took Paul Chamberland and me on a 5,000-kilometre journey across the Alps, down the boot of Italy, across the Adriatic (by ferry), and return via the former Yugoslavia, the Alps again, and home to Brussels—all in three weeks.

OPPOSITE, BOTTOM Promoting Canada in my 1962 speaking tour of West Germany for the Canadian Embassy.

Streifzug durch Kanada

Deutschstämmige Volksgruppe stellt 12 Prozent der Gesamtbevölkerung

Zu einem Filmvortragsabend lädt die Kanadische Botschaft in Deutschland für heute abend in den Hörsaal 13 der Neuen Universität ein. Zwei preisgekrönte Farbtonfilme sollen mit dem zweitgrößten Land der Welt auf dem amerikanischen Nordkontinent näher bekannt machen; außerdem gibt Michael L. Hadley von der Kanadischen Botschaft einen kurzen einführenden Vortrag.

Dieses abendfüllende Programm, das seit dem 1. Dezember läuft, soll innerhalb von rund einem Vierteljahr mehr als 60 deutsche Städte besuchen, um die Freundschaftsbande zwischen den beiden Ländern enger zu knüpfen, die auf so vielfache Weise zusammenarbeiten und doch so weit voneinander entfernt sind. Die gegenseitigen Beziehungen waren von jeher schon recht bedeutend, und heute ist die deutschstämmige Volksgruppe in Kanada mit 12 Prozent an der Gesamtbevölkerung die drittgrößte.

Es war im Jahre 1750, als das Segelschiff „Ann" Deutschland mit den ersten Siedlern für das nördliche Gebiet Amerikas — das heutige Kanada — verließ. Nach abenteuerlicher Fahrt und mehrmonatiger Ungewißheit über das kommende Schicksal legte die kleine Gruppe in Neu-Schottland an und gründete die Stadt Lunenburg. Im Kampf mit den wilden Natur und den teils sehr kriegerischen Ureinwohnern, den vermutlich aus Asien kommenden Indianern, bildeten sie den Grundstock einer der vielen verschiedenen Volksgruppen, die inzwischen zu einer Nation zusammengewachsen sind.

Aus dieser Zeit berichtet der erste Film mit dem Titel „Indianische Legende". Ein zweiter Streifen führt durch das moderne Kanada, durch die verschiedenen Städte mit ihren Kulturzentren und durch die unendlichen Weiten des Landes auf der 6000 Kilometer langen Bundesstraße von der atlantischen bis zur pazifischen Küste durch alle zehn Provinzen. (Um einen Eindruck zu geben: die Provinz Manitoba ist allein so groß wie Frankreich und die Benelux-Staaten zusammen.) Wegen der relativ sehr geringen Bevölkerungsdichte und den noch unerschlossenen reichen Bodenschätzen ist Kanada eines der Zukunftsländer.

Karten für diese „Reise durch den andern Kontinent" sind bei der Straßen- und Bergbahn AG zu haben, die die Veranstaltung hier unterstützt; die Tournee leitet die Home Lines Schiffahrt GmbH. – b -

Michael L. Hadley, von der canadischen Botschaft in Deutschland, wird heute abend über seine Heimat berichten. Foto: Speck

ABOVE "On track by lead marks!" Great Lakes navigator, 1964.

TOP "Our four little elves," dressed up for the Christmas party at Government House, Winnipeg, 1970. From left: Norman, Pauline, David, Michèle.

BOTTOM With Prime Minister Pierre Trudeau at Government House, Winnipeg, 1970.

OPPOSITE, TOP "A Band of Brothers." In 1987, with former submarine skippers and senior officers from Germany's *Kriegsmarine* of the Second World War. From left: Klaus Hänert, U-550; Klaus Hornbostel, U-806; Jochen von Knebel-Doeberitz, flag-lieutenant to Grand Admiral Dönitz; Kurt Petersen, U-541; Schorsch Meckel, chief, operational intelligence; Paul Hartwig, U-517.

OPPOSITE, BOTTOM Kiel Harbour, Germany, in 1988 aboard the 1914-built and restored 3-mast gaff schooner *Anny von Hamburg. In the background is the* German Navy's training vessel *Gorch Fock.* JOCHEN VON KNEBEL-DOEBERITZ

ABOVE "Up periscope. Stand by to surface." Guest officer aboard Canadian submarine HMCS *Okanagan,* 1990.

ABOVE My induction into the Royal Society of Canada with President of the RSC, Dr. Jean-Pierre Wallot (right). Ottawa, 1998.

ABOVE Punting on the Cam, during a sabbatical at the University of Cambridge, UK, in 2000. With Anita (right) and my sister Elizabeth Joan (left).

OPPOSITE, TOP "Making things right." Community-based research and social action with the Restorative Justice Coalition in William Head prison, 2001. Pierre Allard (left), Director of Chaplaincy, Correctional Service of Canada, and inmate Manny Jaimes (right). In a tragic turn, Manny was gunned down in a gang-land slaying shortly after his release.

OPPOSITE, BOTTOM "A restorative justice initiative." The labyrinth on the grounds of Christ Church Cathedral in Victoria, BC, was designed and built by a team of inmates from William Head prison, and cathedral parishioners. 2001. UNIVERSITY OF VICTORIA PHOTO

ABOVE Father Paulo Dall'Oglio welcomes us to the fourth-century monastery of Mar Musa, Syria, in 2001. Here, he had founded a community for Muslim-Christian dialogue. Tragically, he was murdered by ISIS during the Syrian civil war.

OPPOSITE, TOP Anita preparing our workshops with the Honourable Miria Matembe, Minister of State for Ethics and Integrity, Uganda, 2003.

OPPOSITE, BOTTOM With Anita in northern waters, 2008.

TOP With my travelling companion at the edge of the desert in Jordan, 2017.

BOTTOM Reading C.S. Lewis's *Narnia* with granddaughter Alexandria, 2021.

TOP, RIGHT Restorative Justice: taking the Moon Mask home to its creator, Charles August, in 2022. ANITA HADLEY

TOP, LEFT Receiving the Lieutenant Governor's Award for Maritime Achievement from Her Honour Janet Austin, Lieutenant Governor of BC, 21 November 2023.

BOTTOM *Peregrine*'s skipper. DAVID HADLEY

8

A BAND OF
BROTHERS

*You know that age can be
A hill of looking; and the swaying sea
A lifetime marching with the waves of time.*

CHARLES BRUCE, "Eastern Shore"

THE BALTIC SEA was grey and growly as we cast off moorings at
the North German island of Fehmarn and set course for the Danish
archipelago. A fresh northwesterly breeze was curling the tops of the
waves, promising a brisk passage. On my way home from attending
research conferences in Helsinki and St. Petersburg, I had stopped
at Hamburg to join my friend Jochen von Knebel-Doeberitz for a
cruise aboard his 10.7-metre (35-foot) sloop *Aka*. During the Second
World War, Jochen had served as flag lieutenant to Grand Admiral
Karl Dönitz, the architect and driving force behind Germany's submarine war against the Allied forces. The two of us had met during
research for my first book, *U-Boats against Canada*. Now, however,
we were getting the weather gauge of an East German patrol vessel
anchored at the edge of its presumed boundary with West German
sovereign waters. It was July 1987, and no one had yet expressed
any inkling that the wall dividing the two Germanies would soon
collapse. Surprisingly, as we pressed on under taut sails into the
late afternoon light, Jochen chose to pass close alongside his East
German naval brother with the taunting cry: "Comrades, what an
odd-looking flag you've got!" Horrified, I envisioned our spending
the next few days in a Stasi cell. Frequent crossings into the East at

Berlin's famous Checkpoint Charlie had taught me that East Germany's secret police network had an unappetizing reputation for being unpredictable.

Yet I had to admit that the vessel's ensign did look odd, at least from the West German perspective. Like the West, it bore the tricolour of black, red, and gold inherited from the Weimar Republic. But emblazoned upon it was the East's coat of arms consisting of the Communist hammer and compass dividers encircled with ears of rye wheat. Typically, it also bore the international naval symbol of the foul anchor. For the moment, however, we busied ourselves with widening the gap between ourselves and the seemingly indifferent East German patrol. Perhaps someone on board had sensed that radical political change was coming soon, and we simply were not worth the candle.

We shaped our Baltic voyage through the Danish archipelago, taking whatever weather came our way. When mooring for the night, we would dine in one of the region's delightful cobblestone villages, with their whitewashed buildings and cozy inns. Rising early, we would slip back into town to purchase coffee and freshly baked croissants for breakfast, and tasty breads for the day. For one accustomed to cruising the rugged BC coast, with its sparse and spotty coastal culture and indifferent eateries, sailing in these European waters was a gourmet treat.

The passage itself was all a sailor could wish for: blistering breezes under clear skies that sent us creaming to windward, often followed by spirited spinnaker reaches and runs. I remember a particularly testy reach southward along the coast of the Danish island of Langeland, while en route home to Fehmarn. Under a fresh easterly, we had set our huge asymmetrical spinnaker. Having just placed a visual fix on our chart down below, and projected our course and dead reckoning positions, I joined Jochen in the cockpit. Wispy streaks of mist still stood some distance off, but quickly began thickening until we lost sight of land. Still slicing briskly through the water, we felt hugged by silence. Suddenly, we spied a tall island where no land should be. Sunlight breaking through the murk was creating a loom, stretching and raising what appeared to be the southern tip of Langeland dead ahead in the distance. My navigation told me this was impossible. Yet there it was. The unidentified island lay fading, re-emerging, and receding in the mist before us. Then we saw her. Just a couple of miles across our line of advance, the mirage transformed itself into the German naval training vessel *Gorch Fock,* moving under full sail and with a bone in her teeth. Over 1,650 square metres (18,000 square feet) of canvas were driving the fifteen-hundred-ton barque through whisper-thin veils of mist. It was a sight to warm any sailor's heart. The ship's name reminded us of the relationship between literature and life, or in this case, between "pop-lit" and naval culture. We recalled the Battle of Jutland of 31 May 1916. In that famous *Skagerrakschlacht,* as Germans know it, the popular poet Johann Wilhelm Kinau, writing under the pen name Gorch Fock, had died when British naval forces sank his ship, the light cruiser SMS *Wiesbaden.* That clash between the Royal Navy's battle-cruiser fleet and the German High Seas Fleet drew Jochen and me into lively debate, just as it had previous generations of history buffs. The Germans lost eleven ships with over three thousand casualties; the British lost fourteen ships—including three battle cruisers—with over six thousand casualties. So, who won? Statistics don't tell the whole story. For while the Germans had won a tactical victory, the Royal Navy's victory had been strategic. After the *Skagerrakschlacht,* Germany's High Seas Fleet never put to sea again.

THRUSTING HOMEWARD into German waters under the press of quartering winds and sea, we again took up the threads of our many narratives. The atmospherics of our brisk passage cast me back onto my origins. My venture into naval history had begun at a Christmas cocktail party at Admiral's House, in the Canadian naval base of Esquimalt, BC. It was 1978, and I was attending as commanding officer of the naval reserve unit HMCS *Malahat.* Like many others, I had been following two parallel careers: naval officer and academic. On this occasion I met Craig Campbell, the former captain of

HMCS *Clayoquot*. The Bangor-class minesweeper had been torpedoed and sunk by German submarine U-806 off Halifax, on
Christmas Eve 1944. Craig had come upon a page from the submarine's war diary and asked me to translate it.

That enigmatic page drew me into an unchronicled dimension of Canada's war at sea. These official documents—*Kriegstagebuch*,
or KTB in German—contained important tactical data for evaluating a warship's performance while on patrol. The diary's cryptic
entries hinted at a wealth of information that the whole diary would
eventually reveal: a running commentary on U-boat deployment,
tactics, navigation, and weather. Sometimes they contained obser-
vations about the enemy, with the occasional excerpt or paraphrase
of U-boat radio signals. Up to then, the full story of *Clayoquot*'s
destruction had never been told. Nor had anyone yet analyzed the
overarching subject of the operations of German submarines in
Canadian waters. I felt myself drawn into the vortex of a compelling
project. Researching and writing naval history became one of the
most intriguing phases of my whole academic career. As it turned
out, the story was huge. It covered not only the nuts and bolts of
wartime strategy and tactics; it was also about politics, propaganda,
human fates, and myth.

Only a two-pronged approach could winkle out the answers I
sought. I needed one foot in Germany and the other in Canada. The
Canadian side rested firmly in the Directorate of History, a division
of the Department of National Defence, in Ottawa. Its director,
Dr. Alec Douglas, was a former naval officer. A fine academic leader
and team player, he encouraged my research project and welcomed
me warmly into the fellowship of naval historians. In those days, the
directorate occupied the whole second floor of Ogilvie's Department Store, a rather down-at-heel building in downtown Ottawa.
We used to joke that this was the only defence establishment that
required a credit card as official ID. This unlikely treasure trove of
declassified records invited me into an intriguing world of historical
sleuthing. The gold was there. One simply had to dig.

Here I rubbed shoulders with two young scholars who later became senior professors of military history: Roger Sarty and Marc Milner. They became lifelong friends and colleagues. Roger assisted me in my slalom through Canadian official records, and sent me photocopies of documents whenever I needed data and could not travel the long and costly haul from Victoria to Ottawa. Marc shared his wealth of knowledge about the Canadian side of the Battle of the Atlantic. Both men were passionate in their research into untapped or uncatalogued sources and eagerly debated the fine points of evidence. Our working together in the Directorate of History—Dee Hist, as we spoke of it—was colourful, lively, and congenial. When Marc and I finished our books in 1985—my *U-Boats against Canada*, and his *North Atlantic Run: The Royal Canadian Navy and the Battle for the Convoys*—we undertook promotional media tours together throughout Ontario and Quebec. Our appearances on TV and radio opened up a new world to us: the media wanted short, snappy sound bites. We had to simplify a complex story about how German forces had almost brought the Allies to their knees. What is a U-boat? (answer: a submersible torpedo boat). Why did they attack convoys? (answer: to cut Britain's lifelines). While we enjoyed the novelty of the limelight, we recognized that it was more about showbiz than substance.

It was in Ottawa that I met Louis Audette, one of the most memorable Canadian naval veterans. Louis's zestful and often self-ironic retelling of his wartime exploits graced many a dining table. A lawyer turned naval reservist and eventually escort commander, he came from a long line of professionals leading back to the celebrated sailor, shipbuilder, and explorer Pierre Le Moyne d'Iberville. Born in Montreal, New France, in 1661, d'Iberville had famously defeated an English squadron in 1697 during the Battle of Hudson's Bay. That, too, was a tale Louis enjoyed recounting. With bravado and wit, he brought the past alive. Dinner at Louis's home in Ottawa was always a festival of effervescent conversation over whiskey in crystal glasses and exquisite fare served on fine linen with Georgian silver. On several occasions, Louis entertained a small cohort of naval historians including myself, Roger, and Marc. Canadian naval history never had such a lively promoter nor such an avid fan club as we three.

Half a world away from Canada's naval historical research unit in the upper floor of an Ottawa department store lay the North Sea island of Sylt, in the Frisian archipelago of Northern Germany. It was here, in a hangar of a naval air station, that German U-boat veteran Horst Bredow had established the first home of his famous U-Boot-Archiv. Now a charitable national foundation (*Stiftung*), the archive had begun as a private collection of artifacts and memorabilia from U-boat warfare. My correspondence with Horst and subsequent visits to Sylt marked the beginning of a years-long association. He had been a watch officer in the VIIC "Atlantic boat" U-288 in Arctic waters when his submarine downed a British Swordfish torpedo bomber during a rare gunnery duel. Wounded by shrapnel, Horst had to be landed in Tromsø, Norway. In a twist of fate that changed Horst's life, his U-288 again encountered a Swordfish when outward bound from Tromsø. After taking off from the escort carrier HMS *Activity*, the torpedo bomber attacked the submarine with rockets and depth charges. It was 3 April 1944. U-288 went down with all hands. Ashore undergoing medical treatment, Horst suffered the psychological wounds known as survivor's syndrome. "Why, and for what possible purpose, have I been saved while my shipmates died?" he agonized. He found his answer by creating the U-Boat Archive. Its purpose, he would tell his every visitor, was to provide the raw data for finding the truth about the naval war. "The truth"—*Die Wahrheit*—became his watchword. Books that failed to meet his political expectations landed on his blacklist.

Horst always struck me as the most complex and troubled of the many German ex-submariners I met. An obsessive workaholic, he invested all his energy and most of his money in expanding his collection and promoting research and writing on the U-boat war. Politically unable, or unwilling, to accept the cultural changes evolving in postwar Germany, he remained an apologist for many aspects of the Third Reich. To his mind, the 1960s and '70s had ushered in a fatal mix of pop culture, hippies, noisy music, and democratic politics. In "the old days," he would argue with characteristic vehemence, you could expect order and discipline—and respect for national institutions and symbols. Nowadays, he complained, the country was being undermined by anarchists and "chaotic types." They were, to his mind, an undisciplined generation of leftists. It was not worth challenging his opinions.

By the 1980s, the growing international success of Horst's museum and archives was eroding his sharper corners and maturing (or healing) his mindset. His impressive collection offered a unique resource. Not only as a source of hard data but as a meeting place for researchers, writers, and film teams. Many veterans of the wartime German submarine corps saw it as a place of pilgrimage. That explains why the modern-day Federal German Navy for many years kept a respectful distance from the museum. Horst died in February 2015, leaving a lasting legacy to international research and understanding. The government of the day honoured him with the Federal German Cross of Merit for having established what is now called the German U-Boat Museum (*Deutsches U-Boot Museum: Stiftung Traditionsarchiv*).

STEEPED IN salt and seamanship—and in our probing discussions of German naval culture—Jochen and I continued our Baltic voyage. Under taut sails we navigated his sloop past the tip of Langeland and down the long homeward leg to Fehmarn. At the end of our voyage, we returned to Jochen's home in Aumühle, some 30 kilometres (18.5 miles) east of Hamburg (my favourite seaport), where he lived with his gracious wife, Claudia. They resided in a grand home at the edge of the *Sachsenwald*—the Saxon Forest—with its many hiking paths. Jochen and I had often walked here, whatever the weather. The peacefulness of the setting triggered conversations in which our minds met as often as they diverged. Questions of human dynamics invariably took the foreground: the military concepts of duty and allegiance, Germany's tangled and still raw memories of the Third Reich, the Holocaust, the morality of power, and whether the armed forces of any nation can honestly deem themselves to be politically neutral. Jochen was a refined gentleman of the utmost probity. He had been generous in his support of the rebuilding of a village just inside Poland near his former family estate, which German forces had largely destroyed during the war. As we walked and talked, our steps almost invariably drew us to the Forest Cemetery—*Waldfriedhof Aumühle*—and the grave of Grand Admiral Karl Dönitz.

The headstone is stark; a rough-hewn runestone with the name Dönitz chiselled into the rock. Behind it rises a tall, black crucifix, with the tortured figure of Christ outstretched upon it. I later discussed the image with the old admiral's postwar spiritual mentor, the Lutheran pastor Hans-Jochen Arp. Arp had asked the admiral why he would want such a striking grave marker, an unusual choice in Protestant Northern Germany. Dönitz had quietly confessed, "Because He is the only one unto whom I can cleave." Christ had become his centre. To the end of his days, Dönitz faithfully attended Arp's church. At one point, vandals showed their contempt for the man sometimes pilloried as the Nazi admiral by dousing his impressive grave marker with red paint. The vandalism caused unintended ambiguity. Anti-Nazis saw the red paint on the crucifix as symbolizing the blood of the German submariners whom Dönitz had "sacrificed" in the war; others saw it as the blood of Christ that had ultimately redeemed him.

Karl Dönitz remains one of the great enigmatic figures of the Second World War. Widely known as the mastermind behind Germany's submarine operations during the crucial Battle of the Atlantic, he eventually succeeded Hitler just as the shattered Nazi state stood poised on the point of unconditional surrender. He had never aspired to this estate. His government lasted but twenty-three days until dissolved by the Allies on 23 May 1945. The International Military Tribunal at Nuremberg found him guilty of crimes against peace and crimes against the laws of war. He served his full sentence of ten years in Berlin's Spandau Prison. By contrast, Britain's Air Vice-Marshal "Bomber" Harris, who had sent his thousand-bomber raids over civilian targets in Germany—quite wantonly according to some historians—became a war hero. Britain still honours Harris with a commemorative statue outside London's St. Clements Dane, the Central Church of the Royal Air Force. The contrast between Harris and Dönitz raises compelling questions on both sides about victors' justice and the portrayal of war leaders.

On release from Spandau, Dönitz spent his final, reclusive days in Aumühle. To his aging supporters he remained "the lion," the charismatic Grand Admiral. To his detractors, he was a tired old Nazi lackey, "the last Führer," and "the devil's admiral." But in the funeral oration in January 1981, Pastor Arp honoured him as "one of the most grateful Christians I have ever met."

But who was he really? I had long been intrigued by his private personality. Working through archives and interviews, I gathered my evidence. I took my lead from two interpretative frames of reference: Germany's classical dramatist Friedrich Schiller, in particular his trilogy *Wallenstein,* and military historian John Keegan's *The Mask of Command.* Years in the making, my conclusions were published in 2000 in the article "Grand Admiral Karl Dönitz: A Dramatic Key to the Man behind the Mask." Like Keegan, I argued that leadership is a performance in which an actor plays a role. (I had learned this piece of theatre years earlier while observing, and playing, leadership roles in my own navy life.) I went further and placed the character and his role on the dramatic stage of German classical tragedy.

Dealing with Dönitz, I argued, necessitates ignoring the chronological phases of the Battle of the Atlantic as defined by naval historians. Instead, we must follow the psychological phases through which the dramatic protagonist passes, from the opening curtain to the last. Through this lens, we can see how Dönitz changed in each scene, in response to the various crises and responsibilities that shaped him. Each stage of his advance up the chain of command forced him to think and react within the unique "box" into which he had been promoted. With an eye to the partitioned spaces in which bureaucrats work, Germans call this "cubicle thinking"— *Ressortdenken.* Of course, his box got bigger with each promotion, and demanded a wider perspective. Like every dramatic character, Dönitz had a tragic flaw. Cubicle thinking, and his commitment to duty within that box, was his. "Devotion to duty was his life," his daughter once explained. In naval parlance, devotion to duty is a paramount virtue. In tragedy, it can become a "dramatic necessity." The term, according to drama theory, refers to the sum of forces that thrust a character toward her or his irrevocable end. Devotion to duty took its toll on Dönitz.

One time, while hunkered down in the cellar of Stuttgart's Library of Contemporary History, I began sifting through some of the admiral's personal files. Letters he had written and received, casual notes, and memos lay in uncatalogued order. They gave a tactile sense of the man's history. His bold, Teutonic signature—always the single name *Dönitz*—attested to his authority, drive, and mythical stature.

Suddenly, a bundle of forensic photos spilled onto my lap. Fixated by horrific photos of corpses sprawled on the floor of the hangman's cell in Nuremberg Prison, I gasped in disbelief. Brutally graphic, they revealed the final agony of three leading Nazis who had been condemned to death at the War Crimes Tribunal and executed by hanging on 16 October 1946: Hans Frank, the governor-general of Poland; Joachim von Ribbentrop, Hitler's foreign minister; and SS General Ernst Kaltenbrunner, the man ultimately responsible for carrying out the Nazi's Final Solution—the extermination of the Jews in German-occupied Europe. Their deaths were ugly. The hangings of Kaltenbrunner and von Ribbentrop in particular had been botched. Gripped by the moment, I felt no pity. Ribbentrop had remained loyal to Hitler to the end. Kaltenbrunner had defended himself in Nuremberg with sophistry, cunning, and an appeal to the tribunal to appreciate that he had merely followed orders. "I have done my duty by the laws of my country," he confessed in his final moments. Never did he show any insight into the moral depravity of the Nazi regime, nor of what he himself had done in its name. Only Frank, who had converted to Catholicism after his arrest, had shown any remorse.

By all accounts, Dönitz was a charismatic leader and a different kind of man. I gradually came to realize that he was not so much a devil's admiral, as some would have it. He was a bedevilled one. He had fallen—from U-boat deck to prisoner's dock—not because he had been a master of Nazi policy. Rather, he had slipped incrementally into it because of his tragic flaw. He had already fallen to uncritical acceptance of the religion of duty and nationalism, and to the allurements of a criminal regime. In terms of Schiller's classical theatre, he was likely both guilty *and* innocent of all that he had contrived. That was his tragedy and the fate of those whom he commanded.

THE U-BOATS' Admiral Dönitz frequently surfaced during my long associations with former German submariners. They were a resilient and resourceful lot. They had survived war in a naval branch that had suffered the loss of 80 percent of its seagoing personnel. They had had to live with the fact that whatever their personal political stance might have been during wartime, their naval service had been in support of a monstrous criminal regime. My friend Jochen von Knebel-Doeberitz, for example, had survived the sinking of the famous "Golden Horseshoe" U-99 U-boat, skippered by the "Tonnage King" Otto Kretschmer. Both men became prisoners of war in Canada's famous Camp 30 at Bowmanville, Ontario. Here Jochen played a key role, along with other members of the camp's "Lorient Espionage Unit," in a plan to tunnel out of Bowmanville and rendezvous with a U-boat in the Baie des Chaleurs, in New Brunswick. Letter codes passed via the Red Cross in neutral Switzerland arranged the pickup. Indeed, Rolf Schauenburg's U-536 did arrive as planned, but the one escapee who managed to break out with a counterfeited identity had already been arrested on the beach. When I first visited Jochen's home in Aumühle, I found in his bookshelves the very copy of *Dent's Canadian School Atlas* which his group of Bowmanville prisoners had used to plan the escape. Published in 1943, it was the same edition I myself had used in school. After the war, Jochen built a successful career as an importer of lumber from Canada.

The former U-boat men I came to know shared their stories with me once I had gained their confidence. Indeed, many of them appear in my first book on U-boat history. Each one of these men had been shaped by his wartime naval service. On returning to civilian life, most looked back at their sea service as the pinnacle of youthful bravado. Canadian veterans were no different. And, like their Canadian counterparts, a couple of them actually basked in the glories of those days. Their wartime exploits still seemed to define them. Reinhard Hardegen, for example, had been skipper of the famous U-123 during the so-called happy time of 1942, when U-boats seemed invincible. I met him in his home in 1987, and confronted an overly large oil portrait of him in his *Kriegsmarine* uniform and boat-cloak dominating his living room. The portrait exuded the full weight of German heraldry and, I suspected, his politics. The painting distilled a person of deeply rooted traditional values in the prime of his life. A generous host, Hardegen died in 2018 at the age of 105, still driving his car with the vanity plate U-123, which proclaimed him a U-boat ace.

THE GERMAN side of my research into U-boat operations drew upon my ever-expanding network of submariners who had experienced the war at sea. My own naval experience provided the key to their memories and their assistance. My academic credentials, however, made me rather suspect in their eyes. This became clear on my first meeting with the former skipper of U-1232, Captain Kurt Dobratz, in Bremen. In January 1945 he had played the lone wolf, plying the inshore routes of the Sydney-Halifax convoys and generally observing traffic patterns while lurking some four miles off Sambro Light Vessel. He eventually attacked Boston-Halifax convoy BX-141 as it broke formation to enter Halifax Harbour, destroying three major vessels. His action earned him the Knight's Cross. For our meeting, he had suggested the Intercity Hotel across from Bremen's main railway station. Veterans typically preferred to first meet with outsiders on neutral territory. The receptionist directed me to a private lounge where Herr Dr. Dobratz, he explained, awaited me. Now a prominent lawyer in the city-state of Bremen, he cut an imposing figure. Impeccably dressed in a formal black business suit and white silk tie, he was clearly accustomed to command. During the war, he had been something of a rarity among submarine commanders, the majority of whom were lieutenants or lieutenant-commanders. Dobratz had been a four-ring captain. At a time when U-boats were suffering severe losses and skippers were being killed more quickly than they could be replaced, he had been transferred to U-boat service from the Fleet Air Arm. Highly intelligent and gifted, he had adapted seamlessly to submarines, where he was respected and admired for his decisive and daring manner.

By the time I joined Dobratz in the lounge, he had already arranged for coffee. We sat down after formal introductions and began staking out our mutual fields of interest. Like other veterans, he had been badgered by journalists and other writers seeking a sensational story, and he intended to hold court on his own terms. At one point—and it should really have been my opener—I revealed my naval background. I was an officer in Canada's naval reserve, had undergone anti-submarine warfare training, and had commanded a naval vessel. "For God's sake, man," he exclaimed with a whiff of theatrical outrage—"Um Gottes Willen, mein Lieber"—"do you mean to tell me that you are a naval officer and not just another goddamn academic?" With a snap of his fingers, he recast the scenario: "Waiter, cancel the coffee. We're drinking schnapps!" From that point on, the formal tone of our encounter shifted. First tolerated as a mere academic hack, I was now a fellow officer sharing a common seafaring culture rooted in ships, seas, and an understanding of how crews actually work. This notion of a common culture played a key role in helping former combatants to reconcile with one another after the war. Once accepted as a naval man by one former combatant, I was passed along to others. In time I grew close to a number of important participants in the war at sea.

Beneath his crust, Dobratz was a personable, generous, and congenial conversation partner. Etched in his mind was 13 January 1945, the day when the Canadian frigate HMCS *Ettrick* charged down upon him. It was a defining moment in his naval career. The Canadian counterattack brought him literally to within inches of becoming one more statistic in Dönitz's disastrous record of U-boat losses. No longer would the cool and calculating operator regard Canadian tactics as a case of "little Johnny playing at war." Scarcely had he managed to slip inside the protective screen of convoy escorts when he suddenly sighted *Ettrick*. Quickly picking up the U-boat's scent, *Ettrick* had turned to attack. Thrusting full bore upon the intruder, the warship's bow wave projected power and determination. The ship filled his periscope lens. At dangerously close quarters to a merchantman caught in his sights, Dobratz fired and dived deeper. *Ettrick* drove right over his bridge, bending his attack periscope, scarring the bridge combing, and sending U-1232 lurching onto its beam. As *Ettrick* passed almost unscathed overhead, her towed anti-acoustic cat-gear—a cluster of steel bars and cables—ripped off the submarine's net guard. It was a scene right out of the movie *Das Boot* as, certain of their impending doom, the crew cowered under depth charge explosions and huddled against the screeching circular-saw sound of the cat-gear that seemed to be slicing the U-boat's steel hull into pieces.

The attack was witnessed by Canadian skipper Louis Audette, with whom I spent many congenial visits in the 1970s. Standing on the bridge of his escort vessel, the frigate HMCS *Coaticook*, he was one of many "sheep dogs" herding the merchant ships as they peeled off into a single column toward safe haven in Halifax. Louis's account of the Canadians' painstaking pursuit of Dobratz and U-1232 was one of the more sombre of his tales. The torpedoeings were ugly and effective, he recalled. Three days later, Louis and his shipmates picked up the body of an unidentified young merchant sailor. Perfectly preserved, it showed the beginnings of marine growth. The lad had been in the water for some time. Knowing nothing about him, Louis cobbled together a brief ecumenical service in the hope of honouring whatever the dead sailor's origins and traditions might have been. Burial at sea, according to the traditions of the naval service, followed. For many hours afterward, Louis explained, "my ship was quieter than usual... However, a sailor's mind soon finds its way back to its normal channels." Kurt Dobratz and the crew of U-1232 would have understood completely. During my last visit to Kurt and his family in Bremen, he presented me with his U-boat branch badge. Crafted in brass by his chief engineer during the Halifax patrol, the badge bore all the heraldry of a once-proud fleet: a U-boat surmounted by the Reichsadler (Imperial Eagle), clutching a swastika in its claws, and framed in oak leaves. Showing the marks of hasty manufacture under the stress of combat, the rough craftsmanship suggests a certain end-of-conflict malaise. We will all get out of this together, it seems to say. But when? As though in answer, the words of Shakespeare's witches in *Macbeth* intrude: "When the hurly-burly's done / When the battle's lost and won." Dobratz and his crew made it home, and on 2 April 1945—over a month before the war ended—their damaged submarine was decommissioned in the Baltic port of Kiel.

MEN OF the lower decks invited me into their circles as well. These non-commissioned ranks of the Submarine Service maintained a strong mutual loyalty toward one another. Almost every city boasted its *Uboot-Kameradschaft* (U-boat comradeship). Salzburg, for example, the city of Mozart, had a long tradition of naval service reaching back to the days of the Imperial and Royal Navy of the Austro-Hungarian Empire (*K.u.K. Marine*). Günther Reibhorn, my Austrian friend and business colleague from my foreign service days in Germany, provided the initial link. He had long since become a U-boat buff and collector of memorabilia from Austria's naval past. I regularly visited him and his wife, Inge. In Salzburg, I became *"Onkel Mike"* to their three daughters.

Here in Salzburg, I became acquainted with a small group of Second World War veterans who kept their stories alive in a smoky beer cellar in an obscure street near the centre of town. Going down "into the cellar"—*in den Keller gehen*—was colloquial German for "take her down," or "dive, dive, dive." A secret door buzzer granted access to the ancient warriors, who took me aboard as a member of their crew. I dropped by each time I visited town. Beer flowed aplenty as we re-fought old battles, traded "wartime secrets," and shared salty dips. But our conversations could also become serious. When visiting the U-Kameradschaft in Dresden my old friend, ex-submariner Kurt Sommer, confessed: "I've spent my whole life under two dictatorships: Hitler, and East Germany. Thank God the Wall has fallen, and we now live in Western Europe."

During one of my frequent visits to Germany, I met with the former skipper of U-806 who had torpedoed Craig Campbell's ship on that fateful Christmas Eve in 1944. Like Kurt Dobratz, Klaus Hornbostel had been transferred into the U-Boat Arm late in his career. Faced with high U-boat losses, the German leadership had drawn upon talented officers wherever they could find them. Thus Klaus, a gunnery officer with the surface fleet, underwent a rapid transformation during basic training in the Submarine School. In rapid succession, his watch officer's course led directly to a commanding officer's qualifying course, and, shortly after that—his first command. He had had no previous submarine experience. His first officer, a former minesweeping officer, had never served in submarines either. His chief engineer had just completed his first course, while his navigator, a former army signalman, had never been to sea. The challenge was immense, for U-806 was a newer type IXC/40 submarine. It was technologically much more advanced than the earlier type VIIC "Atlantik" boats that had dominated action during the halcyon days of the Battle of the Atlantic. The U-806 crew's ability to master steep learning curves under pressure-cooker conditions impressed me.

Craig Campbell had prepared the path to Klaus Hornbostel for me in his inimitable, forthright way. He had dashed off a note in English that said, in effect, "I'm the guy you sank that Christmas Eve in '44, and I'd love to meet you." Craig spoke about the loss of his ship and crewmen, and indicated that he wanted to make peace. Without that approach, Klaus would likely have let sleeping dogs lie. He was a private, reflective gentleman. Coming to terms with the past is always tough soul work. This was particularly so with Klaus, with whom I shared the impact of his acoustic torpedo against Craig's ship. The impact had curled up the afterdeck like a sardine can, leaving the men caught amidst shattered steam pipes and blocked hatches. Trapped in the twisted wreckage of their aft cabin, two wounded junior officers could only stare out their porthole in horrified disbelief as their ship lurched slowly into an agonizing plunge, taking them down to a grisly death. I don't know whether Klaus was ever able to come to terms with the deaths of those sailors.

Klaus and I had corresponded for some time before I first travelled to his home in Kappeln, a small town in Schleswig-Holstein. The town sits on a narrow arm (*an der Schlei*) of the Baltic Sea. Winter often grips these regions in oppressive Siberian ice conditions. So much so that locals jocularly call the nearby Olpenitz Naval Base "Olpenitz-Sibirsk"—a play on Novosibirsk, one of Siberia's largest cities. On a typical deep-freeze day in January, I took the train from Hamburg's Altona Station to the whistle stop at Süderbrarup, where Klaus awaited me on the icy platform. Dressed like a Russian landowner in his heavy coat and fur cap, he welcomed me warmly. Yet he must have felt anxious, for he knew I wanted to write the story of his encounter with Canadian naval forces off Halifax. We quickly settled into discussions of wartime naval life, of the stress felt by outbound crews setting off on patrol while Allied bombs were dropping on their loved ones at home, and of the tensions between one's professional duty and one's personal desires. I recall our sitting at his dining room table, manoeuvring the cups and salt and pepper shakers around to imitate the tactics used by an attacker against a convoy in a particular battle situation, when his wife, Karla, walked in on us. "Oh, for God's sake, you men," she exclaimed in horror at our war games. "Will you never learn?"

Karla's question struck us to the quick, for too many convenient myths about heroism and honour surrounded us. We never stop repeating them at annual Remembrance Day ceremonies— cheap pieties like "lest we forget," "fallen for king and country," and "fallen on the field of honour." The old German invocation of a "hero's death for people and fatherland," still stings. The reality of war is different: brutal, violent, terrifying, and traumatic. The war poets of the First World War—and many others since—have taught us that. But we seem never to listen.

I LATER captured the Craig–Klaus story for the German naval journal *Marine-Rundschau*. It was an illustrated nautical journal edited by Dr. Jürgen Rohwer, director of the Library of Contemporary History in Stuttgart. I had first met Jürgen at Royal Roads Military College, in Victoria, where he had presented a paper on Second World War convoy battles. My work researching the article for *Marine-Rundschau* convinced me of the much larger story: the operations of German submarines in Canadian waters. That became the subtitle of my first book of naval history, *U-Boats against Canada*, of which the Battle of the St. Lawrence formed a major part. The book underwent a second printing in English and a new edition in German. These publications led to my being invited to give a presentation at the German navy's annual Historical-Tactical Conference, in the famous naval college at Mürwik. In the style of these conferences, I was to mentor a German officer.

The imposing Marineschule Mürwik stands on a hill overlooking the Flensburg fjord. The red brick neogothic structure has been training Germany's naval officers since 1910. It had been founded by Kaiser Wilhelm II in imitation of a thirteenth-century castle of the Teutonic Knights, the Ordensburg Marienburg, which now lies in present-day Poland. By the time of the school's founding, the Imperial German Navy (*Kaiserliche Marine)* had been in existence for almost forty years. Three subsequent German navies would make it their home: the *Reichsmarine* (1921–35); the *Kriegsmarine* (1935–45); and the Federal German Navy, or *Bundesmarine* (1955–89). After the unification of East and West Germany in 1989, their respective navies merged and became known simply as the *Deutsche Marine.*

It was a bitterly cold day in January 1987 when I arrived for the conference. I had taken the train from Altona Station to Germany's northernmost city of Flensburg. The railway tracks lay frozen, as indeed were some of the navigable waters. The thick ice delayed the trains, as rail crews worked painstakingly to clear the tracks. The passengers sought shelter in overcrowded waiting rooms. After a late arrival, a hotel dinner with German naval friends picked up my spirits. After dinner, I decided to walk to the water's edge. The starry sky glistened in the crisp air. Somehow, the atmosphere of that icy evening conjured up for me a panorama of German naval history. Two world wars full of ships and submarines, sailors, and overarching political ambitions slipped past in haunting review. Striking characters strode by in spectral order, while other figures—many of them flawed—strutted and fretted their time upon the stage. I could not help but ponder the fate of Grand Admiral Dönitz, who had ended his brilliant career as Hitler's successor in a defeated Germany. It was here, in the Marineschule Mürwik, that the newly minted *Reichspräsident* (Imperial President) Dönitz had conducted the complex business of surrender until arrested by Allied forces.

I HAD travelled a long road from my schoolboy days in Vancouver to the famous German naval college. I was now joining forces with a young submarine commander of the Federal German Navy to present a joint illustrated paper to the conference. Our theme— the Canadian Navy's hunt for U-806 after its sinking of HMCS *Clayoquot*—was of contemporary interest to both our countries. The difficult bathythermographic conditions in the Baltic contribute to high-reverberation sonar echoes that mirror the waters off Canada's Atlantic coast. Moreover, the Baltic is the operational area for which the current German navy is responsible under its NATO commitments. In short, the high reverberation levels of sonar transmissions always favoured the submarine by frustrating the surface units in their difficult task of search and destroy. To make that point in the keynote address, I played the role of U-806 while my German colleague portrayed the Canadian response. After the discussion that followed, I formally presented a personal gift to Captain Klaus Hornbostel, on behalf of his former opponent Commander

Craig Campbell. Craig had engaged an artist to capture the *Clayo-quot*'s final moments, based on several available reports of the torpedoeing. Craig had autographed the picture with the words "To Klaus Hornbostel, in friendship and respect." As I read out that auto-graphed dedication, the naval audience broke out in spontaneous applause. The occasion marked a keen moment of reconciliation.

Asked later in the conference what he considered his greatest wartime achievement, Klaus modestly replied, "Getting my crew to Halifax and back home safely." It was a huge achievement. His attack against *Clayoquot* had triggered an intense pursuit by more warships than currently exist in the whole of today's Canadian navy. The oceanographic conditions of the rocky Canadian coast played havoc with their search, deflecting the Canadians' probing sonar beams. Creeping along the ocean bottom amidst sonar probes and exploding depth charges, Klaus escaped. When asked about his par-ticular tactics, Klaus at first replied that he had none apart from the desire to escape. But there was much more to it than that. No tactical handbook tells you what to do when pursued by two dozen trained enemy warships. Klaus resorted to intuition: thinking along with his opponent, listening, intuiting, and patiently pre-empting his pursu-ers' movements. Successful tactics are as much art as science.

Years later, I shared the story with the crew in Canadian subma-rine HMCS *Okanagan* as we visited the site of the sinking and tried to retrace the evasive feints of U-806. Armed with my own recon-struction of U-806's movements, and blueprints of the U-boat, I conducted technical briefings for the off-watch personnel. Overhead during the exercise, one of our aircraft deployed sonobuoys to cap-ture our acoustic signature, while two destroyers played war games against us. We "escaped." Coming up to periscope depth under simulated wartime conditions, I put my eye to the lens and made a quick sweep of the area. I could have been in a time machine, for I quickly discerned among the heavy swells two "enemy" vessels: an old coastal tanker and a steam trawler with its ochre-coloured steadying sail. The exercise reminded me of the critical skill sets that successful submariners must possess in abundance. In the brief moment when the lens breaks surface, you must gain an immediate and comprehensive grasp of the situation. After a quick sighting of two distant destroyers, I concluded my visual sweep, and we dived deeper before heading for Halifax.

ON ONE of my research forays into Germany, I met with Rear-Admiral Eberhard Godt, who had become a legendary figure during the U-boat heydays of the Second World War. For it was he who deployed the subs, determined their mission, examined their war logs and adjudicated their patrols. Deliberately mispronouncing his name as Gott (instead of the correct pronunciation of goat), some submariners referred to him as "God Almighty" (*der liebe Gott*). They did so with a mixture of awe, ire, and admiration, for no one could deny his competence. Having joined the Imperial Navy in 1918, he had served aboard the famous light cruiser SMS *Emden* in 1935, at the time under the command of Captain Karl Dönitz, before switching to the newly formed Submarine Service. During the Spanish Civil War, Godt commanded U-25, a Type A ocean-going sub, in support of General Franco's fascist government. He never lost the U-boat skipper's touch. When Dönitz succeeded Admiral Raeder as head of the navy in 1943, Godt assumed tactical command of all U-boat operations.

We had arranged to meet at the Submarine Memorial (*U-Boot Ehrenmal*) in Möltenort, near Kiel, on the occasion of *Einsatztag* (working party), a regular event in which former submariners and naval officers gather to tend to the memorial and care for its surrounding gardens. On arriving, I found a group of naval veterans dressed in gardening gear, watering flowers and polishing memorial plaques. Meanwhile, a jolly group of wives and widows were "manning" the galley, preparing a communal noon meal. Godt had invited me to join the fellowship for some traditional German fare and conversation. It was here that I met Addi Schnee, one of the most famous of the great U-boat aces. Like Godt, he had fought as a submariner during the Spanish Civil War. During the Battle of the Atlantic, he had sunk twenty-one merchant ships and an auxiliary cruiser, earning himself the Knight's Cross of the Iron Cross with Oak Leaves. Even more famously, he had taken Germany's first operational "complete submersible" type XXI to sea in late April 1945, a couple of weeks before Germany's unconditional surrender. Up to that time, U-boats had in effect been little more than submersible torpedo boats. From now on they would outpace destroyers. Schnee's final foray in the type XXI U-boat signalled the new direction in submarine warfare. Our paths would cross many times during my research. Always professional and correct, Schnee was a gentleman's gentleman, in both cultivation and manner. But on *Einsatztag*, at the U-Boot Monument, he looked every bit the local gardener.

Admiral Eberhard Godt, in contrast, never dressed like a tradesman. At least, not to my knowledge. Already well into his eighties, he wore a trim, finely tailored suit that day, with binoculars hanging around his neck. Playing the eminence grise with grace and charm, he strolled about the grounds while casting a mariner's eye over the proceedings. This being our first encounter, he greeted me with practised formality. Correct but reserved, in naval parlance. But over time, our relationship mellowed and became hearty and collegial. In the short time that I knew him I visited him regularly at his home in Kiel. We enjoyed many convivial moments. At first over coffee, and later over congenial glasses of whisky. At one point, I questioned him about the political climate in the German navy in the 1930s and '40s. Popular wisdom held that up until the attempt on Hitler's life on 20 July 1944, naval officers had been forbidden from joining a political party. Of course, I knew that party membership and political convictions were two different things. Godt's pensive response to my question struck home. Carefully placing his whisky glass on the table, he drew himself up and leaned back into his armchair. "We were all Nazis," he confessed quietly. "All of us." He paused for a thoughtful sip while looking me in the eye. "Until one or the other of us began to see what was behind it all—but by then it was too late." I appreciated his companionable honesty. When he died in 1995 at the age of ninety-five, I felt a considerable loss. Godt had been the last flag officer of the *Kriegsmarine* (German navy under the Nazis).

And it was through him that I became acquainted with Schorsch Meckel, a former chief of naval operational intelligence during the war. He came to hold a special place in my story.

I first met Schorsch at the top of the stairs at the exit to the Hamburg-Altona subway. Dapper and affable, he was holding by way of identification a copy of my *U-Boats against Canada*. With its bright red cover, the book stood out like a beacon among the crowd of passengers spilling out onto the Altona exit. He had just contracted with the publisher E.S. Mittler und Sohn to translate my book into German. It was an auspicious moment. I soon came to know Schorsch as a keen-minded man whose sound grasp of German history and culture was outdone only by his profound understanding of the human condition. He knew and could quote English poetry by heart, especially Wordsworth. Yet he felt out of practice and preferred to converse in German.

My visits to Schorsch and his wife, Hanne, invariably took place at their home, with the three of us seated around their hospitable coffee table. The view through their narrow living room window framed the steeple of Altona's *Friedenskirche* (Church of Peace). The scene could have been from a Dutch Renaissance painting. Built at the end of the nineteenth century and partially destroyed by the Allied bombings of 1944–45, the *Friedenskirche* now serves as a sanctuary for refugees and other marginalized people of Hamburg.

The Meckel's living room projected yet another image of the *heile Welt* that I frequently met on my travels among German veterans: the world once again put right after the desolation of war. During my visits to the Meckels, that view of the church steeple betokened a higher moral calling than conflict and aggressive war. But the horrors of war lived on. Schorsch, in the words of Chaucer, was "a verry parfit, gentle knyght," and Hanne a "mirour of alle curteisy." The virtues that they both reflected were more than mere politeness, as the words of Chaucer might suggest today. "Curteisy," in Chaucerian English, embraces a whole world view, a gracious way of being.

Growing up in the prewar years, Schorsch had witnessed the crippling effects on Germany of the 1919 Treaty of Versailles—the

Diktat of Versailles, as the Germans called it—with its forced impo-
sition of crushing war reparations. These economic and political
burdens had fanned the smoldering fires of nationalism and fascism.
Then too, the *Diktat* had virtually dismantled the German Imperial
Navy (*Reichsmarine*) and forbade the building of large vessels. But
submarines, of course, were small. Some were even as small as 250
tons. Thus, as early as 1932, the Naval Command began drafting
covert plans for the construction of submarines. Schorsch had joined
the very first class of submariners in 1933. By August 1935, he was
in command of a brand new U-3, a 250-ton type IIA coastal submarine. Familiarly referred to as a "canoe" (*Einbaum*), these single-hull
boats were capable of laying mines along British shores, and could
dive to a depth of a hundred metres. When war was declared in the
fall of 1939, Schorsch was commanding a type IIB *Einbaum* in the
North Sea. Rapidly promoted, he eventually served as Staff Officer,
Operational Intelligence, on the staff of Admiral Karl Dönitz. With
the creation of the postwar German Navy (*Bundesmarine*) in 1955,
he served as Germany's naval attaché in Washington, DC.

Schorsch and Hanne formed an impeccable translation team
for the transformation of my book for the German market. Their
meticulously crafted translations ran through successive drafts. I
admired their technique of pondering the context, always choosing
the right nuance and resonance. They were especially good at sens-
ing the syntactical rhythms of each sentence. They kept their eyes
on the target audience. In their hands, my *U-Boats against Canada*
became a German book. I had the good fortune of visiting them on a
couple of occasions to discuss their progress. In writing my book for
a Canadian audience, I had wanted, among other things, to counter
popular gossip and journalistic fantasizing about wartime events.
For that reason, I had on occasion provided too much technical
detail: navigational coordinates, for example, instead of impres-
sionistic descriptions. In the most colourful language, Schorsch
persuaded me to cut such passages and recast them for the German
version. His critiques were always memorable and to the point. His
exhortation "*Kein Schwein will das wissen!*"—"Who the hell wants to

know that?"—became an operating principle in all my later editing and teaching.

I have always regretted that Schorsch did not live to translate my *Count Not the Dead: The Popular Image of the German Submarine,* for it is my best piece of literary history. In his absence, the publisher had fobbed the task off on an inexperienced German student of American literature—with appalling results. Translation is a complex and exacting art. Perhaps none has expressed this better than Peter Mark Roget, in the preface to the first edition of his *University Thesaurus,* published in 1852. This "arduous task," as he put it, involves nothing less than "transfusing, with perfect exactness, the sense of the original, preserving at the same time the style and character of the composition, and reflecting with fidelity, the mind and the spirit of the author..." In every respect, my anonymous German translator was hopelessly out of his depth. Adding insult to injury, the publisher neglected to register the work as a translation from my original English, thus implying that the German was mine. And if that were not enough, and against my advice, the German publisher changed my title to the racier *Myth of the German Submarine Service* (*Der Mythos der deutschen U-Waffe*). The word *Mythos* is a heavily freighted, brooding term in German. It evokes notions of irrational tradition and experience. The German title thereby conjures up tones and inferences more incendiary than my original title. I have never felt so betrayed.

Readers of the German version would not have understood what I had actually written. My story, had it been competently translated, would have exposed them to a version of nautical narratives they would not have seen before. With the exception of salty veterans of naval warfare—and the occasional poet—few German writers had ever taken up the literary theme of the sea. And whenever they did, it was mostly in a romantic vein. Throughout my years of reading German history and studying in archives, I had also been indulging in German novels, memoirs, and pulp-trade hits about the war at sea. My book illustrated the propaganda value of what they had written. It offered an historical account of how *Trivialliteratur,* as the pulp-trade is known in German, both shapes and reflects social and cultural reality. Indeed, I found that such literature not only reflected political culture, but helped create it. Schorsch, for whom I had the greatest respect and admiration, would have done the work justice.

In June 1987, as the former Allied countries were commemorating the Normandy landings of 6 June 1944, I thought of the Meckels' home, with its inspiring view of the *Friedenskirche*, and telephoned them from Victoria. They were having coffee with friends when I called, but with his speaker phone switched on, Schorsch and I chatted about the events that were filling our TV screens. The celebrations marked the final great assault on Fortress Europe. At one point, I expressed regret that no representatives from Germany had been invited to the ceremonies. Whatever significance the Normandy landings may have had in terms of military strategy, I suggested, the operation had launched the inevitable collapse of the Nazi era, with all its evils. All the more reason, I proposed, that representatives of the new, democratic Germany—our trusted NATO partner—should attend. Not so, Schorsch responded. "The Allies and their successors have earned the *right* to celebrate. We have not." His comprehensive grasp of his country's history was always incisive.

ARCHIVAL SWEEPS through Germany during the U-boat phase of my academic career regularly took me to three principal sources: the U-Boot-Archiv at Sylt, and later Altenbruch; the Federal and Military Archives in Freiburg im Breisgau; and the Library of Contemporary History in Stuttgart. I comfortably settled into each of them. Horst Bredow even allowed me to live in the guest room of the Archives during my frequent visits to Germany. Alone at night amidst the memorabilia and uniformed mannequins of past eras, it could be spooky.

Where the U-Boat Archiv was run by non-professional volunteers and was privately funded, the Freiburg archives were federal, and the Stuttgart library was administered under the State of Baden-Württemberg. Each bore the stamp of its leadership: Bredow's obsessively driven personal style in the north, and the professional academic style of the archives in the south. The latter were supervised by Dr. Manfred Messerschmidt, the senior historian in Freiburg from 1977 to 1988, and Dr. Jürgen Rohwer, director of the Library of Contemporary History from 1959 to 1989. Productive scholars, both Messerschmidt and Rohwer published internationally recognized standard works of military and naval history. In Freiburg, for example, you could find virtually all of Germany's military and naval records from 1867 to the present, and have ready access to specialists for consultation. It was here that I studied all the official papers bearing upon the conduct of the Battle of the Atlantic. At the end of an exhausting ten-hour day of intense sleuthing I would stroll to the quaint Hotel Schiff in the quiet village of St. Georgen. A couple of pints and a hearty dinner never failed to restore me. Except for the evening's culinary indulgence, I led an ascetic existence.

Stuttgart drew me not only for its contemporary records but for the opportunity to visit my old friend Jürgen Rohwer. His encyclopedic knowledge of the history of warfare, coupled with his voracious appetite for new research and a profound human empathy, made for challenging conversations. Admittedly, I always found myself on the learning end of any of our discussions. Whether meeting me on his home turf or at the international conferences we attended in Helsinki, St. Petersburg, Flensburg, or Athens, he was a hearty colleague and companion. Always his own man, he was colourful. Himself a naval veteran, he enjoyed his own tacit jokes about military dress codes. Professorially dressed in sartorial splendour—loud tie and socks, wrinkled slacks, and casual lounge jacket—he stood out among the blue naval uniforms and straight-cut business suits worn by the naval college set. His quiet sense of humour could break into infectious laughter when lampooning human folly. Not surprisingly, his contacts with the leading pacesetters in his country were many and varied. He referred to them as *Akteure* ("players") on the stage of history. Ultimately, his wide network of players led to his acquiring the private papers of Grand Admiral Dönitz for the Library of Contemporary History.

My hearty and collegial relations with the many U-boat men whom I came to know were overshadowed by the course of German history leading up to the Nuremberg Trials. As members of Germany's wartime naval forces—and hence instruments of the Nazi state—these men had fought on the wrong side of history. Yet, as Commander Craig Campbell once confessed, one's choice of sides depended upon fate; it hung, he argued, upon the roll of some cosmic dice that determined where one was born and how one had been raised. Craig often said that had he himself been born and raised in Germany, he, too, would have found himself thrust into the German navy. His words underscored the stark tragedy of war. In some perverse sense, war—even a war of aggression—can appear to young recruits as a moral highroad.

Throughout the 1960s and 1970s the words Holocaust and Shoah—the Hebrew word for utter devastation—came into common parlance in Germany. Each of these words pointed to the traumatic past through which German veterans had lived. Arguably, their sea-going warfare had kept them far from land, and away from the evils of concentration camps and territorial conquest. Their experience at sea had been transformative and bonding, and marked at times by flashes of gallantry, just as it had been for Canadian sailors. Combatants on both sides had been given responsibilities beyond their years, and had risen to the challenge. The average age of a German submarine commander on combat patrol was twenty-eight; after 1943, due to harrowing losses, the average age dropped to twenty-three. Some skippers had been as young as twenty years old—the average age of Spitfire pilots during the Battle of Britain.

On one occasion, Jürgen and I were discussing the Germans' preparations for the Allies' Normandy landing of June 1944. In anticipation of the inevitable invasion of Europe, Hitler had put Field Marshall Erwin Rommel in command of what became known as the Western Wall, the whole west coast of Europe, from the Baltic to Southern France. Known in both the Axis and Allied camps as "The Desert Fox," Rommel had earned a reputation for detailed planning and decisive action. His naval advisor in Normandy was

Admiral Friedrich Ruge, an officer of depth and experience. Normandy buckled under the full brunt the Allied invasion on 6 June
1944. The Allied victory is a matter of public record. So, too, the
downward spiral of events on the German side that followed. On
20 July 1944, military members of the Resistance failed in their
attempt to assassinate Hitler and were brutally executed. Then,
on 14 October 1944, the Nazi leadership, suspecting that Rommel
had aligned himself with the German Resistance, forced Rommel
to commit suicide. It was a cynical and sadistic act of dictatorial
power. Rommel was fifty-two years old. His naval advisor, Admiral
Friedrich Ruge, escaped the clandestine carnage and lived to teach
at Tübingen University and write his memoirs. To my deep gratitude,
Jürgen arranged for me to meet the admiral at his home in Tübingen,
an hour and a half by bus from Stuttgart.

Ruge was an extraordinary individual. He had capped his service in three successive German navies between 1914 and 1945
by serving with distinction as the senior admiral of the fourth, the
postwar *Bundesmarine*, from which he retired on 21 July 1961. The
previous day, 20 July, had been historically significant. It marked
the seventeenth anniversary of the assassination attempt on Hitler's
life. Throughout the carnage of the Second World War, Ruge had
met several of the key figures of German military history—big Nazis
like Hitler, Himmler, and Heydrich. He had also known Admiral
Wilhelm Canaris, Chief of Intelligence, who served as a double
agent while siding with the Resistance. Ever the gentleman and
scholar, Friedrich Ruge received me as a guest in his home. Over
sherry, we staked out our common interests before my hosting him
for luncheon at a local *Wirtshaus*.

We had only just met, yet we found ourselves comfortably
addressing a number of ethical issues that had woven their way
through his recent autobiography, *In Vier Marinen* (*In Four Navies*),
published in 1979. He distinguished two key strands in the weave:
the military ethic of duty (*Pflicht*) and the comradely continuity of
Germany's successive navies. The key principle was "duration in
constant change"—*Dauer im Wechsel*—the title of a philosophical

poem by Goethe. Against that background, another force emerged in our conversation: the cancerous growth of Nazism throughout German society during the 1930s and '40s, and how it transformed peoples' sensibilities and perspectives. These threads impinged upon the ultimate notion of what it meant to take the "sacred oath" required of all military personnel during wartime, and later of all civil servants and academics. The oath professed unconditional obedience, not merely to the office of the imperial chancellor, which Hitler held, but to the very person of Hitler himself. In taking the oath, one swore to lay down one's life "as a brave soldier" for him alone. Some regarded the oath as irrevocable, even if you had sworn allegiance to the Devil himself. This wasn't just a German phenomenon, Schorsch Meckel had reminded me. He readily cited the Romantic poet William Wordsworth, for whom duty was the "Stern Daughter of the Voice of God." Yet for others, Schorsch among them, Hitler's immoral and evil actions had nullified the oath.

Ultimately, it was rarely a question of either-or. Helmut Schmidt, West Germany's sixth head of state from 1974 to 1982, and perhaps the most gifted chancellor up to that time, addressed the issue after his retirement. He had served in a "Flak" anti-aircraft battalion of the German Air Force from 1937 to 1945. Like many U-boat men, he regarded his military service as an oasis, free from Nazi ideology. During the war years, he rejected the myth-mongering of Nazi writers and quietly coveted Remarque's pacifist novel *All Quiet on the Western Front*. Nazi officialdom, by contrast, regarded Remarque's work as defeatist and "un-German." Against this background, Schmidt dismissed the question of the oath as essentially irrelevant to the far greater moral issue. You can never "master" the past or even "come to terms" with it, as the then-current term *Vergangenheitsbewältigung* suggested. The past, he insisted, cannot be overcome. Germans must rather examine and evaluate the past in order to draw factual and moral conclusions that could set the nation on a moral track into the future. As I moved among my German veterans, I found that precisely this kind of soul work was well underway.

Friedrich Ruge recognized the motivations on all sides of the argument. In considering the complexities of ethical ambiguity, he argued in his retirement address of 21 July 1961 that it should be possible to serve in the armed forces of a dictatorship—as Field Marshal Rommel had done—without sharing in the state's moral depravity. It all depended, he argued, upon a soldier's being guided by noble motives for the good of his people, and not by private ambition. Admiral Ruge understood these difficulties and complexities, for he had lived them himself—and had reflected on them. As I climbed back aboard the bus to Stuttgart, this modest and thoughtful grand old man of German naval history waved me off. I knew I had touched greatness. He died quietly in 1985 at the age of 91.

POLITICS AND ethics were far from my mind as I linked up with the Federal German Navy's high-speed Tiger-class attack-boat crew at their squadron's home base in Olpenitz, in Northern Germany. I was joining a group of German naval veterans aboard the small, super-charged craft in order to experience the tactical exercises of a modern naval force. Designed for surface-to-surface naval combat on the North Sea and the Baltic, these 265-ton vessels carried four Exocet missiles and a wide range of electronic warfare equipment. Today, Germany's new navy was exercising its defence of the Baltic on behalf of NATO. The growling of engines revving up gave us a foretaste of the thirty-six-knot chase that was to come. Twisting and yawing in close flotilla formations, the boats in their modern-day combat exercises reminded me that this was seafaring with a compelling, visceral edge. It was a young man's game. It always had been.

As our engines roared, I thought of the war years from 1939 to 1945, and the coastal combat between German and Allied torpedo boats in the English Channel and in the Mediterranean. With their high-octane, fifteen-hundred-horsepower gasoline engines—the motor torpedo boats (MTBs) had three, and Fairmiles four—they could attain speeds of forty knots. Variously armed with torpedo tubes, pom-pom guns, depth charges, Oerlikons, and machine guns, they were the "stallions of the sea." Matched against the German

Schnellboote (the Allies called them E-boats, or Enemy-boats) these were the lively warhorses driven by the young of both warring sides. Close-quarters action along the coasts of Holland, Belgium, and France proved to be dangerous adventures. The sea and the ships shaped not only the identity of these young sailors, but the mythologies of their respective naval forces. The thrilling lore of both sides had formed part of my own naval training in the 1950s. Now, as I headed out into the Baltic under the competent leadership of a new generation of German sailors, I felt uplift and camaraderie. For at the end of the day, we shared a common naval culture—though with a very different history.

Seafaring under such battle conditions sharpens a sailor's mind to the exigencies of war. Life at sea can be both intense and short. Young sailors quickly realize that their lives will be irrevocably changed by the experience. One such mariner was Gordon Stead, a naval reservist from Vancouver. He had commanded a motor launch, or ML, at the height of the Siege of Malta, in 1942, one of the most crucial theatres of war. Like other boats of its class, the ML was a floating powder keg, for it carried 22,700 litres (5,000 gallons) of high-octane fuel. Stead meditated on this in his 1988 memoir *A Leaf Upon the Sea*. The sea, he writes, "imposes terms that are quite different from those permitted by the land. Mariners must first learn to live with every mood and hazard of a temperamental element. The menace of the enemy is just one more reason for being sharp. When the enemy appears, he comes in small packages." And then, with that pragmatism common among sailors, he adds, "the object of the exercise is to put the threatening package out of action. Once that is done, the people from the package become survivors to be rescued, since they no longer bear upon the outcome." Stead's memoir quietly records the "lengthy periods of tension, sudden shocks of fear, and instants of high excitement—albeit tempered by the joys and challenges of being at sea." But, he adds, "they do not inflame the blood." With compassionate realism, he recalls how "there can be pain and suffering, but no vast scenes of carnage. And, ordinarily, there is no call for hatred." Such is the fellowship of the sea, even in time of war. German sailors understood that as well.

Ghosts of the past surround me as I write these lines. I am reminded of the youth of both sides, and their lusty singing of nostalgic songs and barroom ballads. All of them full of bravado and adventure, gallows humour and theatrical joie-de-vivre. The Germans, for example, had their "Torpedo-Boat Song," with all the prerequisites of youthful derring-do and swagger. Despite its clichés, sailors sang it through two world wars. Standing on guard in peacetime "like a tamed dragon," they answer the clarion call of the trumpets of war. They bid a "final farewell" to loved ones at home, and dash "full steam ahead into the clamour of battle." Then, with the enemy in sight, they "knife through the waves like the Sea God's stallions." The song offers a hackneyed cornucopia of devil-may-care dash, death-wish, and danger. So, too, the Canadians' "Maple Leaf Squadron" captures the pathos and the pity of war: "So we're off to the wars where there's death in the making, / Survival or sacrifice, fortune or fame; / And our eyes go ahead to the next wave that's breaking, / It's the luck that's before us adds zest to the game." My generation of naval trainees was likely the last to sing these museum pieces. Germans had stopped singing theirs by 1945. The silence on both sides augurs well for us all.

9

MAKING
THINGS RIGHT

Nourish your soul with just a drop of
water, and it'll net you a river in return.

DONNA MORRISSEY, *Pluck*

THE SYRIAN desert stretched out dry and barren below the ancient monastery of Deir Mar Musa al-Habashi, some eighty kilometres (fifty miles) north of Damascus, Syria. After a long climb along the narrow, winding path up the cliff face, we had reached the upper walls, where we were greeted by Father Paolo Dall'Oglio, a quietly charismatic Italian Jesuit. Far beneath us, a dust storm was beginning to swirl. We looked down as twisting pillars of sand cast a pall over the bleak landscape. The hot afternoon suddenly grew chill. Yet, like the fulfilment of some ancient Biblical promise, the penetrating desert heat returned as soon as the storm subsided. The deep valley below us conjured up the harsh and long-past world of the prophets Isaiah, Jeremiah, and Amos. It underscored the dangers awaiting those who challenge the wilderness. It evoked the valley of dry bones in the Book of Ezekiel, and the eternal question confronting the prophet in that story: "Mortal, can these bones live?"

First known as the monastery of St. Moses the Abyssinian, Mar Musa has dominated this austere scene since the middle of the sixth century. Among the oldest in Syria, it was one of over 150 monasteries throughout the ancient Byzantine Empire that once dotted the Holy Lands of present-day Syria, Jordan, Palestine, Israel, and Turkey. Situated in harsh and unforgiving terrain, these monasteries

offered a haven to ascetic monks. Just why they would choose to
live in such austere circumstances raises many complex issues. But
we find a recurrent theme in the writing of the most famous of these
ascetics, the itinerant John Moschos, who died in 619 BCE. As his
now classic work *The Spiritual Meadow* explains, "by living in utter
simplicity and holiness, the monks were returning to the conditions
of the Garden of Eden, in harmony with both the natural world and
its Creator." Just as the work of Moschos guided the travel writer
William Dalrymple during his journeys in 1994, so Dalrymple's brilliant travelogue *From the Holy Mountain* enriched our reflections in
2001. Most of the monasteries described by these writers have lain
in ruins for centuries.

Mar Musa, however, has weathered waves of decay and human
intransigence, only to arise again in response to visions of peace and
then face violence and neglect once more. For years, the site had lain
in ruins until Paolo brought new life to it in the 1980s and founded a
monastic community dedicated to Muslim-Christian dialogue. Born
in 1954, the year I had joined the navy to learn how to wage war,
Paolo believed that the life of dialogue meant far more than conversations about personal points of view. Dialogue was about what
Judaic philosopher Martin Buber had taught about "I-Thou" relationships and their potential for reconciliation and peace. As Paolo
intuited it, dialogue meant seeing in the "Others" not objects to be
feared or despised, but fellow human beings, in all their vulnerability, needs, and strength. Paulo's openness to other religions was
existential; an immediacy of living that engaged the whole human
being. He recognized that principles like dialogue, love, openness,
and justice transcended mere personal preference. Indeed, he himself experienced what he called "double belonging." As the title of
his book suggests, it was possible to be in love with Islam and still
believe in Jesus. His later years saw him steeped in Sufism, a mystical
tradition of Islam that nourished a spirituality of inwardness. People
from different faith traditions found Mar Musa an oasis of peace.

It was April 2001, and I had come to Syria with a small group of
scholars and like-minded friends expressly to meet him. Led by my

colleague, Dr. Erica Dodd, an Arabic-speaking scholar of Islamic art, we had come not only to experience the monastic community, but to examine its magnificent frescoes and wall inscriptions in Arabic, Syriac, and Greek, which she had been studying. In this atmosphere of trust, Paolo nurtured a vision of a spiritual life engaged in the pursuit of peace. Or he did so, that is, until his kidnapping and murder in July 2013 at the hands of Islamic State insurgents. Some say he walked to his death in the jihadi-controlled area of Raqqa, firm in the belief that ISIS would engage in rational discourse. His murderers in ISIS had seen him as "the enemy Other," an object to be hated and scorned. I still see that embattled retreat alone, on a cliff in the desert. I have never been back there since, and perhaps never will. Yet hope, however improbable, remains.

As I write these lines, Mar Musa rises above a shattered Syria, a suffering people, a desolate wasteland. Since 2011, an ugly, multi-factioned civil war has taken a half-million lives and forcibly displaced more than half the country's population. As always, these barren statistics don't tell the whole story. Figures tend to dehumanize the real people behind them. I remember fondly the people I met in Syria: the roadside cobbler who mended my shoes and offered me tea while he worked in the early morning sun; the mother and young daughter at the dusty street corner who showed me how to bake flatbread in their earthenware *tannur*; the baker in a little back street who gave us bread for our journey, but would not accept payment; and the little lad who dashed from his squalid mud hut to wave cheerily at us as our van rumbled across the trackless, rock-strewn desert that was his home. Over them hovers the memory of Father Paolo, a victim of ISIS and the cult of terror.

So, I wonder: is Mar Musa, with its vision of peace and its practical mission of dialogue merely a vestige of the past? Is the monastery no more than a cry from Ezekiel echoing down the years since the sixth century BCE? Or is it a signpost for people of goodwill today? Behind such reflections, I hear the insistent rhythms of the old 1930s gospel spiritual "Dem Bones," that took up the story of Ezekiel when he visits the valley of dry bones and prophesies that they will live again.

The composers gave it a modern, jazz-driven beat: "Dem bones, dem bones gonna walk around ... Now hear the word of the Lord!" As I trod the Syrian desert, the extraordinary assertion that restoration and recovery are possible undergirded my thoughts about justice. I had encountered broken worlds, had witnessed shattered lives and unhinged relationships. I had recognized the potential for repair and reconstruction, even after prolonged violence and long years of hurt. I had recognized the human need for making things right and overcoming the burdens of wrong. By 2000, many threads had come together for me, including the real message about renewal and criminal justice, to which "Dem Bones" seemed to point.

It was about a year before my formal retirement from the University of Victoria in 2001. I was serving as acting director of the Centre for Studies in Religion and Society and had just received an invitation for the centre to join a Vancouver-based initiative entitled "Satisfying Justice." The catchy title intrigued me. Was it a question of satisfying the terms of some abstract notion of justice? Or was it rather about seeking a form of justice in which all the stakeholders—victims, offenders, the judiciary, and society itself—could find satisfaction? And what did it all have to do with religion? The fact that the committee was led by a Mennonite reassured me of the potential for productive interfaces between our research centre and the wider community, both secular and religious.

By that time, the CSRS, as we called our centre, had been running for almost ten years. Our research explored how, in a post-religious age, religious traditions and theological insights continue to shape human reality and experience. The tremendous creative energy which religious traditions had released—for good or ill—was a matter of historical record. As I prepared for my new research relationships, I faced a steep learning curve. The concept of restorative justice was new for me. Its proponents were putting forth an alternative justice paradigm: that crime is not so much an offence against the state and its legal statutes as it is a violation of people and relationships, a disruption of the peace of community. Like a photographer, we had to change the lenses through which we viewed our complex world. That's precisely what Howard Zehr of Eastern Mennonite University challenged us to do in his groundbreaking book *Changing Lenses: A New Focus for Crime and Justice*. An excellent portrait photographer, he had also published two collections of portraits, *Doing Life: Reflections of Men and Women Serving Life Sentences* and *Transcending: Reflections of Crime Victims*, that reflect on the human dimensions of suffering, spirituality, and transcendence.

Anxious to root my research in experience, I decided to go to jail. Like most citizens, I had little notion of the penitentiary system. Images of prisons from the media and movies had influenced me deeply. I gleaned my first impressions of prison while still a schoolboy in Marpole, when, especially on foggy days, the spectral image of Okalla Prison sometimes haunted our district. First opened upriver in New Westminster in 1912, it gained a reputation as one of the more notorious of Canada's correctional institutions. All executions in the province took place behind its secretive grey walls, while local newspapers and the popular imagination stoked stories about violent criminals and cruel hangings. Okalla stood for seventy-nine years as a stark reminder of the retributive approach to criminal justice. Amidst this lore, I nursed a naive hunch of one day becoming a prison chaplain, though I hadn't the slighted idea what that might entail. Sunday school ideas of what the church called "cure of souls" had taken root. We also learned that visiting those in prison was central to doing the Lord's work. Now, as I prepared to join the Restorative Justice Coalition at William Head prison, near Victoria, I realized that such inadequate and distorted images would soon be changed radically.

Founded by lawyer David Hough, the William Head Coalition consisted of inmates and local citizens jocularly known as outmates. At each gathering, the group explored new understandings of how the restorative principles of accountability and "making things right" could mesh with established practices in criminal law. In fact, as Judge Barry Stuart had frequently affirmed, they can and do so seamlessly. As chief judge of the Territorial Court of the Yukon, he had found that restorative justice, and especially principles drawn from Indigenous practices such as peacemaking circles, could together meet all justice objectives. They could also create collaborative partnerships that in turn healed trauma and helped build safe communities. Indeed, the principles and processes of restorative justice could actually transform people, their passions, and their potential. Like others, I eventually preferred to call the process transformative justice.

The Restorative Justice Coalition of William Head held its first meeting behind the prison's barbed wire in July 1998. Inmates and outmates usually met in the chapel. In time, I enjoyed the privilege of meeting privately with individual inmates like the late James Henry, whom I had befriended. An Afro-Canadian "lifer" from Montreal, he had been both victim and victimizer. Bullied and marginalized by the predominant white culture, he responded with violence. Years later, he began to regain his self-esteem in our coalition circles. By sitting in a circle after the fashion of Indigenous styles of community healing, we modelled the value and equality of each member. We practised attentive listening and respectful speaking. Most of the inmates had struggled through an often-violent life on the assumption that you only got respect by instilling fear in others. Now, given a safe place in which to explore their potential, they gradually came to understand that you gain respect by means of your moral stature—by valuing differences. Here, the dialogical principle came into play: seeing in "the other" a fully human person. We chose different themes for each week. Inmates themselves regularly suggested themes and took turns acting as moderator. What is justice? How do you manage anger? What would you want to say to your victim if he or she were here? It was astonishing to see how easily both inmates and outmates warmed up to accepting each other despite the bumps, warts, and past histories.

Over time we found ourselves bonding into a community. Inmates began to share dimensions of their lives they had long kept hidden. They felt free to laugh, and to weep. Whatever we shared, we held in trust. Viewed from the outside, we may have seemed a strange community: former drug dealers and bank robbers, muggers, and murderers engaging in sensitive discussions with business people, bureaucrats, teachers, and tradespeople. But our community was genuine. We based it on mutual concern, shared vulnerability, and, over time, respect and affection.

As my experience broadened, I began sharing in Sweat Lodge ceremonies led by the prison's Anishinaabe spiritual advisor, Lloyd Haarala. I found the Sweat Lodge a powerful rite. For Indigenous inmates it offered a spiritual homecoming. For the non-Indigenous, a fresh path toward an inner life. As a spiritual ritual for cleansing body, mind, and soul, it bore none of the cultural baggage of the mainstream religions. Set apart on the prison grounds close to the sea, the lodge itself looked like a domed Lapland tent. It consisted of deerskin stretched over bent saplings, in the centre of which lay a firepit. Outside, a fire-keeper heated stones in a wood fire. Silently, and virtually naked, we took our places around the firepit and sat shoulder to shoulder with our "brothers" in complete darkness. Coping with the intense heat and the close proximity of others in the confined space, we were utterly alone with our thoughts. Throughout the sweat, Lloyd spoke about the sacredness of life, about the great work of the Creator in bringing all things into being. He talked about the interrelatedness of things, animate and inanimate alike. Knowing each of us well, the Elder asked about our sorrows and needs, about our demons. He asked why we were making the journey into this sacred place. The Elder sought honesty and urged us to speak from the heart.

Being hunkered down almost naked in a circle reduced us— whatever our past or our station in life—to our basic humanity. The experience was transformative and affirming. It helped inmates and outmates alike to work their way toward a healing future. Nor would I myself be the same after the experience. After what seemed like an eternity, the doorkeeper opened the flap that separated us from the outside world. We slipped out quietly for a few minutes to inhale deeply the fresh, cool air before returning for the next round of teaching and meditation. Tragically, Canada's Indian Act of 1876 had forbidden the curative practice of Sweat Lodges. Lifting the ban in 1951 had arguably helped Indigenous People to take a significant step on the elusive road to recovery.

Our social engagement with one another during meetings of the Restorative Justice Coalition spawned a buzzword among the inmates. They wanted to "give back to society." The question was how? Eventually our circle hit upon the idea of organizing a public conference within William Head prison. No one had ever done this inside a prison before. But we did, in November 1999. With the ready engagement of staff—the security issues alone were huge—we planned the program and catering, and invited speakers and some ·sixty guests to spend a day with us in prison. Afterward, we edited and published the proceedings. By inviting the public to participate in our conference we had made a unique contribution to Canadian penal history.

This first of what would become a series of annual conferences began by tackling two big questions: What is the role of forgiveness in healing the harms caused by crime, and how do we support the reintegration of inmates into society after their release from prison? We invited four experts to address the issues: two victims from the outside community and two lifers who had committed murder. What better experts, we thought, than those who had actually suffered the pain of criminal acts. After each presentation, small groups composed of insiders and outsiders discussed the issues and reported the results of their deliberations to the plenary. Major threads like compassion, forgiveness, healing, and repentance worked their way into the weave. The latter—repentance—posed a challenge. It meant nothing less than a radical change of direction in life. This in turn pointed toward new possibilities for changing the way we do the justice business.

The conference at William Head Institute showed us the potential for the transformation of persons, relationships, and communities, and indeed of social structures. And so it was for every annual conference that followed. During one these, our guest speaker, Judge Barry Stuart, shared his experience of peacemaking circles. Always personable and low key, he stood amidst the inmates in his jeans, runners, and T-shirt, and took his audience by surprise. Equally surprising was the critical response of lifer James Henry, the only Afro-Canadian in the prison. I had been mentoring James in how to respond to a speaker's remarks in a perceptive and measured manner. So it was that James replied to Barry. With a twinkle in his eye, my lifer protegé and friend set the stage: "Well, your Honour—Barry. I've stood before many judges before. But I have never, ever told a single one of them exactly what I think." To which Barry replied, "Well, then, friend James, here's your chance. Have at me." I knew our restorative approach was on the right track when I witnessed the warm-hearted and insightful repartee between the two men. I know it marked a highlight in James's tough life.

I had long felt the importance of socialization in the prison context. Keeping prisoners cooped up does nothing for their eventual reintegration into the day-to-day society beyond the prison walls. A special opportunity arose through my membership in Victoria's Christ Church Cathedral. The parishioners had been inspired by an idea proposed by Sister Judi Morin, the prison's Roman Catholic chaplain, to build a labyrinth on the cathedral's south lawn, where she enjoyed practising her Tai Chi. I took the idea to the inmates and met with an immediate response: "Why not make it a joint parish-prison enterprise?" And so the project began. We first created a joint planning team from the two populations. Its initial task was to design the labyrinth and develop criteria for its size, materials, construction, and the skill sets required. Everyone needed to understand the concept, for a labyrinth is not a maze where you can get lost, as the popular mind (and some dictionaries) would have it. Indeed, a labyrinth is a contemplative path of pre-Greek origin that combines two concepts: the circle and the spiral. Laid out on the ground, it represents a meditative, prayerful journey in search of inner peace and wholeness. On reaching the centre, the walker returns along the same contemplative path to re-engage with the external world.

The symbolism of the labyrinth struck the inmates as huge. They took up the challenge. For here, they could participate in an ancient art form whose structure afforded a deeply personal and unfettered approach toward integrity. Parishioners then joined them in the prison for several design sessions. Together, these diverse groups became partners in a community initiative that ultimately included staff and equipment from the City of Victoria.

The construction took place through the spring of 2000. Inmates on escorted day passes and those in the work-release program worked alongside parishioners on the construction site. The interpersonal dynamics on the site revealed close teamwork and companionship. In fact, as one of the inmates observed, passersby casting an eye over the work crew could never tell who was in jail and who was not. They simply saw a happy group of people engaged in a creative enterprise. Our video documentary *Journey to the Centre* shows as much. All participants celebrated the labyrinth's completion by walking the contemplative path together.

But how can you give back to society if you have never ever taken anything away? How do you deal with forgiveness if you have done nothing that needs forgiving? And how do you reconcile with a society you have never wronged? These were the tough questions that "A.J." invariably asked. He had found the weak link in the restorative justice movement's argument about the possibility of making things right. We struggled with our answers. An articulate Anishinaabe, Allan J. Woodhouse had been jailed for murder in 1974 and for decades had stoically maintained his innocence. Though some of us at first suspected him of denial, he gained our trust and respect, and we began to understand. We recognized his controlled, slow-burning anger just beneath the surface. We witnessed his dignity in defeat and admired his compassion for the struggling underdog. Prison, he argued, was "a complete waste of time." A man of upright bearing and logical persuasion, he had schooled himself in the law. We needed a person like A.J. in our midst if we were to remain honest and on track. While his forthright arguments led us to suspect his innocence, Canada's judicial system continually crushed his hope for a meaningful review. The authorities twice rescinded his application for parole. Yet both he and Innocence Canada (an advocacy group for the wrongly accused) persisted.

His great day finally came, years later. On 18 July 2023, Chief Justice Glenn Joyal of the Court of King's Bench, Winnipeg, declared A.J. and his co-accused, Brian Anderson, innocent, and acquitted them both. Almost fifty years had passed since their convictions as murderers. In giving his decision, Judge Joyal said, "your stories are stories of courage and resilience." According to Manitoba's Attorney General, the men had been victims of a miscarriage of justice triggered and sustained by the systemic racism against Indigenous People that permeated all levels of our legal system, from police to investigators and prosecutors, and to the Correctional Service of Canada. As the Crown prosecutor put it when the judge announced the acquittal, "our justice system failed."

Today, A.J. lives on modest means, while officialdom argues about meaningful compensation. But as the Attorney General confessed in his apology to the two men, there is "nothing that can be said that will bring back the years of lost freedom or the time away from family and friends." While the acquittal marks A.J.'s first steps to freedom and reconciliation, it also marks the re-victimization of the family of Ting Fong Chan, who was murdered in 1973. The Attorney General expressed it well: "This miscarriage of justice compounds the suffering of the Chan family as well, and as Attorney General, I regret and recognize this hardship." For half a century the Chan family had believed that justice was being done, but it was not.

I am glad to have known A.J. during those days at William Head and delight in being able to meet him now on the outside. But I look back upon them with the deepest regret, for I never really understood the depths of his anguish, frustration, and sorrow. Nobody can restore the freedom that was so cruelly taken from him. Yet, as I told him after his acquittal, I hope that all those who wronged him—governments, the judiciary, and the Correctional Service of Canada—now do their utmost to make things right by recompensing him to the full. Indeed, I expressed hope that the individuals who had personally wronged him would find the moral courage to confess their faults and reach out to him in reconciliation. That would mark society's first steps toward restorative justice. It was now up to society to give back to those it had victimized.

STORIES OF Canada's residential schools permeated our "in-circle" gatherings. Indigenous inmates recalled their harrowing experiences of being taken from their families and subjected to years of abuse. Many of them blamed the "white man's system" for their ruined lives. Yet, bit by bit, we came to grasp what had really happened under the colonial regime. We looked forward to the work of the Truth and Reconciliation Commission and welcomed its multivolume report in 2015. It had been seven years in the making. In this context, I met Charles August, a member of the Nuu-chah-nulth First Nation in Ahousaht, who was then serving time. We first crossed paths in a prison healing circle, where we had shared with each other our stories, our hopes, and our fears. Often in these sessions, our Indigenous spiritual leader Lloyd Haarala would lead us in the wisdom of his Anishinaabeg People, while the prison chaplain Judi Morin, of the Sisters of St. Anne, led us in the wisdom of her faith, and mine. Interfaith dialogue—listening to the voices of others—lay at the heart of the process.

In his gentle way, Charles August shaped my experience of restorative processes. Torn from his family at the age of seven, he had been psychologically and sexually abused. Released from residential school at the age of fourteen, he had left as a frightened, bewildered, and angry lad. His path was not unusual. Like others, his hurt, anger, and loss of identity led to conflict with the law and repeatedly landed him in prison. I tried to foster Charles's well-being, especially when he faced difficulties. On hearing one day that he had landed in solitary, I rushed to William Head prison and was allowed to visit him. (Solitary confinement ended officially on 30 November 2019, though the media continues to report its use under other names.) Solitary is a lonely, soul-destroying experience that can break an inmate. But once released back "into the population," as inmates put it, Chuck, as we affectionately called him, set himself a project that pulled him out of his despair. He spent the rest of his time in prison becoming a traditional Nuu-chah-nulth wood carver.

I would often see an inspired Chuck working on his Moon Mask project. I saw how he shaped and loved the mask, ever deepening its expression of profound sorrow. I watched him nurture it into being. He gave it that special living quality that only a fine work of art can express. I came to realize that, in expressing both meditative sadness and indwelling hope, Chuck had created an interior self-portrait. Then came a prison Potlatch, complete with the arrival of families, a ceremonial feast, and smudging, songs, and stories. Once forbidden by Canadian governments bent on destroying Indigenous cultures, the ceremony was being celebrated in the most unusual of places—in a prison, behind barbed wire. During the celebration, Chuck had held his carving closely in his arms. Then he did something unexpected, extraordinary, and generous: he invited me to join him in front of the Potlatch, where he presented me with the mask. That gracious act taught me much. It revealed his people's rich tradition of gift giving. For among his people, a gift establishes a relationship. It says to the recipient that this object that is mine is now yours; but it's still mine, just as it remains yours. We are linked by affection, respect, and good will.

Chuck's masterful carving watched over me and my family in our home. That's how Indigenous lore would put it. The Moon Mask would grace the walls of my study for many years, while Chuck and I went our separate ways and eventually lost contact. The mask constantly reminded me of a man who had struggled against enormous odds, and of the strength of Indigenous spirituality and trust. Yet I knew that the artwork was mine only to hold for a while. I was its caretaker and nothing more. I had to find him and return it. Twenty years after the Potlatch and Chuck's release into an independent life, I managed to trace him through his people on Flores Island, off the west coast of Vancouver Island. Our telephone conversation crackled with the joy of re-encounter. The Moon Mask was going home, into the hands of the gifted artist who had made it.

Our Feast of Restoration ought to have taken place immediately. But the COVID-19 virus intervened, and we had to wait a year, until July 2021. Meanwhile, horrific discoveries at former residential schools had cast another shadow over our plans. Scarcely two weeks earlier, the Tk'emlúps te Secwépemc Nation near Kamloops,

BC, had located the suspected unmarked graves of 215 children on the grounds of the former Kamloops Residential School. Similar discoveries quickly followed at sites in British Columbia and Saskatchewan. New stories of residential school traumas filled the news and led to the Orange Shirt Movement proclaiming "Every Child Matters." When the day finally came, we set out for our reunion with Chuck. At every kilometre along the road from the old growth forest at Cathedral Grove in MacMillan Provincial Park to Chuck's home in Port Alberni, an orange T-shirt hung from the trees.

In the best of all possible worlds, we would have marked our Feast of Restoration in the Port Alberni Native Friendship Centre. We would have burned Sweet Grass, offered tobacco, smudged, and sung songs. But it was now serving as a COVID-19 vaccination unit. At Chuck's suggestion, we went to a local family restaurant, where the four of us, Chuck, Lorna, Anita, and I, squeezed into a booth and ordered his favourite meal: thick mushroom omelettes with heaping hash browns followed by creamy cheesecake and rounds of coffee. A feast! The largely non-Indigenous patrons must have found us a culturally odd foursome. Their glances suggested as much. But we didn't care, for we were doing soul work. Our meal finished, we presented the Moon Mask to Chuck in a moment of tearful, hushed rejoicing. And then the stories began.

Chuck again spoke of his seven years in residential school, the abuse, and his feelings of loneliness and worthlessness. He spoke of prison and recounted his healing, his happy involvement in the Friendship Centre, and how he now visited local schools to recount his experiences. He had shown great courage in opening up his world to others. For my part, I told the story of his carving the mask and what he and his artwork had meant to me. As I spoke, both he and Lorna wept—and smiled. I ended the story I had written for the occasion with these words: "Your mask has come home to you, my brother. Thank you for your precious gift, which I now place into your hands. May the Creator watch over you and your people. Always." We were both at peace. In the language of restorative justice, we had made things right. Albert Schweitzer once said that when you reach "that point in life where your talent meets the needs of the world, that is where God wants you to be." If that is so, then this chapter of my life marked a pinnacle.

HAVING LIVED inside the restorative justice model, it was time to press on with scholarly investigation into the spiritual roots of restorative justice. I began by inviting a diverse group of religious scholars to prepare papers examining how the religions they studied related to criminal justice. I asked them to address the issue in terms of texts, traditions, and current practices. In what ways, I asked them, could their faith traditions contribute toward healing the harms caused by crime? I specifically chose scholars who had not yet examined those relationships and practices.

While the scholars wrote, I approached experts in the criminal justice system—police, members of the judiciary, inmates, and parolees among them—to critique the final papers. What better experts, I thought again, than those who had felt the pain. With a large research grant from the Social Science and Humanities Research Council of Canada, I hosted over thirty of these experts at an eight-day retreat at the Anglican Church's summer camp in Sorrento, BC, where we held intense and closely led discussions of the draft papers. Here we shared camp-style living while partaking in a rich program of activities that included shared meals and debates; Tai Chi led by a proponent of Chinese religions; meditation in a Christian chapel under the leadership of our Sikh participant; an Indigenous Sweat Lodge and Sweet Grass smudge; and healing circles under the spiritual guidance of the Skwlāx Peoples (known in the year 2000 as the Little Shuswap Lake Band). I was moved by the variety of personal interactions I observed during our woodland walks together: a judge and a former lifer strolling in deep discussion, a policeman and a parolee readying a canoe, an Indigenous psychologist teaching chess to a young victim of crime. Our experience of communal living and open discourse reminded us that spirituality is more than an awareness of "holy" feelings. It is, as

Diana Eck had written in her 1993 book *Encountering God*, "the disciplined nurturing of inner spiritual life."

My journey in quest of justice took us in 2000 to Robinson College in Cambridge, UK. Here we lived in a small flat in the college, participated in its fellowship of discussions and dinners at High Table, attended lectures and special events in various colleges and centres of the university, and availed ourselves of the libraries. We also used our academic quarters as a home base for travelling throughout the UK—especially for visits to historic sites and prisons. By this time, I was transitioning away from formal academic research to a more personalized program of travel, learning, and teaching that Anita and I shared together. My book *The Spiritual Roots of Restorative Justice* would appear in 2001, yet already its insights had gone some distance in showing how the principles of forgiveness and reconciliation might be implemented in pluralistic, multifaith societies. But I knew I needed more comparative experience in prison culture. Furthermore, I was also developing an academic interest in the problem of evil. This was not solely a philosophical or theological problem. It also encompassed a practical dimension. I regarded it as the litmus test for determining whether there are limits to restorative justice, with its components of accountability, healing, and restoration.

I began to realize that nothing so shatters a victim's sense of a personal moral order—of identity, integrity, security and well-being—as the visceral experience of evil. Indeed, evil challenges our bedrock assumptions about the world. I wanted to address the concept of forgiveness for a number of reasons. I found forgiveness constantly arising in the discourse about restorative justice and the process of healing after trauma. Victims and offenders spoke about it; sometimes they agonized about it. So, too, did the professionals. I began to see that forgiveness is at best a problematic virtue, if only because it is so widely misunderstood, particularly in the context of a major traumatic experience. In short, forgiveness was a messy business. It was, in Stephen Cherry's telling words, "healing agony."

During three residential terms at Robinson College over a span of twelve years, I kept returning to the theme of evil. Whether I was examining the history of the Holocaust or cases of serial killers, I repeatedly came up against the same sordid reality. The appalling depths of human violence and depravity know no bounds, and radical evil is an insidious malevolence that leaves victims without hope. My study of evil proved such a sickening business that I could take it only in very small doses. The sadistic perversions of serial killers and of political regimes like those of Stalin, Hitler, and Pol Pot were too gruesome to counter as a daily diet. They all shared a common thread: unrepentant and remorseless iniquity in which God—however understood—did not intervene in any practical way to rescue victims. Nonetheless, the problem of evil—especially in its most depraved forms—was central to my work on criminal justice and, more particularly, to restorative justice.

Yet even in the most abject circumstances of grieving, restoration is possible. My Quaker friend Marian Partington, from Wales, whom I hosted at William Head prison, has shed much light on this and shared her path of recovery. Her kidnapped sister, Lucy, suffered horrific sexual depravities and brutality from her tormentors before being murdered and ignominiously buried among their other victims. Twenty years passed before police discovered her remains. As Marian records in *If You Sit Very Still,* her 2012 account of her journey from horror to wholeness, "the movement toward comprehension is neither logical nor straightforward. Essentially, it involves "becoming less self-centered," thus making space for "the experience of empathy for oneself and for others." For her, the struggle against immense pain and loss involves "sitting still within the mystery beyond human comprehension. It involves getting out of the way. Ultimately, it may involve becoming forgiving." Marian acknowledged her indebtedness to the various spiritual lineages of the East and West, which offered "guidance, strength, wisdom and discipline" for overcoming grief. She had tapped into the roots of restorative justice as I have known them, and understood what they demanded of her.

Gradually, I gained a sufficient hold on the issues to integrate them into my work on criminal justice. My visits to prisons in the UK afforded opportunities to engage with players in the field. We spoke with prison governors, custodians, prisoners, and members of the group known as the Board of Visitors, an independent prison watchdog and reporting agency. All shed light freely on life on the inside. Their stories were as diverse as their locales and their roles within the prison system. Architecturally, the prisons were a study in contrasts. From austere Victorian to polygonic to military-camp retreads and country homes rejigged as Borstal institutions. They were uniquely fascinating and very photogenic. Yet, rarely did life within their walls offer much hope that "dem bones, dem bones gonna walk around."

An exception was Tim Newell, the governor of HMP (Her Majesty's Prison) Grendon, a prison officially described as a "democratic therapeutic community." At Grendon, staff members had two overarching responsibilities: safeguarding the prisoners and caring for their welfare. The whole culture of the institution focused on helping them to develop positive attitudes to life. Grendon provided facilities for training and education, and opportunities for fostering healthy family relationships. Tim himself was impressive. We first met him in May 2000. A Quaker, he believed in the presence of God in every prisoner and argued that prisons should always be a place of last resort. Hence, when the state does resort to prisons, they should be safe places for healing. In the final analysis, he insisted, "the human spirit has hope even in the most soulless situations." Tim had arranged for us to meet with a few of his "residents," in order to discuss restorative justice. With its emphasis on accountability, healing, and respect, the model offered them hope. They warmed to exploring the theme. They acknowledged in Tim and his staff the very mentors they needed for growth.

As a governor, author, and lecturer, Tim himself was always deepening his own understanding of justice issues. In recognition of his many achievements, he received the Order of the British Empire (OBE). A couple of years later, I hosted him at William Head, where he attended the Salmon House, a program that supports Indigenous inmates to reconnect with their culture. Tim discussed his approach with a large number of inmates. He capped his visit by joining the Sweat Lodge. There, we underwent the four gruelling cycles of ceremonial sweats. As the rites drew to a close, the leader, Lloyd Haarala, bestowed upon Tim a great Indigenous honour by giving him the Ts'msyen name Spirit Bear.

THE GROWING expertise that Anita and I had been developing in restorative justice led to a unique opportunity to teach in Uganda, first with the International Christian Medical Institute (ICMI) and then as consultants with Miria Matembe, the Minister of State for Ethics and Integrity. We flew to Uganda via Vancouver and London just three days after the horrific attacks of September 11, when al-Qaeda terrorists hijacked airliners loaded with fuel and passengers and crashed them into the twin towers of the World Trade Center, in New York. The airports now lay virtually empty. We arrived in Heathrow during the night to await our connection and found our new world eerie and unsettling.

Yet, we looked forward to our nine-hour onward flight to Entebbe—and found it spectacular. Bright sunshine and clear skies accompanied us. From a height of 34,000 feet, we could pick out the whole map of Europe stretching beneath us. We flew from London in a broad, curvilinear route from Brussels to Paris, then headed toward Switzerland and the Alps. Memories of our adventures during Expo 58 came flooding in as we reminisced about our courting days: meeting Anita's French relatives; our strolls together along the Seine; and my epic scooter adventure with Paul Chamberland through the mountains of Switzerland, down through Italy, across the Adriatic, and up the rugged Yugoslavian coast. In the space of minutes, our flight was traversing distances that once had taken us days. Now our route took us down the western coast of the whole boot of Italy: Genoa, Livorno, Naples, and over the Straits of Messina from Sicily to the boot-tip of Calabria. Crossing over the deep-blue Mediterranean, we flew toward the Libyan desert, with its miles upon miles of rolling sand dunes, and onward into dusk and early evening. Soon, while floating silently over the Sahara Desert, we could see isolated lights beckoning and twinkling far below in the deepening dusk. Villages, probably, or groups of Bedouins settling down for the night.

New friends greeted us in a well-worn Toyota van for the ride into Kampala. As we bumped our way along the rutted, red-dirt road into town, unaccustomed sights assailed us. We saw brightly clad people—many of them heavily laden—ambling along in a moving frieze; and neighbours visiting one another by lantern light in the doorways of their humble shacks, while behind them jalopies and trucks weaved their way among the potholes on a highway unmarked by lanes. Driving in Uganda, we found, was something of an obstacle course. As one wag quipped, you could always tell the drunk drivers. They're the ones who drive straight—because they never see the holes. Flushed with fresh impressions, we slept well that night. But the dawn came upon us suddenly through the haunting mists of morning. It was nature's unique ritual on the equator, the first of many stupendous early mornings in Uganda: silent, deep-hued, poised in the rising heat, and smelling of moist, red earth and the fragrance of bougainvillea. Sometimes, mornings also brought the chatter of monkeys in the nearby eucalyptus, jackfruit, and mango trees.

Uganda, "the pearl of Africa" in Churchill's famous words, is a land of aching beauty and striking contrasts. Its history has been scarred by tribalism, colonialism, violence, oppression, dictatorships, civil war, and revolution. It is marked by poverty and a range of complex challenges in the areas of health, education, and the economy. With the right political will, Uganda could become the bread basket of Africa. Yet despite its troubled history and continuing problems with widespread corruption, it was a land offering hope and compassion. The hurly-burly of its public life along with its stoic conviviality, overwhelming poverty, and great generosity of spirit punctuated our daily experience. Underlying it all was a religious fervour that pervaded every facet of life.

Faith, we found, was outgoing, vital, and existential. Even the names of commercial enterprises bore witness to living faith traditions: Ave Maria Hair Salon, Hail Mary Take-Away, Holy Trinity Secretaries, Jesus Is Alive Family Shop, God's Grace Internet, Glory Be to God Gift Shop, God's Mercy Taxi, and Back to God Medical Centre. Garish signage on the windshields of smoke-belching *matatus*—the jalopy buses that hogged the overcrowded highroads and rutted byways—proclaimed the omnipresence of God: "Allah is Great," "Jesus Lives," "The Holy Spirit Calls." These abundant signs, conspicuously displayed in the pulsing hustle-and-bustle of crowded markets and taxi parks, underscored a cacophony of interwoven narratives. While some 82 percent of Ugandans count themselves as Christian (predominantly Roman Catholic, Anglican, and Pentecostal), animists and voodooists can be found among them. All emphasize the spiritual journey that Ugandans see themselves taking under the hand of Providence—from birth through travail to death, with its promise of an afterlife. African mythology also bears witness to a whole people's pilgrimage in search of the Kingdom of God. In this light, the nation's motto "For God and my country" enunciated a palpable set of moral priorities. Sometimes these priorities were observed in the breach. Widespread corruption prevailed—and still does.

At the request of ICMI, we had created a course entitled "The Human Condition in the Modern Age: The Literary Record of Faith, Philosophy, and Science." Aimed at adult learners, the course offered a critical survey of our changing understandings of the world and of our relationships to one another. But we had been ill-advised in developing our course, for it stressed the colonial heritage in which they had been brought up under British rule. Once on the ground, however, we rewrote it. We shifted the course away from the exploration of traditional Western ideas; we focused instead on material that drew upon the students' experiences as Africans. Together we sought out works by Ugandan writers and thinkers that reflected voices from their own transitioning culture. These new and emerging African voices evoked emotions, memories, and ideas that resonated with the students' own experience.

Our students were professional people—nurses, midwives, doctors, health care administrators—who in childhood had been accustomed to learning by rote. I think of Vivian, a widow who had founded a home for child mothers. Abused and rejected from their homes because of their unwanted pregnancy, these young, school-aged girls lived without hope until Vivian took them in. Vivian was supporting her two young sons while still committing to her charitable work. Another student was Sister Judith, a nursing sister and nun who had ministered in northern Uganda among the dispossessed victims of the vicious Lord's Resistance Army. And there was Sister Edith, a head nurse at Mulago Hospital, who took her responsibilities in stride despite limited equipment and support. Over thirty men and women attended our class, each one of them having known poverty, despair, serious illness, social inequality, and heavy responsibility. Yet they had hope, and they worked hard to succeed, knowing that their families and their country needed them.

Once our students began to discover their country's rich cultural heritage, they engaged with it enthusiastically. Alexander Muigai's poem "The Troubled Warrior" drew them into the life of a troubled youth who leaves home to fight against a tribal enemy in response to "the will of my fathers." John Ssemuwanga's poem "The Blind" explored faith and suffering by asking a blind man how he copes with his debilitating infirmity, and how he can possibly relate to a God who cast him into outer darkness. In another poem, "Dual Piety," Ssemuwanga challenges Uganda's colonial religious heritage and ponders his own spiritual dilemma. He finds himself torn between two faith traditions—the faith of the English missionaries and his own exiled Indigenous religious traditions. Our course dealt head-on with the tragedy of the AIDS epidemic. Most of our students had lost a family member to AIDS, yet they rarely if ever spoke of it. So we introduced them to Julius Ocwinyo's "AIDS – Death," a poem rich in provocative questions. Always pressing the boundaries of moral outrage, the Ugandan poet asks whether this "dreadful virus" is how a loving God cares for his creatures. Most of our students had lived in poverty and suffered much. They taught us much about living reverently. We came to care about them deeply.

ON RETURNING to Canada, we committed ourselves to designing a practical course on ethical decision making. Mukono Christian University, which housed the ICMI program, required a course specifically focusing on Christian ethics. We kept the title, but approached the subject with a wider lens. Thus we based our approach on the model of adult education known as andragogy, which draws on the knowledge and expertise of adult learners. Recognizing the variety and depth of the students' skills, education, and training, the course would introduce them to key principles of situational ethics. It would make use of case studies drawn from the hospitals and clinics where they worked. The case studies would be broadened to include environmental and political issues from Ugandan life.

We returned to Uganda a second time, and emphasized our approach both in the preface to the course pack and frequently throughout the course: "*You* are the expert," we told them. "We aim at engaging *your* knowledge and insights to shape the course according to *your* professional needs. We are simply guides through your own landscape of ethical decision making." The method involved determining the facts of any given case and then identifying the stakeholders. The students especially enjoyed what we called the "brainstorming" phase, where they got into a huddle with colleagues to discover the best ethical alternative and how to implement it. They took pleasure in the workshops and discussion groups—as did we.

By the end of the course we had shared and learned so much together that we had become friends. But we also regarded them as much more. In professional terms, they were not only partners in learning. They were potential trainers in ethics. Most of them were supervisors in hospitals and clinics, with responsibility for passing their new skills on to others. Did it work? We believe it did. One case comes quickly to mind. During a tea break one day, a student came to me with a real-life problem. He was a health inspector in an outlying village that had become mired in an ongoing dispute. It turned out to be a case of tribal rivalry and political corruption that was resulting in black-water pollution of the river and lake where fishing had once thrived. The dispute was causing a major health issue. "Can these bones live?" my student quoted to me the familiar question. In short, we helped him write it up as a case study, which he presented to our class of experts for resolution. They beavered away at it intensely, punctuating their deliberations with guffaws and joyous slaps on their thighs. As a group they helped the health inspector to choose the best solution. Many weeks later we received a jubilant email: he had solved his community's problem.

ONE STEAMY morning we found ourselves heading across Kampala in a jalopy taxi to meet the Honourable Miria Matembe, Minister of State for Ethics and Integrity. As we drove up the great hill to the directorate and checked in at the guard box attended by armed military, we faced a scene right out of a Graham Greene novel. A large, colonial building stood baking in the morning sun, while a lackadaisical army guard in rumpled uniform and gumboots checked the appointment book with his sullen sergeant. Shadows of intrigue and subterfuge percolated about me. So, too, the odour of power. Eventually, the guard waved us on to a parking place in front the building, as I pondered the taxi driver's ominous warnings. On the way up the narrow road the driver had been grumbling about "that woman Matembe." She was the most powerful woman in Uganda, he said, which was true. She wanted to root out corruption wherever she found it, which was also true. Indeed, she detested male violence against women so much she would gladly "cut the balls off any man" who crossed her path. Not a little intimidated, I informed the driver that I hoped to take back to Canada everything I had brought in.

My sense of intrigue heightened as I climbed the staircase to the upper floor and entered the vestibule. The minister's bodyguard confronted me. Doudie, as I came to call him, was a heavy-set, finely

suited man with a welcoming smile like a pounce-ready Cheshire
cat. The slight bulge in his breast pocket hinted at a palm-sized pis-
tol. Yes, she was ready to see us, he said, as he stood up and adjusted
his jacket. And suddenly, there she was, an imposing woman at an
impressively large desk. We settled in to stake out the field of our
common interests. Or rather, she staked out the field with zest and
pizzazz, while I sat transfixed, trying to get a word in edgewise. She
was vivacious, vociferous, and volatile about her passions. So much
so, in fact, that her colourful rhetoric and emphatic gestures pinned
me to my chair as though I myself were responsible for Uganda's
problems. She was on the warpath against corruption and violence
against women. Her country's moral inertia angered her. In a culture permeated by these self-inflicted "diseases," she argued, she
needed all the help she could get. And that invitation brought me to
life as I put my suggestions on the table. As we rose to leave after a
challenging hour, she tempered the tone by asking us whether our
hometown of Victoria was anywhere near Vancouver, where her
sister lived. Her question modulated our discussion to a personal
level, eventually leading to a friendship that survives to this day. And
Doudie, with his irrepressible grin and bulging jacket, accompanied
us over many a mile.

Anita and I subsequently worked with Miria on a special initiative funded by the World Bank. We travelled widely throughout
Uganda, presenting interactive workshops on ethics for public servants. Miria hosted them all, and saw to it that all ranks attended our
sessions. Her imposing presence rattled the cages of conventional
thinking. The Ugandan establishment regarded her as brash, brazen,
and a threat to the status quo. Some among our captive audiences
felt hopeful about the initiatives and took the teaching seriously.
Others felt imposed upon and out of sorts. The press sought out
enticing bits for its media mill.

In mid-February 2003, we launched the initiative in Kampala
with a day-long introduction to ethical decision making. Senior
government administrators and a large cohort from the Criminal
Investigation Division attended. Having had her staff organize
the teaching tour, Miria's role was ostensibly to present us to the

audience and make a few inspirational remarks. Yet every time we hit a new town on our tour, she would begin the day with a long harangue about the evils of corruption, the laziness of workers, and the brutishness of so many men toward women. No wonder that she became known by her critics as "big mouth," and by her supporters as "every dictator's worst nightmare." Cowed, and perhaps humbled, by her blistering jeremiads, so liberally peppered with Biblical quotations, her audiences scarcely stirred.

By the time our own turn came on this opening day, we had had to trim and short-circuit much of what we had planned on saying. Quickly placing the program into context, we laid our cards on the table. We hoped to explore with them how best to fulfill their responsibilities as managers of public services and the public purse. For many, this was incredibly difficult at a very personal level. Firstly, as Miria readily admitted, civil servants were badly paid. And yet their inadequate salaries had to help feed, house, and raise not only their own immediate families but also impoverished or orphaned relatives ravaged by the HIV virus. We wanted to give them some tools to help them make decisions that supported the common good. Thus, we explored with them the critically important concepts of integrity, honesty, impartiality, and fairness. We introduced them to such neglected notions as the precautionary principle, the fiduciary principle, the common good, and equal consideration of interests. In short, we offered them just enough to whet their appetite and then offered a couple of case studies on which they could hone their skills, under our guidance. When we bade them farewell at the end of the day, we thanked them and said, in effect: you have seen how ethics work; you are the experts in your administrative units. Go now and work accordingly, and teach your colleagues how to do the same.

Kampala's *The New Vision* newspaper for 15 February 2003 had a heyday. "Gov't to spy on corrupt officers," ran the headline. Beneath it stood a photo of me (a white-faced *muzungu*) and Miria Matembe in our new role as spymasters. "The Directorate of Integrity," the article read, "is to recruit 'contacts' in government offices to infiltrate cartels of corrupt officers." It would do so with "consultants hired from Canada . . . experienced in fighting corruption and abuse of office." And if all else failed, it said, the Canadian Army might help. For the ministry was drawing not only upon the expertise of "professor Michael Hadley and his wife Anita from the University of Victoria," but also from "other officials from the Royal Roads Military College" (where Anita actually taught). Testy times for a white-faced person in a sea of black to saunter about the streets of Kampala. Lurking along the roads, I felt like a hired gunslinger coming to clean up the town, though I didn't relish thoughts of a shoot-out at the O.K. Corral. I kept a low profile.

Since those earliest days of attempting to help enlarge Uganda's vision, we have remained close friends with Miria. On my recommendation, the University of Victoria awarded her the honorary degree of doctor of laws (LLD) in June 2007, for her pioneering work in constitutional law, women's liberation, and the formation of the Pan-African Parliament. She had been an inspirational member of the country's Constituent Assembly, or Parliament, that formulated Uganda's first post-revolution Constitution under President Yoweri Museveni. Promulgated on 8 October 1995, the Constitution embodied crucial safeguards for the rights of women. Miria's 2002 book *Gender, Politics, and Constitution Making in Uganda* and *The Struggle for Freedom and Democracy Betrayed*, published in 2019, showed us what a dangerous game we had been playing in working with her in Uganda. Violence lay just beneath the surface. Miria explains her survival through her evangelical faith: "God is on my side." Yet, for all that, I view her situation with grave and growing concern.

ALONGSIDE OUR focus on ethics and integrity, we pressed on with restorative justice. The notorious Luzira Prison called. A grim and decaying maximum security prison built by the British in the nineteenth century to hold seventeen hundred prisoners, it now holds over eight thousand under inhumane conditions. We had already presented a workshop of restorative justice for local citizens and for the Kampala Police. All were quietly receptive, though a police officer confessed that at the end of the day, "the Bible still says you gotta punish." For him that settled the issue. And indeed, Luzira dished out punishment in spades. The Ugandan representative of

Prison Fellowship International, Sophie Osaya, arranged for us to spend the day visiting the men in the "condemned section," the Ugandan version of death row. She had clearance for us to attend a Sunday service with the two hundred prisoners who usually took part each week. The mere thought of such a visit caused us anxiety. How dangerous would it be, I wondered, to enter death row with two women? Yet we weighed the venture and decided it was too important not to attend. Early morning mist greeted us at the austere entrance to the fortress, where crisply turned-out guards met us. The prison had been built like a set of nested stone quadrangles set one inside the other and separated by what looked like dry moats, each with its own security checkpoint. There could be no escaping from the innermost quadrangle, where the condemned men lived.

Anita's journal records our impressions: "We found ourselves in a courtyard crowded with men in threadbare white shorts and T-shirts . . . men of all ages, some quick to come forward in greeting, others initially more reticent." We responded by offering our hand in peace and giving our names. Human contact was as simple as that. Anita's journal continues: "From the first courtyard, where the Muslims were beginning to gather for prayer, we stepped into a long narrow exercise yard known to the prisoners as 'St. John's Chapel.' It was a hive of activity. With no soap and very little water, men squatted on the beaten earth to wash clothes in plastic basins and hang them up in the boiling sun to dry. Others sifted beans through their fingers, picking out the maggoty ones in preparation for an eventual meal." The man whom I took to be the prison chaplain conducted us toward a slightly elevated dais from which he would lead the prayers and singing. As we strolled among the prisoners, he turned to us and announced, "Oh, by the way, you are both preaching today." When I asked him how long he had been serving as prison chaplain, he smiled and replied, "Oh no, I'm not a chaplain." And then, with a sweep of his arm across the assembled prisoners, he added, "I am one of *them*."

A condemned man awaiting execution like the others, he had been their chaplain for twenty years. As I learned later, Chris (Cris)

Rwakasisi had been Minister for Internal Affairs—which meant internal security—during Milton Obote's second regime from 1979 to 1985. According to Amnesty International, that period harboured a police state even crueller than that of Idi Amin. Cris's political life had grown out of a tangled and violent—albeit colourful— skein of intrigue, kidnapping, murder, revolution, and counter-revolution. He had been a flamboyant strongman, a persuasive public speaker. He was known in his heyday for being surrounded by wealth, power, and beautiful women. By the time I met him in Luzira Prison he had long been a born-again Christian. He would receive a presidential pardon in 2008.

Cris began the service by addressing Anita and me in front of the men: "Just look at us. Many of us have committed violent crimes. Some of us are innocent but had no money to bribe the lawyers. Others are simply crazy." The ragged young lad with threadbare vestments who served as Cris's acolyte had a distant, vacant stare. Again, Anita's journal picks up the narrative. Cris opened the service with the words "this is the *only* day; this hour is the *only* hour. It is good that we are here in the House of the Lord." As I heard these words, I looked up at the only piece of sky that could be seen. The huge gap in the roof was surrounded by barbed wire. No windows shed light on us. Nothing even hinted that beyond us lay Lake Victoria, the largest body of water in all of Africa. No bird flew over the narrow, stifling place in which we were gathered. Yet, despite their precarious situation, the prisoners did not pray for themselves. They prayed for others also in danger: the women and children of war-threatened Iraq. As Cris stood to address his fellow prisoners, he turned quickly toward us. Drawing our attention to two impeccably attired guards, he said, "If we wished to harm you, those two men could do nothing to help; nothing at all... They have come to hear the Word of God." The guards nodded their assent.

I did preach, if that is the correct word for what I offered that day. The Good News I brought was about restorative justice that can heal the trauma of violence. It was a message they had never heard before. Anita "preached" as well, from a woman's perspective in that womanless place. She spoke about the dignity of every human being, of human love, and of God's love, which in Tim Newell's words can heal "in the most soulless of places." The scene after the long and eclectic service was simple. The prisoners brought us a couple of biscuits and a battered thermos of tea. "You must wash, for we are dirty," Cris said as the altar boy stepped up to us and bowed. The inmates were sharing with us their greatest luxuries: an old piece of soap, fresh water to wash our fingertips, and a biscuit. Anita recalled the scene in her journal: "Looking into the eyes of that condemned youth, I saw reflected in them the face of Christ." The Eucharist has never looked the same to us since that profound experience. Anita concluded her journal entry with this: "The prisoners we visited survive in the bleakest of conditions: filth, overcrowding, malnutrition. That they continue to scrub their tattered rags for 'Sunday best'; that they offer one another hope, encouragement, consolation, even teaching for the illiterate among them; that they pray for the world beyond their own hell on earth . . . all this attests to the strength of the human spirit in the most appalling circumstances."

HUMAN SUFFERING in Uganda did not confine itself to the poor and imprisoned. We found it also among the dying when we visited Hospice Uganda, in Makindye, just outside Kampala. Founded in September 1993, the centre had become a pan-African model for palliative care. My own involvement in hospice began in 2009 as part of an international research project at UVic's Centre for Studies in Religion and Society. Entitled "Religious Understandings of a Good Death in Hospice Palliative Care," the project took as its starting point three principles proposed by the founder of hospice care, Dr. Cicely Saunders: pain control, family and community involvement, and engagement with a dying person's spirituality. While the first two principles—pain control and family involvement—had been well studied since their formulation in the 1960s, the third— spirituality—had not. The three principles were key components of Cicely Saunders's concept of "total pain." She had recognized that pain—particularly in cancer patients—is both multifaceted and multidimensional. It embraces the physical, social, psychological, and spiritual aspects of human suffering.

At the time we visited, Hospice Uganda had no facilities for live-in patients. Dying patients came to hospice primarily for diagnosis and intermediate care. In Uganda, over half the population of over thirty-one million have no contact with a health worker. Most live in rural areas, and one child in every five is an orphan. Thus, the hospice staff would set up roadside clinics and travel to outlying districts to care for the dying. In fact, most patients preferred to die at home close to their family and ancestors. The poet Abago Mary Nyar' Obote captures the sentiment in her poem "Take Me Back Home": "There where my heart is / There where my grave will be." The challenges for holistic palliative care in Uganda are huge. We saw dying patients brought in by motorcycle over rugged, rural roads. We witnessed patients in deep physical pain, and we shared in the prayer life of nurses during the patients' final hours.

A final image of those days remains rooted in memory. We had accompanied two nurses—one Muslim, the other Christian—to the squalid home of a refugee family. The mother lay on the mud floor in the final stages of breast cancer—incontinent, in pain, and a in state of despair. The father, broken by sorrow and anguish, spent whatever money he could get on liquor. By default, the couple's twelve-year-old daughter had become the head of the family. Hospice came, bringing the mother a bed. The nurses, gentle in every way, washed her and administered morphine. The husband wept and pleaded for money, while his ten-year-old son quietly swept rainwater out of their hut. We faced a scene of utter misery. On the wall hung the sole piece of decoration: a plaque proclaiming that "Jesus is the Lord of this home." At the nurses' bidding, we joined them in prayer. The woman's death under hospice care was the best that could have been managed that day.

BEFORE RETURNING home to Canada, we treated ourselves to a holiday on Bushara Island in Lake Bunyoni, near Uganda's border with Rwanda. Dawn in Uganda always stirs with gentle promise as mists rise from the heating red earth and quickly evaporate under an intense blue sky. It began in silence and burst with a shout. As I stepped out of our safari tent into the warm morning air, I heard the voices of school children rippling across the water. The crystal clarity of their distant chirping teased my spirits into an upbeat mood. Thrusting their dugouts across the silent water with rhythmical strokes of their rough-hewn wooden paddles, the children eased their way into the morning sun toward school. So lilting and effortless, it seemed. So steeped in tribal traditions thousands of years old. It was a paradise of colour, motion, and sound. What might their lives become?

From Kabale, some 400 kilometres (250 miles) southwest of Kampala, we had crossed the lake to Bushara Island in modern motorized canoes. These were reasonably comfortable tourist boats and not the traditional shallow-draft canoes used by the local people. Hollowed from eucalyptus logs and propelled by either a team of paddlers or a single boatman standing in the stern, these traditional boats are tricky for the inexperienced to manage. But I had known boats all my life and simply had to have a go.

Once established at our camp, I arranged with a local guide to borrow one of the canoes. I couldn't resist trying to paddle one myself. Was the lake safe from crocs, hippos, and snakes, I asked? "No problem," the guide assured me with an inscrutable smile. "Lake clean." So it was that I strolled through the island's tall grass, hearing what sounded like the faint rustle of snakes in the underbrush near the water's edge. There, standing bolt upright in the stern of the tipsy-looking dugout, a local boatman stepped gracefully ashore, handed me his oar, and wished me "God bless." Little did I know that we *muzungus* had a reputation for incompetence with these craft. The locals expected me to become a cropper too, and couldn't wait for my cry for help.

As I coasted the island in the afternoon sun, I sensed hidden eyes peering from shore for that fateful moment when I would twist and turn in what they called "the *muzungu* circle." But I had quickly gotten the knack, despite my preoccupation with keeping a sharp lookout for the telltale snout of a crocodile or the ears of a hippo. I should have trusted the guide: "No worry, lake clean, God bless." On my return, they greeted me as a fellow boatman. I felt, dare I say it, redeemed.

At the end of our stay, we returned to the mainland by canoe and steeped ourselves in traditional culture. Setting off from the island's dock, we found ourselves surrounded by twenty or thirty traditional canoes, each laden with produce and piles of smoked fish crucified on splayed sticks, plying their way back and forth among the markets of Kabale district. They reminded me of the singing, laughing children I had heard on that first morning. Here, however, the chatter and laughter of the marketplace filled the air, as did the colour of costumes and wares, and the brilliant sunshine rippling off Lake Bunyoni. Uganda was indeed a country of vibrant and intriguing contrasts. Glancing up toward the sunlight, I caught sight of an airliner seemingly suspended thousands of feet overhead. Its momentary suspension above us reflected the coexistence of two disparate worlds: the ultra-modern world of global travel and the earth-bound traditional life of East Africa.

Like others of my generation, I have lived through many paradigm shifts. The extraordinary explosion of human knowledge lies at the root of these changes, most strikingly on the scientific and technical level but also in the spiritual realm. Yet each shift has carried the threads of previous paradigms, from which it creates new patterns and takes on its own aura of orthodoxy. Today, our human species can actually envisage a blending of relativity theory and quantum science that might lead to a unified field theory of the universe and reality. All evidence suggests that we no longer live on a lonely planet in a steady-state universe. We live in a breathtaking, rapidly expanding universe. Indeed, our physical reality embraces the likelihood of an awe-inspiring multiverse that challenges far beyond the human imagination. I find it exciting. Yet, I also empathize with those like the character Meg in P.D. James's novel *Devices and Desires*. Approaching an old church tentatively at first, Meg attends Morning Prayer and Evensong with a tiny band of faithfuls. As James puts it, "this daily ritual, the beautiful, half-forgotten cadences, seducing her into belief, gave a welcome shape to the day." Is it possible, I wondered, to live with a foot in each world? How might we reconcile these two visions? A clue lies in the wisdom of the Syrian monastery of Mar Musa and in Father Paolo's principle of "double belonging." Experienced on an existential level, this approach would allow us to live fully in both these worlds. One can live in both realms with intellectual honesty and without triggering moral dissonance. In any event, as in music, dissonance forms part of harmony.

SIMILAR THOUGHTS accompanied me in 2016 as we crossed the desert wilderness of Jordan by camel. I had ridden the ill-tempered "ships of the desert" before, once during a visit to Tangiers, and again in Syria, among the ruins of Palmyra. But this ride was on a much grander scale. The colour and variety of the Jordanian desert recalled the descriptive accounts of T.E. Lawrence. Known as Lawrence of Arabia, he spoke of the desert as "a pathless sea of sand." Anita and I had spent the previous night with a group of pilgrims among the Bedouins in Wadi Rum. We had partaken of their warm hospitality and enjoyed a fine meal prepared in the *zarb*, an oven-like pot that they had set to cook in a pit dug in the sand. Night had come upon us quickly in our splendid isolation, and the resplendent sky embraced us as it had done so many times before at sea. Far from the loom of land as we were, the stars and constellations stood out in palpable proximity to us. The enormity of the cosmos set human life in context and called to mind those memorable lines of William Blake: "To see a world in a grain of sand, / And a heaven in a wild flower, / Hold infinity in the palm of your hand, / And Eternity in an hour." Spending time with the Bedouins in the extraordinary desertscapes of Wadi Rum is an unforgettable way of stripping the soul to its basics.

Lawrence of Arabia, too, had experienced the cosmic dimension, perhaps not far from the spot where we were sojourning. He spoke in his 1922 memoir *Seven Pillars of Wisdom* of "the sweep of open places, the taste of wide winds, the sunlight, and the hopes" that pressed him onward. He pondered the intoxicating "morning freshness of the world-to-be." Throughout his "whirling campaigns" in the desert war of 1916–18, he had felt "wrought up with ideas inexpressible and vaporous, but to be fought for." Reflecting on the Book of Revelation (21:1), he recalled the sheer joy of working "for a new heaven and a new earth."

Postwar politics had cut Lawrence's dreams short. Embittered, he wrote: "When we achieved and the new world dawned, the old men came out again and took our victory to remake in the likeness of the former world they knew." Perhaps it was ever thus. In the wake of the First World War, statesmen had carved up the Middle East in their own likeness, and in the years following the Second World War, Allied leaders reshaped a desolated globe to suit their own vision of a fair balance of power. And now, in today's globalized, multicultural world, narrowly nationalist right-wing movements would turn the clock back to some former idealized world that quite probably never existed. The Taliban have retaken Afghanistan and created a medieval state, Israel continues to capture Palestinian lands, the United Kingdom has broken free of the European Union in hopes of recreating a "Merry England," and Russia, in its savage war against Ukraine, hopes to recreate the former greatness of the Russian Empire. In 2011, Canadian monarchists took a retrograde step by restoring the word "Royal" in the Canadian Navy's title. And on the demise of the British monarch in 2022, Canada declared her son King of Canada. So, too, traditionalists in every sphere of influence focus on the past. Lawrence of Arabia would not have been surprised, and nor am I.

Likewise in the spiritual realm, where at the first whiff of creative change after Vatican II, successive popes began to backtrack. They relegated updating of the Church and *aggiornamento* to the shadows. And in the Anglican tradition that shaped my early years, many leaders and their followers still perpetuate outdated systems of thought. Rather than opening their doors and windows to the sounds of our contemporary world, they cloister themselves in the "sacred sounds" of the distant past. We are our tradition, a cathedral dean recently announced; we are like a rower in a rowboat, always keeping an eye on the past so that we know who we are and where we have come from. To this, I reply: Not so. We are our wisdom. We are like sailors under taut sails, aware of all that is going on around us while looking ahead, so that we know where we are and where we shall be.

Yet, if the Spirit is active in creation, then surely the faithful should be listening for direction not just from the voices that are over two thousand years old. They should also listen to the contemporary voices of those who have been up to the mountain top, voices like Martin Luther King Jr., Mahatma Gandhi, Óscar Romero, Dalai Lama, Mother Teresa, Dorothy Day, Gustavo Gutiérrez, Thich Nhat Hanh, and Sallie McFague. The list goes on. To remain relevant and alive faiths must evolve, both liturgically and substantively. Indeed, their health and viability depend upon younger generations being open to new categories and dimensions for expressing their truth claims. Forward-looking prophets might speak, but traditionalists hold fast. As an ancient Arabic saying puts it, "The dogs bark, and the caravan moves on."

Our desert crossing continued. We packed up next morning and prepared to cross Wadi Rum. Snuffling and snorting, a large group of camels were kneeling by our tents, soaking up the early morning sun and cautiously eyeing our approach. My own "ship of the desert" allowed me to slip into the high-backed saddle. With a sudden lurch, it rose to its feet, and we set off. Rolling to the rhythm of the camel's loping gait, I cast my eye toward the tall rock formation in Wadi Rum known as the Seven Pillars of Wisdom, a name derived from the Book of Proverbs. A passage from that book says that "Wisdom has built herself a house, She has erected her seven pillars." In this passage, Wisdom—traditionally personified as female—is preparing a great feast. She will invite only the wise. A humbling prospect indeed.

Weeks later, as we flew home via Europe to the West Coast of Canada, I again watched the vast sands of Africa stretch out below me. My mind cast back to the Syrian monastery of Mar Musa, where I had once watched a sandstorm swirling below me. Now, as it did then, the scene evoked images of the prophet Ezekiel's valley of dry bones. It raised a question: would these bones ever live again? Would it ever be possible in this transient world of mistrust and violence to restore what has been lost, to establish peace and sustain hope? Would it ever be possible to establish the tracks that will lead us to a just future? Lawrence of Arabia once wrote of the Middle East nations that "the fringes of their deserts were strewn with broken faiths." He was referring not only to religious faith, but to faith in the possibility of a just world, and confidence that we could rebuild a world once it had been broken.

I trust that Ezekiel had gotten it right when he claimed to have heard the Lord say to him, "I shall put my spirit in you, and you will live." And even if he hadn't, I still feel the hope proclaimed in that syncopating, ragtime rhythm of the 1940s hit song "Dem bones, dem bones gonna walk around." That's precisely what jazz trumpeter Louis Armstrong affirmed with his foot-stomping Dixie beat: "Oh yeah, man, oh yeah."

10

HOME PORT
A CODA

Tho' with great difficulty I am got hither,
yet now I do not repent me of all the trouble
I have been at to arrive where I am.

JOHN BUNYAN, *The Pilgrim's Progress*

OLDTIMER LAY alongside her sun-drenched dock under azure skies when I first walked the yacht basin in Oak Bay fifty years ago. With her gaff-rigged sails all stowed, brass glinting, and lines flaked down on the whitening teak decks, she was as tiddly a vessel as any you'd find gunkholing along these shores. Hunkered down at her helm, one hand on the binnacle and lord of all he surveyed, sat a weather-beaten old sailor. He was contemplating the gentle tugging of his vessel against the morning breeze. Shore-bound but hopeful, he was still her skipper, ready to cast off one more time, before it was too late. He had become an old-timer like the seasoned vessel he clearly loved. He seemed to hold that pose each time I strolled along the floats with an eye to having a boat of my own some day. Yet his days of sea fever were not quite over; he could still relive past adventures and envisage new horizons. That image has been my companion all these years. What he then was, I have now become: a voyager still taking the weather gauge, as they used to say in the tall ship days. I, too, have reached my home port, yet I still feel outward bound.

The expression home port has special meaning for mariners. It suggests you can slip outside the discipline of sea service, double up your moorings, and hook onto shore power. Nobody expects you to pipe the side or attend to the niceties of nautical society. You can cease the hectic pace of life. I have learned that retirement itself is a homecoming. I can let the wind fill my sails and voyage in spirit in any direction and at any time I like. I can indulge in the great writing and musical compositions I first encountered in earlier years. I can steep myself in the literatures and cultures I have come to know and love, and deepen my grasp of them. A host of thinkers and writers from many disciplines walk with me. They press against the often-rigid boundaries that our customary habits of mind proclaim as truth. Books have been our companions on life's journey. Writers from many nations and languages, from ancient times to the present day, share our home. They bestir themselves again in my old hands. I read them quite differently now, for I have gathered a lifetime of experience.

Indeed, each waypoint along the road I travelled in its own way has given me a taste of homecoming: safe anchorages and snug coves; soaring cities and cozy cabins; monasteries, mosques, and wayside chapels. Each afforded glimpses and intimations of the ultimate end to my journey. My spiritual life, though profoundly shaped by the Christian experience, has also been moulded by cross-cultural and multifaith encounters. I am indebted to the Buddhists I visited on Lantau Island and in Kyoto, the Baha'is in Kampala, the Jews at Jerusalem's Wailing Wall, the Muslims in the Grand Mosque of Damascus, the Irish in Monasterboice, and the monks of St George's monastery (Deir Mar Georges) in Homs. My life has been enriched and disciplined by my intellectual pursuits. I have evolved, as have others of my so-called silent generation. I have changed from colonial to cosmopolitan, from unilingual to polyglot. My inclinations toward a larger vision of life stayed with me all along. As Frederick Buechner put it in his book *Longing for Home*, "We carry inside us a vision of wholeness that we sense is our true home that beckons us."

I have lived and loved language and literature. For they reveal the synergies that give texture and expressive depth to human life. No matter the genre—from traditional epic to lyrical and dramatic—they have drawn me into lost and luminous worlds of the imagination and allowed me to engage in the tragedies, comedies, and private emotions that shape us. We are not only a tool-making species, *homo faber*, as anthropologists once led us to believe. Nor are we solely experimenters and experiencers, as Alan Lightman insists in his glorious romp *The Transcendent Brain: Spirituality in the Age of Science*. We are also storytellers, visionaries, and myth makers. Our stories—beginning with the earliest myths of origin, like the Sumerian *Epic of Gilgamesh*, from the third millennium BCE, and the Jewish Bible's fifth-century BCE Book of Genesis—still engage me. The literary records of many cultures afford me multiple perspectives on the family of humankind. Characters like Goethe's Faust, Schiller's Wallenstein, Shakespeare's Hamlet, Dostoevsky's Raskolnikov, Kazantzakis's Christ, and Crummey's Moses Sweetland plumb the depths of the human psyche. Often in disturbing detail. Tolstoy's *War and Peace*, Remarque's *All Quiet on the Western Front*, and Kevin Major's *No Man's Land* confront me with our tragic passion for violence and war. Deeply textured portraits of bygone societies still fascinate. Meanwhile, a rich tapestry of multicultural narratives evokes the emerging soul scape of my home country, Canada.

Thankfully, in all this rummaging about in the human soul, I have never lost my taste for humour. It's a refreshing kind of emotional chaos that puts an over-earnest world into perspective by standing it on its head. Humorists of every hue—social critics, political cabaretists, satirists, and cartoonists—have dared to save us from ourselves. I count myself among the saved. Characters from Simplicissimus to Max and Moritz and beyond have been high priests of laughter. Or mentors of mirth. Here at home, Roch Carrier's bittersweet tale *Le Chandail* (*The Hockey Sweater*) teased out the tensions between Quebec and English Canada in an endearing way that reconciled us to our oft conflicted past. As for humour just for the helluvit, I still delight in the escapades of the Polish lad in Zygmunt Nowakowski's *The Cape of Good Hope* (*Przylądek Dobrej Nadziei*), whom I first encountered in my undergraduate days. Dressed in white breeches, he tosses a slab of raw beefsteak onto the wooden saddle of his rocking horse so that he can experience what riding is "really" like. Reality is often more than we bargain for.

Literature, I have found, is the fascinating record of who we once were, are now, and might have been. Indeed, in every age the creative imagination affords us glimpses of worlds that might yet emerge. Some, like the science fiction world envisioned in Jules Verne's *Twenty Thousand Leagues under the Sea* (1870), and George Orwell's dystopian novel *1984*, published in 1949, were actually realized in my lifetime. Other worlds, like the theocratic Republic of Gilead depicted in Margaret Atwood's speculative fiction *The Handmaid's Tale* (1985), lurk on the horizon—in all their abject horror. All of them I now recollect in restive tranquility. They all bear witness to the human condition, even in its abject rejection of compassion.

Written in a wealth of languages, each literary tradition has its own distinctive metaphors for expressing human experience. The power of each metaphor has drawn upon the perspectives and the values of the cultures in which it arises. Transposing one national experience into another relies upon dedicated translators. Theirs is a daunting and often impossible challenge. The emotional associations and resonances of one language cannot always be transposed effectively into another. How precious, therefore, to read a work in the original. As Goethe's young scholar Wagner avows in *Faust*, he continues to study in hopes of "knowing it all" from the inside. The ancient *libido sciendi* lies deep in the genes and doesn't seem to be fading.

Taken together, literary works have helped me to navigate the shoals and shallows, as well as the salvific heights, of the human condition. They have offered persuasive hints about humanity's redemptive possibilities and attest to the beauty, fragility, and uniqueness of our endangered world. Indeed, literature bears witness to the great mystery of life itself. That we're given the chance to live within this mystery is its own reward and is ultimately the best we can do to authenticate our journey. We are, after all, only guests on this earth, and our knowledge is provisional.

This notion resonates with my reflections on the existentially challenging infrared images transmitted in the summer of 2022 by the James Webb telescope. The images reveal a cluster of galaxies whose light has taken 4.6 billion years to reach us on our fragile blue planet. Indeed, we may possibly be looking at galaxies formed within a few hundred million years of the Big Bang. Our forebears in this search for scientific truth—those like Ptolemy, Al-Farghani, Kepler, Galileo, Newton, Einstein, and Hubble—would be no less awed than I. They and their confreres had always worked at fine tuning their understandings. Though we will likely never hold the final answer in our hand, we can always deepen our relationship to it. By so doing, we reach out for the shores of wisdom. Amidst this swirling multiverse, our earth seems the only piece of rock inhabited by sentient beings. That makes it—and us—unique, and calls for humility.

A writer from my undergraduate days of studying French first brought this point home to me. An adventurer, fighter pilot, and philosopher, Antoine de St. Exupéry was a writer of ever-broadening horizons. A prized first edition of his philosophical tale *Le Petit Prince* graces our shelves. More profound than the children's tale it purports to be, it helped us introduce our four youngsters to the big questions in life. His young protagonist made big concepts like compassion, gentleness, simplicity, authenticity, responsibility, and hope feel uncomplicated, and completely natural. The book revealed, among other things, the importance of looking beneath the surface of things to find their meaning. It offered metaphors for the interior life in order to equip young readers—and grown-ups too—to confront the world with courage. The engaging little prince himself seemed to point to the essence of relationships, particularly when speaking of the solitary rose that shared his life on his tiny, barren planet, no larger than a house. His solitary rose, he explained, had only four thorns to protect it from the world, so he alone was responsible for it: "*Tu sais... ma fleur... j'en suis responsable.*" Responsible,

too, for the asteroid on which he lived. The little fellow and his fragile planet are us.

Our own journeys too, had begun just as innocently. Born into
a world we had not chosen, into a time we had not foreseen, our
own childhood once lay before each of us. It flickered between trust
and insecurity, innocence and anticipation, reality and imagination.
The poet Rainer Maria Rilke captures this remarkable perspective
in his poem "*Das Karussell*" (The Carousel), conceived in Paris in
1906, in the Jardin du Luxembourg. Ostensibly an exploration of the
inner nature of the park's merry-go-round, it was actually a focused
meditation on childhood. Rilke's poem captures fleeting pleasures of
childhood—its self-conscious smiles, blurred emotions and perceptions, and often fragile joys. The poem reminds me of my own young
ones—indeed, of my own tentative passage out of childhood. Each
time Anita and I strolled through the Luxembourg Gardens on our
visits to Paris, the carousel materialized before us with its brightly
painted menagerie of lions, tigers, and horses—and the mysterious
white elephant, whose eternal recurrence marked the passage of
time. Brilliant in conception and execution, "*Das Karussell*" defies
precise translation. But its imagery turns and spins with its youngsters throughout timeless memory.

Shakespeare, too, understood the world of childhood in his own
day, in sixteenth-century England. But how differently from Rilke
did he foresee our final stage. He saw the drama of human life ending in ravaged old age: a "second childishness and mere oblivion /
Sans teeth, sans eyes, sans taste, sans everything." Shakespeare not-
withstanding, this phase of life can be quite a lovely place, despite
hints of our increasing frailty and decrepitude. It's a place in which
self-importance, haste, and obligation play no role (unless, of course,
you have children and grandchildren). It's where you can devote the
most precious gifts of all—time, well-being, and relationships—to
appreciate deeply the world and the roads we travel. The interwoven
threads of life—music, literature, immediate experience, science,
and faith—shape the means to that end. Indeed, as philosopher

Martin Buber reminds us: being old is a marvellous thing provided we haven't unlearned what it means to begin (*Altsein ist ein herrlich Ding, wenn wir nicht verlernt haben, was anfangen ist*). New beginnings, in my case, have meant not only setting off on my own in new directions, but sharing the lore with others and nurturing my children. Steeped in family history, C.S. Lewis's *The Chronicles of Narnia* captured the lively imaginations of our four youngsters. The epic adventure, set in a fantasy land of talking fauns, dwarfs, a wicked witch, and a redeeming lion, held them enthralled as they cuddled up on the sofa, all ready for bed. Now into their sixties, they still recall the sanctuary of a safe and cozy home in which they could experience adventure. The spirit of their deceased younger brother is never far away. The value of the Narnia stories lay in Lewis's imaginative use of symbol and myth to explore the depth and breadth of a moral universe. This was metaphysics for young beginners.

With similar metaphors and parables, our family's well-thumbed copy of Tolkien's *The Hobbit* led our four to further lively adventures and speculations. Launched to great acclaim in 1937, in the midst of my generation's so-called silence, it has never been out of print. The story is set in the fictional world of Middle Earth, and recounts the travels of the home-loving hobbit Bilbo Baggins. Together, as we had done with *Narnia*, we explored unknown worlds through our children's eyes. Bilbo Baggins's journey (though he didn't realize it at the time) was a pilgrimage. The book's ancient maps laid out the challenges: the Grey Mountains, the Withered Heath, Mirkwood the Great, the Desolation of Smaug, the Running River, and of course "a vast, red-golden dragon." Eventually, Bilbo does return home—but as a thoroughly transformed hobbit. Might the author have been inspired here by Martin Buber? I've often wondered. Buber had written that all journeys have a hidden destination that the traveller cannot foresee (*Alle Reisen, haben eine heimliche Bestimmung, die der Reisende nicht ahnt*). The original German hints at presentiment, vocation, direction, guidance, and homecoming, all in one.

And so, I end my days as I began them: in a tower overlooking the sea. Pachena Point Light shaped my life and opened it to the breadth of the teasing, taunting Pacific Ocean. Now, in my condo, I overlook a busy stretch of Victoria Harbour and beyond it to Esquimalt Naval Base and the Sooke Hills. It's the same harbour I travelled while aboard "old faithful," the ss *Princess Maquinna*, in the 1930s, and aboard the Canadian Pacific Steamships' Princess ships *Joan, Kathleen, Charlotte,* and *Nora* in the 1940s and '50s. In these same waters I transited in command of HMCS *Porte Quebec* and *Porte de la Reine* in the 1970s. From my armchair, I've witnessed the daily sailings of the ferry *Coho* nigh on twenty years, while cussing the noisy aircraft of Harbour Air stirring up the waters. Yet each flight reminds me of flying with my father in the 1940s, enjoying the intense anticipation of growling full-throttle takeoffs and skillful three-point landings. You wouldn't live here if you didn't enjoy a working harbour.

When the strong westerlies send cat's paws and whitecaps racing into the inner harbour and thrashing against the docks below my living room window, I raise my favourite tipple to my lips and play old Uncle Richard's game from his storied home in Newfoundland well over a hundred years ago: second-guessing the ship handlers as they struggle to get their vessels alongside in a beam wind. "Hell, Lord, Damn, Susan!" he'd shout to draw his wife's disinterested attention to some outrageous manoeuvre of an inbound schooner in Harbour Grace. "Hell, Lord, Damn, indeed!" I echo to him back down the years. And like old Richard, I insist on engaging my indulgent wife, who might look up from her book to acknowledge my foolish ways. For I still dream of taking the helm of some wayward vessel, or of showing some youngster how along-sides really ought to be done, whatever the weather. But not one of those vessels in the harbour, I hear old Uncle Richard whispering to me down the years, could have made it back alongside without me.

But what became of the little boy from Pachena? Or the young musician who played on Britain's vaudeville stage, the professor in search of wisdom, or the pilgrim in search of Ultimacy. What became of the writer, the husband, father, and grandfather?

The final pages of *The Hobbit* give a hint. "He took to writing poetry and visiting elves; and though many shook their heads and touched their foreheads and said 'Poor old Baggins!' and though few believed any of his tales, he remained happy to the end of his days, and those were extraordinarily long."

SIGNING OFF...

Then the moon, silvery and alone, shines down
Upon the sand—pure, strange, sea-dust of Time.
LOUISE MOREY BOWMAN, "Sea Sand"

REFLECTING ON one's life is like taking a wonderful old book off the shelf from time to time to dust off and browse through at leisure. We indulge in some pages, skip over others in familiar haste, and perhaps doze over the youthful dalliances and artless devices that no longer define us. We find that a few moments of life can command paragraphs and pages, and years but a brisk flourish of the pen. It is all a matter of meaning. Thankfully, a memoir is never the whole story. Heaven help us if it were otherwise. In gathering my reflections, I've been something of an armchair detective. The more I sifted the clues, the clearer became the tracks, with their peaks and valleys. I have made my case with just a few of these.

The roads I have travelled have challenged and enriched me, and unexpected insights have caught me by surprise. A lifetime of family and fellow rovers has nourished me. Indeed, the paths where we walked, and the places where we tarried, have become sacred. Life itself, I have learned, is less a game of chance than a sense of direction, with intimations of a destination. Testing the truth of one's path is like evaluating a fine old musical instrument. Though you master all the concepts that best describe it—its theory and history—the decisive step remains. You still must master the discipline of playing it. Only then will it reveal its secrets. I cannot adequately define the ultimacies that have drawn me and shaped me. No creed can contain them. Yet I know them intimately. My life has been full of meaning. I could not possibly ask more. T.S. Eliot's dramatic character Thomas Becket speaks for many of us: "I have had a tremor of bliss, a wink of heaven, a whisper..."

The story is over. The weaving is woven. The journey is almost done—yet the road goes ever onward. Stephen Cherry got it right in his *Barefoot Ways*: "Thank God, then, not only for memories, but for the mind's kind wisdom for forgetting."

ACKNOWLEDGEMENTS

Sometimes I sit on the old wooden bench on
the dock facing the sea, and after making sure
there is no one watching I peer intently into the
mist, searching for the ghost I know is there.

LOU BOUDREAU, "Schooner Magic"

MY REFLECTIONS owe their life to all the actors—family, friends, mentors, and fellow rovers—who played a part in shaping my journey. All of them have been my companions on the road, though they may long since have forgotten their part in the show, or that they even passed my way. Life, after all, consists of synergies and weavings that form the relationships we call community, and I acknowledge the enterprise.

I am indebted to my editor, Leslie Kenny, a friend and colleague from my time in the Centre for Studies in Religion and Society, University of Victoria. Her collegiality, incisive insights, and wise counsel form part of the weave. I likewise acknowledge the publishing team of Heritage House: Lara Kordic, Nandini Thaker, Monica Miller, Kimiko Fraser, Setareh Ashrafologhalai, and Sara Loos. I am grateful to my good friend the Very Rev. Herb O'Driscoll, from whom I have borrowed the technique of "weavings," and to Arthur W. Delamont for teaching me how to live and play inside the music. I thank Chris Best for permission to draw upon my early thoughts published in his books on the Vancouver Kitsilano Boys Band. I am indebted to my Winnipeg friend and colleague the late Dr. Jack Thiessen, for having introduced me to the Mennonite world. Likewise, I fondly remember my friend and business associate throughout our travels in Germany and Austria, the late Dr. Günther Reibhorn, who opened up unexpected perspectives on Europe in peace and war. So, too, I acknowledge the many other storytellers who shaped my understanding over the years: my colourful uncles Captain Llewellyn Sheppard and Sergeant-Major Harold (Frank) Hadley; the Canadian veterans of the Battle of the Atlantic Craig Campbell, Louis Audette, and Hal Lawrence; and a host of Second World War German naval officers—Admirals Eberhard Godt, Friedrich Ruge, and Paul Hartwig, and Captains Schorsch Meckel, Klaus Hornbostel, and Kurt Dobratz among them. My work in Canada and Germany would not have been possible without the friendship and encouragement of Dr. Alec Douglas, Prof. Dr. Jürgen Rohwer, Horst Bredow, and the former flag-lieutenant to Grand Admiral Dönitz, Jochen von Knebel-Doeberitz. My career shift into the Centre for Studies in Religion and Society owes much to Bishop Remi De Roo, the centre's conceptual founder, and to Dr. Harold Coward, its founding director. I thank their successors, Dr. Conrad Brunk and Dr. Paul Bramadat, for having invited me to continue my productive association with the Centre.

I especially acknowledge my indebtedness to my family: my parents Winnifred and Norman Hadley, and my sister, Elizabeth Joan. My children have always been a source of encouragement and insight, and sometimes of high family drama. In order of their appearance on stage I heartily thank Pauline, David, Michèle, and Norman. My grandchildren rounded out the talented travelling troupe: Tess Walton, Madison Watson, Luke Hadley-Beauregard, Olivia Hadley-Beauregard, and Alexandria Hadley. Finally, and most especially, I thank my wife Anita, my soulmate for sixty-five years. Neither this manuscript, nor any others I've written, would have been possible without her love and inspiration, her encouraging criticism, and her constant companionship. To all of these stars of my stage, I dedicate this book.

AUTHOR'S
SELECTED WRITINGS

Hadley, Michael L. "The Ascension of Mars and the Salvation of the Modern World." In *The Twenty-First Century Confronts Its Gods*, edited by David J. Hawkin. Albany, NY: State University of New York Press, 2004, 189-208.

——*Count Not the Dead: The Popular Image of the German Submarine.* Montreal and Kingston: McGill-Queen's University Press, 1991.

——*God's Little Ships: A History of the Columbia Coast Mission.* Madeira Park, BC: Harbour Publishing, 1995.

——"Grand Admiral Dönitz (1891–1980): A Dramatic Key to the Man behind the Mask." *The Northern Mariner/Le Marin du Nord* 10, no. 2 (April 2000): 1-21.

——*The Justice Tree: Multifaith Reflection on Criminal Justice.* Victoria, BC: Centre for Studies in Religion and Society, 2001.

——"Maritime Nation or Maritime Narrative: The Humanist Case for Canada." *The Northern Mariner/Le Marin du Nord* 27, no. 4 (October 2017): 339-53.

——"The Pacific Gateway and West Coast One-Fifty: Nautical Contours of Celebration." Guest editorial on the 150th anniversary of British Columbia's joining Confederation. *The Northern Mariner/Le Marin du Nord* 31, no. 4 (Winter 2021), iii-x.

——"Resistance in Exile: Publication, Context and Reception of Stefan Andres' *Wir sind Utopia* (1942)." *Seminar: A Journal of Germanic Studies* 19, no. 3 (September 1983): 157-76.

——"'Rückwärts schauende Propheten': U-Bootgeschichte im dienste der Zukunft." In *Hinter dem schwarzen Vorhang: die Katastrophe und die epische Tradition*, edited by Friedrich Gaede, et al. Tübingen: Francke Verlag, 1994, 217-29.

——"Spiritual Foundations of Restorative Justice." In *Handbook of Restorative Justice: A Global Perspective*, edited by Dennis Sullivan and Larry Tifft. London and New York: Routledge, 2006, 174-87.

——ed. *The Spiritual Roots of Restorative Justice.* Albany, NY: State University Press of New York, 2001.

——*U-Boats against Canada: German Submarines in Canadian Waters.* Montreal and Kingston: McGill-Queen's University Press, 1985.

——*U-Boote gegen Kanada: Unternehmungen deutscher U-Boote in kanadischen Gewässern.* Translated by Hans and Hanne Meckel. Herford: E.S. Mittler, 1990. Paperback, Hamburg and Berlin: Ullstein, 1997.

——and Godfrey Agupio. "The Ugandan Way of Living and Dying." In *Religious Understandings of a Good Death in Hospice Palliative Care,* edited by Harold Coward and Kelli I. Stajduhar. Albany, NY: State University of New York Press, 2012, 191–210.

——and Richard H. Gimblett, eds. *Citizen Sailors: Chronicles of Canada's Naval Reserve 1910–2010.* Toronto: Dundurn Press, 2010.

——and Richard H. Gimblett, eds. *Le Marin-Citoyen: Chroniques de la Réserve Navale du Canada 1910–2010.* Toronto: Dundurn Press, 2010.

——and Anita Hadley, eds. *Spindrift: A Canadian Book of the Sea.* Vancouver: Douglas & McIntyre, 2017.

——and Rob Huebert, et al. eds. *A Nation's Navy: In Quest of Canadian Naval Identity.* Montreal and Kingston: McGill-Queen's University Press, 1996.

——and Roger Sarty. *Tin-Pots and Pirate Ships: Canadian Naval Forces and German Sea Raiders 1880–1918.* Montreal and Kingston: McGill-Queen's University Press, 1991.

BIBLIOGRAPHY OF
WORKS MENTIONED

Abella, Irving, and Harold Troper. *None Is Too Many: Canada and the Jews of Europe, 1933-1948*. Toronto: University of Toronto Press, 1983.

Acorn, Milton. *In a Springtime Instant: Selected Poems*. Oakville, ON: Mosaic Press, 2015.

Adachi, Ken. *The Enemy That Never Was: A History of the Japanese-Canadians*. Toronto and Vancouver: McClelland & Stewart, 1976.

Anglican Church of Canada, General Synod. *The Book of Alternative Services of the Anglican Church of Canada*. Toronto: Anglican Book Centre, 1985.

Atwood, Margaret. *The Handmaid's Tale*. Toronto: McClelland & Stewart, 1985.

Barzun, Jacques. *Science: The Glorious Entertainment*. Toronto: University of Toronto Press, 1964.

Bauer, Walter. *Der Weg zählt, nicht die Herberge: Prosa und Verse* (The Path Matters, Not Where You Tarry: Prose and Verse). Hamburg: Tesslof, 1964.

Best, Christopher. *The Life and Times of the Legendary Mr D: The Story of Arthur W. Delamont and his Champion Vancouver Kitsilano Boys Band*. Vancouver: Warfleet Press, 2013.

Bible, The Holy. New Revised Standard Version. Nashville, TN: Thomas Nelson, 1989.

Birney, Earle. *The Collected Poems of Earle Birney*. Toronto: McClelland & Stewart, 1975.

Bithell, Jethro. *An Anthology of German Poetry 1880-1940*. London: Methuen, [1941] 1956.

Blake, William. *Selected Poems*. Edited by Peter H. Butter. London: J.M. Dent, 1994.

Bloch, Michael. *Ribbentrop*. London: Transworld Publishers, 1992.

Bonhoeffer, Dietrich. *Gesammelte Schriften* (Collected Writings). 4 vols. Munich: C. Kaiser, 1958-61.

Book of Common Prayer. *See* Church of England.

Borchert, Wolfgang. *Draußen vor der Tür und Ausgewählte Erzählungen. Mit einem Nachwort von Heinrich Böll* (Outside the Door and Selected Tales. With a Postcript by Heinrich Böll). Hamburg: Rowohlt, [1956] 1964.

Borradaile, Osmond, and Anita Borradaile Hadley. *Life Through A Lens: Memoirs of a Cinematographer.* Montreal and Kingston: McGill-Queen's University Press, 2001.

Boudreau, Lou. "Schooner Magic." In *We Belong to the Sea: A Nova Scotia Anthology, edited by Meddy Stanton.* Halifax, NS: Nimbus Publishing, 2002.

Bowman, Louise. "Sea Sand." In *Moonlight and Common Day.* Toronto: Macmillan, 1922.

Brecht, Bertolt. *Flüchtlingsgespräche* (Refugee Conversations). Berlin und Frankfurt am Main, 1961.

Bruce, Charles. "Islands," and "Eastern Shore." In *The Mulgrave Road: Selected Poems of Charles Bruce,* edited by Andy Wainwright and Lesley Choyce. Porters Lake, NS: Pottersfield Press, 1985.

Buber, Martin. *I and Thou. (Ich und Du.* Leipzig: Insel-Verlag, 1923). Translated by Ronald Gregor Smith. Edinburgh: T.& T. Clarke, 1952.

Buddha. *The Teachings of the Compassionate Buddha.* Edited, with a commentary by C.A. Burtt. New York: Mentor Books, 1955.

Buechner, Frederick. *The Longing for Home: Recollections and Reflections.* San Francisco: Harper, 1996.

Bunyan, John. *The Pilgrim's Progress. From This World to That Which Is to Come.* [...] Part II. London: Printed for Nath. Ponder at the Peacock in the Poultry near Cornhil, 1678.

Cameron, Silver Donald. *Wind, Whales and Whisky: A Cape Breton Voyage.* Toronto: Macmillan, 1991.

Carr, Emily. *Klee Wyck.* With a foreword by Ina Dilworth, Centennial Edition. Toronto and Vancouver: Clarke, Irwin & Company, [1941] 1971.

Carrier, Roch. "Le Chandail." In *The Hockey Sweater and Other Stories.* Toronto: Anansi, 1979.

——*The Expanding Prison: The Crisis in Crime and Punishment and the Search for Alternatives.* Toronto: Anansi, 1998.

Cayley, David. *George Grant in Conversation.* Concord, ON: Anansi, 1995.

—— *The Phenomenon of Man.* Translated from the French by Bernard Wall. With an Introduction by Sir Julian Huxley. London: Collins, 1959.

——*Barefoot Ways: Praying Through Advent, Christmas and Epiphany.* London: SPCK, 2015.

Cherry, Stephen. *Healing Agony: Re-Imagining Forgiveness.* London and New York: Continuum International Publishing, 2012.

Chichester, Francis. *Gipsy Moth Circles the World.* London: Hodder and Stoughton, 1967.

Chiles, James A., and Josef Wiehr. *First Book in German.* Revised Edition. Boston, New York, Toronto: Ginn and Company, [1935] 1948.

Church of England. *The Book of Common Prayer and Administration of the Sacraments* [The Finger Prayer Book]. Miniature edition. \ Oxford: Oxford University Press, Amen Corner [1549], n.d. [ca. 1907].

Conrad, Joseph. *Lord Jim*. London: Dent, 1923.

Conrady, Karl Otto, ed. *Das Große deutsche Gedichtbuch von 1500 bis zur Gegenwart* (The Great German Poetry Book from 1500 to the Present). Munich and Zürich: Artemis und Winkler Verlag, 1991.

Cox, Harvey. *The Secular City: Secularization and Urbanization in Theological Perspective*. New York: Macmillan, 1965.

——and Daniel Callahan. *The Secular City Debate*. New York: Macmillan, 1966.

Dall'Oglio, Paolo. *Amoureux d'Islam, et Croyant en Jésus* (In Love with Islam, Believing in Jesus). With the collaboration of Églantine Gabaix-Hialé. Paris: Les Éditions de l'Atelier, 2009.

Dalrymple, William. *From the Holy Mountain: A Journey in the Shadow of Byzantium*. London: HarperCollins, 1998. *See also* Moschos, John.

Dehmel, Richard. *Lebensblätter: Gedichte und Anderes* (Pages from Life: Poems and Miscellany). Berlin: Verlag der Gemeinschaft Pan, 1895.

De Roo, Remi. *Chronicles of a Vatican II Bishop*. Montreal and Toronto: Novalis, 2012.

Dönitz, Karl. *Zehn Jahre und Zwanzig Tage* (Ten Years and Twenty Days: Memoirs 1935-1945). Koblenz: Bernhard & Graef, [1958] 1985.

Donne, John. *Devotions on Emergent Occasions* [1624]. Ann Arbor: University of Michigan Press, 1959.

Dyck, Arnold. *Verloren in der Steppe* (Lost in the Steppes). Steinbach, MB: self-published by the author, 1944.

Easton, Alan. *50 North: An Atlantic Battleground*. Toronto: Ryerson Press, 1963.

Eck, Diana. *Encountering God: A Spiritual Journey from Bozeman to Benares*. Boston: Beacon Press, 1993.

Eichner, Hans. *Wem kein Bogen gesetzt. Mit einem Nachwort versehen von David G. John* (Collected Poems, with a postscript by David G. John). Vienna: Theodor Kramer Gesellschaft, 2021.

Eliot, T.S. *Murder in the Cathedral*. London: Faber & Faber, [1935] 1938.

Esslin, Martin. *Brecht: A Choice of Evils; His Work and His Opinions*. London: Eyre & Spottiswoode, 1959.

Fiedler, H.G., ed. *Buch deutscher Dichtung von Luther bis Liliencron* (Book of German Poetry from Luther to Liliencron). Oxford: Universitätsverlag, [1916] 1951.

Fry, Elizabeth. *Memoir of the Life of Elizabeth Fry, with extracts from her journal and letters*. Edited by Rachel Elizabeth Cresswell. London: C. Gilpin, J. Hatchard & Son, 1847.

Garner, Hugh. *Storm Below*. Toronto: Collins, 1949.

Geibel, Emanuel. *Ein Münchener Dichterbuch* (A Munich Poetry Book). Stuttgart: A. Kröner, 1863.

Gibbs, Philip. *No Price for Freedom*. Stratford Place, London: Hutchinson, 1955.

Goethe, Johann Wolfgang von. *Faust*, Teil I, in *Goethes Werke*, Bd. 3 (Goethe's Works in 14 Volumes). Edited by Erich Trunz. Hamburg: Christian Wegner Verlag, 1964.

——*Wilhelm Meisters Lehrjahre* (Wilhelm Meister's Apprenticeship). In *Goethes Werke*, Bd. 7 (Goethe's Works in 14 Volumes). Edited by Erich Trunz. Hamburg: Christian Wegner Verlag, 1964.

Grahame, Kenneth. *The Wind in the Willows*. London: Methuen, 1933; New York: Grosset & Dunlap, 1966.

Grant, George. *See* Cayley, David.

Greene, Graham. *The Power and the Glory*. Harmondsworth: Heinemann, [1940] 1971.

——*Christ in India: Essays Towards a Hindu-Christian Dialogue*. New York: Scribner, 1966.

Griffiths, Bede. *The Golden String*. London: Catholic Book Club, 1954.

Grillparzer, Franz. *Der Arme Spielmann* (The Poor Street Musician). Ansbach: Insel-Verlag, [1848] 1957.

Hadley, Anita. *See* Borradaile.

——*Heine: A Verse Selection*. Edited by G. W. Field. London: Macmillan, 1965.

Heine, Heinrich. *Selected Poems*. Edited by Barker Fairley. Oxford: Clarendon Press, 1965.

Horwood, Harold. *Tomorrow Will Be Sunday*. Garden City, NY: Doubleday, 1966.

Huxley, Aldous. *The Perennial Philosophy*. New York: Harper & Row, [1944] 1970.

James, P.D. *Devices and Desires*. London: Penguin, 1989.

——*The Last Temptation of Christ*. Translated from the Greek by P.A. Bien, New York: Simon Schuster, 1960; New York: Bantam, 1961.

Kazantzakis, Nikos. *Zorba the Greek*. Translated from the Greek by Carl Wildman. New York: Simon and Schuster, 1952; New York: Bantam, 1965.

Keegan, John. *The Mask of Command*. London: Jonathan Cape, 1987.

Kokubo, Hideo. *See* Adachi, Ken.

Koran. *See* Qur'an.

——*Brüder und Knechte* (Brothers and Slaves). Stuttgart: Evangelische Buchgemeinde, 1965.

——*Lebens-Zeichen: Meditationen, Bilder, Reden* (Signs of Life, Meditations, Images, Talks). Freiburg, Basel and Vienna: Herder, 1978.

Kramp, Willy. *Die Welt des Gesprächs* (The World of Dialogue). Zürich: Im Verlag der Arche, 1962.

Kretschmer, Otto. *See* Robertson, Terence.

Küng, Hans. *Does God Exist? An Answer for Today*. Garden City, NY: Doubleday, 1980.

——*Theology for the Third Millenium: An Ecumenical View.* New York: Doubleday, 1988.

Langewiesche, Wolfgang. *Stick and Rudder: An Explanation of the Art of Flying.* New York: McGraw-Hill, 1944.

Lawrence, T.E. *Seven Pillars of Wisdom: A Triumph.* New York: Doubleday, 1936.

Lersch, Heinrich. *Das dichterische Werk: Mensch im Eisen* (Poetic Works: Man in Iron). Berlin And Stuttgart: Deutsche Verlags-Anstalt, 1937.

Lewis, C.S. *The Complete Chronicles of Narnia.* 7 vols. Harmondsworth: Penguin Books, in association with The Bodley Head, London: 1950-55.

Lightman, Alan. *The Transcendent Brain: Spirituality in the Age of Science.* New York: Pantheon Books, 2023.

MacLean, Alistair. *H.M.S. Ulysses.* London: Collins, 1955.

Major, Kevin. *No Man's Land.* Toronto: Doubleday Canada, 1995.

Mann, Thomas. *Tonio Kröger.* School edition edited and introduced by John Alexander Kelly. New York: Appleton-Century-Crofts, [1925] 1931.

Marsh, Charles. *Strange Glory: A Life of Dietrich Bonhoeffer.* New York: Vintage Books, 2015.

Masefield, John, "Sea Fever." In *Ballads and Poems.* London: E. Matthews, 1918.

Matembe, Miria. *Gender, Politics, and Constitution Making in Uganda.* With Nancy R. Dorsey. Kampala: Fountain Publishers, 2002.

——*The Struggle for Freedom and Democracy Betrayed: Memoirs of Miria Matembe as an Insider in Museveni's Government.* Kampala: Fountain Publishers, 2019.

McMurray, Kevin F. *Dark Descent: Diving and the Deadly Allure of the Empress of Ireland.* Camden, ME: International Marine Publishing, 2004.

Milner, Marc. *North Atlantic Run: The Royal Canadian Navy and the Battle for the Convoys.* Toronto: University of Toronto Press, 1985.

Miłosz, Czesław. *The Captive Mind.* Translated from the Polish by Jane Ziolonko. New York: Alfred A. Knopf, 1953; Vintage Books, 1955.

Monsarrat, Nicholas. *The Cruel Sea.* New York: Knopf, 1951.

Morrissey, Donna. *Pluck: A Memoir of a Newfoundland Childhood and the Raucous, Terrible, Amazing Journey to Becoming a Novelist.* Toronto: Viking, 2021.

Moschos, John. *The Spiritual Meadow.* [n.p. early 7th century]. Translated and introduced by John Wortley. Kalamazoo: Cistercian Publications, 1992. *See also* Dalrymple, William.

Mowat, Farley. *The Boat Who Wouldn't Float.* Toronto: McClelland & Stewart, 1969.

Newell, Tim. *Forgiving Justice: A Quaker Vision for Criminal Justice.* Quaker Home Service, 2007.

Nossack, Hans Erich. *Der Untergang: Hamburg 1943.* (The Destruction: Hamburg 1943). Photos by Erich Andres. Postscript by Erich Lüth. Text Suhrkamp: 1948. Harburg: Ernst Kabel Verlag, 1981.

——*The Cape of Good Hope.* Translated from the Polish *Przylądek Dobrej Nadziei [1931]* by Kate Zuk-Skarszewska. London: Minerva, 1941.

Nowakowski, Zygmunt. *Przylądek Dobrej Nadziei* (The Cape of Good Hope). London: Alma Book Company, 1957.

O'Connell, Robert. *Of Arms and Men: A History of War, Weapons, and Aggression.* New York: Oxford University Press, 1989.

Orwell, George. *Animal Farm.* London: Martin Sacker and Warburg, 1945; Penguin Books, 1951.

——*Nineteen Eighty-Four: A Novel.* New York: Harcourt, Brace, [1949] 1959.

Partington, Marian. *If You Sit Very Still: A Sister's Fierce Engagement with Traumatic Loss.* Kingsley, UK: Jessica Publishers, 2016.

Pirandello, Luigi. *Six Characters in Search of an Author.* London: Methuen, 1979.

Poe, Edgar Allan. "A Descent into the Maelstrom" [1841]. In *The Complete Works of Edgar Allan Poe.* Edited by James A. Harrison. New York: Crowell, 1902.

Procter, Adelaide Anne. "A Lost Chord." In *The Poems of Adelaide A. Procter.* Introduced by Charles Dickens. New York: J.W. Lovell, 1884. *See also* Sullivan, Arthur.

Purdy, Al. "Reaching for the Beaufort Sea." In *Beyond Remembering: The Collected Poems of Al Purdy.* Madeira Park, BC: Harbour Publishing, 2000.

Qur'an. The Meaning of the Holy Qur'an. New edition with Qur'anic text (Arabic) by Abdullah Yûsuf 'Alī. Beltsville, Maryland: Amana Publications, 1997.

Raban, Jonathan. *Passage to Juneau: A Sea and Its Meaning.* New York: Pantheon Books, 1999.

——*Die Nacht von Lissabon* (The Night in Lisbon). Cologne: Kiepenheuer & Witsch, 1962.

Remarque, Erich Maria. *Im Westen Nichts Neues* (All Quiet on the Western Front). Berlin: Propyläen Verlag, 1929.

Rilke, Rainer Maria. *Rilke Poems.* Edited by G.W. McKay. New York and Oxford: Oxford University Press, 1965.

Robertson, Terence. *The Golden Horseshoe: The Wartime Career of Otto Kretschmer, U-Boat Ace.* Introduced by Jürgen Rohwer. London: Greenhill Books, [1955] 2003.

Robinson, John A.T. *Honest to God.* London: SCM Press, 1963.

——*The New Reformation?* London: SCM Press, 1965.

Robson, Peter A., and Betty Keller. *Skookum Tugs: British Columbia's Working Tugboats.* Photographs by Robb Douglas, and foreword by Stephen Hume. Madeira Park, BC: Harbour Publishing, 2002.

Rodger, N.A.M. *The Wooden World: An Anatomy of the Georgian Navy.* London: Collins, 1986.

Roget, Peter Mar. *Roget's University Thesaurus.* Edited by G.O. Sylvester Mawson. New York, Cambridge: Barnes & Noble, [1852] 1963.

Ross, Rupert. *Returning to the Teachings: Exploring Aboriginal Justice.* Toronto: Penguin Books, 1996.

Rostand, Edmond. *Cyrano de Bergerac: Comédie en cinq actes* (Cyrano de Bergerac: Comedy in Five Acts). Paris: Librairie Charpentier et Fasquelle, 1914.

Ruge, Friedrich. *In Vier Marinen: Lebenserinnerungen als Beitrag zur Zeitgeschichte* (In Four Navies: Memoirs as a Contribution to Contemporary History). Munich: Bernard & Graef Verlag, 1979.

St. Exupéry, Antoine de. *Le Petit Prince* (The Little Prince). Montreal: Beauchemin, and New York: Reynal & Hitchcock, 1943.

Sakamoto, Unosuke. *See* Adachi, Ken.

Salomon, Ernst von. *Der Fragebogen* (The Questionnaire). Reinbek, Hamburg: Rowoht, [1951] 1961.

——*Werke in Drei Bänden* (Works in Three Volumes). Munich: Carl Hanser Verlag, 1966.

Schiller, Friedrich. *Wilhelm Tell*. School edition edited and introduced by Robert Waller Deering. Boston: D.C. Heath, [1894] 1915.

Schmidt, Helmut. "Politischer Rückblick auf eine unpolitische Jugend" (Political Retrospective on an Unpolitical Youth). In *Kindheit und Jugund unter Hitler* (Childhood and Youth Under Hitler). Introduced by Wolf Jobst Siedler. Berlin: Wolf Jobst Siedler Verlag, 1992.

Schull, Joseph. *The Far Distant Ships: An Official Account of Canadian Naval Operations in the Second World War*. Ottawa, ON: Queen's Printer, 1952.

Schweitzer, Albert. *Aus meinem Leben und Denken* (My Life and Thought). Hamburg and Frankfurt: Fischer Verlag, 1952.

Shakespeare, William. *William Shakespeare: The Complete Works*. Edited by Charles Jasper Sisson. Longacre, London: Odhams Press, 1960.

Shields, Carol. *The Stone Diaries*. Toronto: Vintage Books, 1993.

Skelton, Robin. "Last Song" and "Yellowpoint." In *One Leaf Shaking*. Victoria, BC: Porcépic Books, 1996.

Stanton, Meddy. *See* Boudreau, Lou.

Stead, Gordon W. *A Leaf Upon the Sea: A Small Ship in the Mediterranean, 1941–1943*. Vancouver: University of British Columbia Press, 1988.

Steinbeck, John. *The Grapes of Wrath*. New York: Viking, 1939.

Storm, Theodor. *Gesammelte Werke: Gedichte, Novellen, Briefe* (Collected Works: Poems, Novellas, Letters). 6 vols. Herrliberg-Zürich: Bühl Verlag, 1945–47.

Sullivan, Arthur, and Adelaide Anne Procter. *The Lost Chord: Song, with Pianoforte and Harmonium Accompaniment*. Score by Arthur Sullivan, 1877, and lyrics by Adelaide Anne Procter, 1858. Toronto: Anglo-Canadian Music Publishers' Association, 1885.

—— *The Lost Chord* [1877]. Musical score arranged for brass band by Scott Richards. Crans-Montana, Switzerland: Éditions Marc Reifft, 2019. *See also* Procter, Adelaide Anne.

Teece, Philip. *A Dream of Islands*. Victoria, BC: Orca Book Publishers, 1988.

——*A Shimmer on the Horizon*. Victoria, BC: Orca Book Publishers, 1999.

Teilhard de Chardin, Pierre. *Le Milieu Divin: An Essay on the Interior Life*. London: Collins, 1960.

Tennyson, Alfred Lord. "Crossing the Bar." In *Poems of Alfred Lord Tennyson*. Edited by Charles Tennyson. London and Glasgow: Collins, 1954.

—— "Ulysses." In *Poetical Works of Alfred Lord Tennyson, Poet Laureat*. London: Macmillan, 1899.

Thatamanil, John. *Circling the Elephant: A Comparative Theology of Religious Diversity*. New York: Fordham University Press, 2020.

Thomas, Dylan. *Collected Poems*. London: Dent, 1952.

Thucydides. *The War of the Peloponnesians and the Athenians*. Edited and translated by Jeremy Mynott. Cambridge: Cambridge University Press, 2013.

——*Impressionen und Reflexionen: ein Leben in Aufsätzen, Reden und Stellungnahmen* (Impressions and Reflexions: A Life in Essays, Addresses and Commentaries). Stuttgart: Evangelisches Verlagswerk, 1972.

Tillich, Paul. *Philosophie und Schicksal: Schriften zur Erkenntnislehre und Existenzphilosophie* (Philosophy and Fate: Writings on Epistemology and Existentialism). Stuttgart: Evangelisches Verlagswerk, 1961.

Tolkien, J.R.R. *The Hobbit: Or There and Back Again* [1937]. 19th printing, London: Allen & Unwin, 1967.

——*The Lord of the Rings* [1954, 1955]. London: Allen & Unwin, 1968.

Vassanji, M.G. *The In-Between World of Vikram Lall*. Toronto: Anchor Canada, 2003.

Verne, Jules. *Twenty Thousand Leagues under the Sea*. Introduced by Felix Riesenberg. Original illustrations by Anton Otto Fischer. Chicago, Philadelphia, and Toronto: John C. Winston Company, 1932.

Voltaire, François-Marie Arouet. *Traité sur la Tolérance (1763): suivi de la Lettre sur la Tolérance (1689) de John Locke* (Treatise on Tolerance: Followed by the Letter on Tolerance by John Locke). Paris: UPblisher, 2016.

Wagamese, Richard. *What Comes from Spirit*. Vancouver: Douglas & McIntyre, 2022.

Whalley, George. *The Collected Poems of George Whalley*. 2 vols. Kingston, ON: Quarry Press, 1986.

Wiebe, Rudy. *Peace Shall Destroy Many*. Toronto: McClelland & Stewart, 1962.

Zehr, Howard. *Changing Lenses: A New Focus for Crime and Justice*. Scottsdale, PA, and Waterloo, ON: Herald Press, 1990.

——*Doing Life: Reflections of Men and Women Serving Life Sentences*. Scottsdale, PA, and Waterloo, ON: Herald Press, 1996.

——*Transcending: Reflections of Crime Victims*. Scottsdale, PA: Good Books, 2001.

INDEX

Brunk, Conrad. *See* Centre for
Studies in Religion and Society
Brussels, 5; and international pavilions, 105–106; World Fair, 5, 62,
103–119
Buber, Martin, 150, 278–89, 237
Bunyan, John, 273
bureaucracy, 120–41; and existential frustration, 143; and Public
Service, 120; and questionnaires,
137–38; and training for, 121–23

Campbell, Craig, 205 f., 218–19. *See
also* veterans
Carr, Emily, 64
Carrier, Roch, 275
Centre for Studies in Religion and
Society, 239 ff.; and Conrad
Brunk, 179; founding of, 166 ff.;
and Harold Coward, 179; and
Remi de Roo, 166 ff.
chance, 1–2, 4–5; as apophany, 103;
as fate, 229–30; and vocation, 182.
See also grace *and* serendipity
Chardin, Pierre Teilhard de, 170. *See
also* theology, process
Chaucer, Geoffrey, 195, 225
Cherry, Stephen, 284
Chichester, Francis, 188. *See also*
seniors
childhood, 2; in art and poetry, 278;
and fear of air raids, 32; school,
26 ff.; understandings, 25 ff.; in
wartime 25–36. *See also* Hadley,
children
Christianity, 2, 274; and
Benedictines on peace and prayer,
112–13; hospitality, 116–17, 118;
and nostalgia, 96; religionless, 149; Salvation Army, 46;
and social gospel, 145. *See also*
theology
Church, of England: and colonialism,
28–30; Lutheran, 210, 225; and

renewal, 270; United, 20. *See also*
Anglican Church; De Roo, Remi;
and Vatican II
Coleridge, Samuel Taylor, 88, 187
Columbia Coast Mission, 9, 193,
197; and John Antle, 176; and
Rollo Boas, 184–85
compass, *See* boxing the compass
Conrad, Joseph, 1, 9
Cook, Capt. James, 27
Correctional Service of Canada. *See
also,* justice, and Woodhouse, A.J.
Coward, Harold. *See* Centre for
Studies in Religion and Society

death and dying: and commemo-
ration, 95, 219–20; from AIDS,
257; for one's country, 137; at sea,
216–17. *See also* hospice
Dall'Oglio, Paolo, 236; and
double-belonging, 237. *See also*
monastery, Mar Musa
Delamont, Arthur W., 5, 40–63. *See
also* Kitsilano Boys Band
De Roo, Remi. *See* Centre for Studies
in Religion and Society
development, 2, 101
dialogue living: principles of, 135;
and journey, 279. *See* Buber,
Kramp
Dobratz, Kurt (U-1232), 214–17. *See*
veterans, German
Dodd, Erica, 238. *See also* monastery,
Mar Musa
Dönitz, Grand Admiral Karl, 203,
229; and "Bomber" Harris,
210–11; faith of, 210; grave of,
210; identity of 211–13; and War
Crimes Trials, 210, 212, 229
Donne, John, 10
Douglas, Alex, 206
duty: as voice of God, 232. *See also*
Third Reich, religion of; oath to
Hitler

Moss-Empire chain, 49–50; and
professional stage, 51–55, 280.
Verne, Jules, 199
veterans: Austrian, 217–18;
Canadian, 205–208, 214; Louis
Audette, 216 ff.; Craig Campbell,
205–206, 218–19, 222–30; Alan
Easton,189–90 ; Gordon Stead,
234, and George Whalley, 190;
German, 97, 138, 208–35; and
Kurt Dobratz, 214–17; Eberhard
Godt, 223–24; Reinhard
Hardegen, 214; Klaus Hornbostel,
218–19, 222; and Schorsch Meckel,
224 ff., and Friedrich Ruge,
231–33; and Helmut Schmidt, 232
Victoria Harbour, 280
von Knebel-Doeberitz, Jochen and
Claudia, 203 ff., 209, 213. *See also*
veterans, German

Wagamese, Richard, 6
Wagner, Richard: and *Flying
Dutchman*, 40. *See also* Kitsilano
Boys Band
war, 2–4, 5, 11–12, 147, 275; as anni-
hilation, 132; atomic, 3; Cold
War, 200; crimes of, 135; Cuba
missile crisis, 3; fear of, 70–71;
mines and minesweeping, 82–83;
Normandy Invasion, 228, 230;
Passchendaele, 3; Plains of
Abraham, 27, 56; reality of, 219;
Stalingrad,133–34; submarine

warfare and war diary, 206; and
survivors, 134 ff.; in Syria, 238;
Vimy Ridge, 27; Ypres, 3, 95
war poets: Wilfred Owen and
Sigfried Sassoon, 95
warships: HMCS *Clayoquot*, 206,
218–19; *Coaticook*, 216–17;
Deutschland, 190–92; *Fortune*,
82–83; and gate vessels, 84
ff., 280; *New Glasgow*, 77–81;
Olympias, 90–91; *Ontario*,
55; *Oshawa*, 76–77; *Quebec*,
57, 72–76; HMS *Vienna*, 83;
Wiesbaden, 205
Whitehead, Alfred North, 170.
See also theology, process
Winnipeg, 142 ff.
wisdom, 23, 100; inter-religious
146, 150; multifaith, 148–49;
popular, 224; as *sapientia*, 269,
280; and situational awareness,
5, 188; 270–71, 277; and William
Blake, 269
Woodhouse, Allan, J., 245–46. *See
also* justice, Restorative
writing: craft of, 2, 6, 283, 284;
and Bede Griffiths, 145; and
metanarrative, 59–60; as
weaving, 1, 5–6

youth: spirit of, 94, 118, 153; in war,
230, 233–35. *See* Kitsilano Boys
Band
Zehr, Howard, 240

ABOUT
THE AUTHOR

MICHAEL L. HADLEY is an award-winning writer, interdisciplinary scholar, yachtsman, retired naval officer, international traveller, and lecturer. He is the author and editor of books on naval and maritime history, including *Spindrift: A Canadian Book of the Sea* (co-edited with his wife, Anita Hadley) and *Citizen Sailors: Chronicles of Canada's Naval Reserve, 1910–2010* (co-edited with Richard H. Gimlett), and his work has won such prestigious awards as the John Lyman Prize of the North American Society for Oceanic History and the Keith Matthews Award of the Canadian Nautical Research Society. He is a Professor Emeritus at the University of Victoria and a Fellow of the Royal Society of Canada. In November 2023, he received the Lieutenant Governor's Award for Maritime Achievement.